MAINSTREET CAPITALISM

Essays on Broadening Share Ownership

in

America and Britain

Edited by

Stuart M. Speiser

New Horizons Press
New York, New York

New Horizons Press is an imprint of
the Council on International and
Public Affairs, Inc., 777 United
Nations Plaza, New York, New York
10017 (212/972-9877)

Library of Congress Cataloging-in-Publication Data

Mainstreet capitalism.

    Bibliography: p.
    1. Stock ownership.   2. Stock ownership—United States.
3. Stock ownership—Great Britain.   I. Speiser, Stuart M.
HG4528.M35   1988   332.63'22'0941   88-27819
ISBN 0-945257-02-3

Typeset and printed in the United States of America

MAINSTREET CAPITALISM:
Essays on Broadening Share Ownership in America and Britain

EXPLANATORY NOTE

Because the contributors to this volume are widely dispersed across the face of the globe, it did not prove possible to contact all of them in order to obtain complete bibliographical data on sources used in the text. Consequently, some sources are lacking or incomplete.

By the same token, some changes were made in the final editing process that could not be checked with individual essayists.

The publisher takes full responsibility for the form of the essays as they appear in this book.

CONTENTS

1

EDITOR'S INTRODUCTION

This is a collection of essays submitted in response to calls for papers on the following topic:

> In 5,000 words or less, devise a plan for spreading ownership of [America's] [Britain's] productive assets broadly among the people, and reviving the economy. without confiscation or increased taxation.

The North American essay competition was sponsored by the Council on International and Public Affairs, offering prizes of $5,000, $2,500, and $1,000 respectively for the three best essays. There was a parallel competition in Great Britain, sponsored by the Wider Share Ownership Council, with prizes of £2,000, £1,000, and £500. The competitions ran for the calendar year of 1986.

Since so many high-quality papers were submitted, choosing the winners proved to be a difficult task. In order to get the full flavor of the competition and to include all the useful ideas submitted by the entrants, I found it necessary to include in this volume the complete texts of many more than the winning essays, and to excerpt from a number of others.

At the close of the 1986 competition, I had planned to try to synthesize the lessons learned from all of the papers submitted. However, I found that the essays opened up so many promising new paths of inquiry, and also revealed so many important questions to be pursued, that it would be both presumptuous and premature to attempt a synthesis now. Instead, I have decided to be content with publishing the cornucopia of promising new ideas in the hope that they will be used by participants in future essay competitions—including those planned in the United States and Great Britain for 1988—so that we can carry the discovery process one step further before attempting a definitive synthesis.

The wording of the topic was chosen carefully. Spreading the ownership of productive assets broadly among the people brings into play the concept of *universal* capital ownership, and rules out such microeconomic plans as employee ownership. Unfortunately, it is not possible to spread capital ownership *broadly* among the people through employee ownership. While most Americans are employed, the great majority would not gain any benefits from holding shares in the enterprises for which they work. The relatively few companies that remain successful, the shares of which retain market value over a working life span of 40 years, employ only a fraction of our population. Most of our people work for themselves, for government agencies, for entities that do not issue shares that are traded, or they do not work at all. Employee ownership brings no benefit to the unemployed, the very poor, and those who are not fortunate enough to be long-term employees of continuously successful companies. Furthermore, employee ownership has been facilitated by tax benefits, which amount to a tax subsidy to the most fortunate sector of our society—those who have steady employment with strong companies. To that extent, it decreases the funds available to help the disadvantaged sector: those who have the least desirable jobs or no jobs at all.

Nevertheless, employee ownership has opened the door to a more equitable economic system in both nations. Therefore, the relationship between employee share ownership plans and the broader universal plans that will deliver capital ownership outside of the employment relationship is an important part of this essay competition. Obviously, those who seek to democratize the ownership of capital would be well advised to build upon the solid foundation of employee ownership that has been laid in the United States and, more recently, in the United Kingdom.

By ruling out confiscation and increased taxation, the topic called upon the essayists to produce a plan that will not redistribute wealth at the expense of its present holders and that will not increase the tax burden on productive people. The term "productive assets" is broad enough to include shares of companies, whether large or small; income-producing real estate; and all other items, ownership of which carries with it the right to receive income.

Thus, the topic calls for a blueprint of a Universal Share Ownership Plan—"universal" in the sense of being open to all citizens and "share" in the sense of shares of company stock or shares in ownership rights to other property. The essayists were provided with a guide to past thinking on this subject in the form of *The USOP Handbook* (Speiser, 1986). This handbook was something like a smorgasbord, in that it put before the essayists many of the ingredients that might be used in an ideal plan of universal capital ownership. The essayists were free to pick and choose among the various dishes and indeed were encouraged to brew their own concoctions.

The earliest American writings on this subject were contributed by the San Francisco lawyer Louis O. Kelso, who proposed the Financed Capitalist Plan under which all Americans who did not have the savings to become capitalists would be enabled to buy shares in our major successful companies through credit arranged by the federal government (Kelso, 1958, 1961, 1967, 1987).

In conjunction with my 1984 book, *How To End The Nuclear Nightmare*, I sponsored an essay contest designed to spur worldwide discussion of universal share ownership and its chances of lessening Soviet-American tensions (Speiser, 1984). Ward Morehouse, President of the Council on International and Public Affairs, agreed to have his organization administer the contest, for which I donated a $10,000 prize. The contest, which closed on December 31, 1985, brought hundreds of entries from all parts of the United States and many foreign countries. The eventual winner was Professor Jon D. Wisman of the Department of Economics at the American University in Washington, D.C. (formally published, 1988). At the presentation ceremony hosted by the Council, the principal speaker was The Rt. Hon. David Howell, Conservative Member of Parliament and formerly a minister of the Thatcher cabinet, who has written and lectured widely on the need for the broadening of both work and ownership. The overall quality of the entries was so high that the Council decided to publish a collection of the papers, edited by Professor Kenneth B. Taylor of the Department of Economics at Villanova University (Taylor, 1988).

In order for readers of this book to understand the terminology used in the essays that follow, it is necessary to give some of the history of the concept of universal share ownership as expressed in prior writings which were available to the contestants. The term USOP (Universal Share Ownership Plan) was coined in the 1986 publication, *The USOP Handbook*. In that book, I described a particular form of USOP, previously called "SuperStock," and which I renamed the "Kitty Hawk Model" of USOP. SuperStock, derived loosely from Kelso's Financed Capitalist Plan with considerable modification, and Kitty Hawk Model or KHM are used interchangeably by the contestants, depending upon which name they like better or which previous book they happened to read. SuperStock and KHM are one and the same plan which I will describe briefly below. SuperStock/KHM is one possible way of approaching the design of a USOP. It is not a finished or ideal plan, but it does present a framework for discussion because it demonstrates many of the problems and potentials of USOP.

Before our brief review of SuperStock/KHM and other possible forms of USOP, it is worth noting that there are three basic types of plans for broadening share ownership. Plans in the first group, which we shall call Type A, are based on the employment relationship. Type B plans are based on savings enhanced by tax relief, and Type C covers the broadest plans, opening ownership to all citizens regardless of their employment status and their savings or lack thereof.

Type A Ownership: Based on Employment

Ownership of a piece of the action by a firm's employees is the simplest and most attractive method of broadening ownership, but as noted above, it is not possible to spread capital ownership broadly among the people through employee ownership. It brings no benefit to the unemployed, the very poor, and those who are not fortunate enough to be long-term employees of continuously successful private companies. Therefore, the great majority of Americans who need the help that share ownership can bring are simply not in a position to achieve it through employment. Nevertheless, it is important to study the great progress that has been made through employee share ownership recently; it has started the process of broadening ownership and it can serve as a foundation for the Type C plans needed to achieve real diffusion.

Building a Bridge from ESOP to USOP

Seven million Americans are already owners of employee shares, and ESOP receives across-the-board political support. How, then, can we build on this foundation to achieve our goal of universal share ownership?

One possibility arises out of the principal shortcoming of employee ownership. ESOPs and similar plans have been criticized because they tend to put all the workers' eggs in one basket. It is not uncommon for an ESOP to be substituted for a pension plan, thus making the retirement nest egg of the employees, as well as their living standards during their working lives, dependent on the financial performance of the employing company. Commentators from the political left, right, and center have pointed out this shortcoming. USOP could overcome this problem by providing that under certain conditions, ESOP shares could be converted to USOP shares. This would give employees the lifetime security that is missing in the ESOP-type scheme. It would also make employee ownership much more saleable to employees, for then employers could bargain for the replacement of pension plans by ESOPs without endangering the workers' future security.

The convertibility feature has two important facets. First, it serves as a safety net for those employees who are depending upon ESOP shares in their retirement years; and second, it is a potential means of getting the best out of ESOPs by limiting convertibility to those plans that contain the features most likely to enhance worker productivity and security.

Employee Convertible Debentures

The idea of Employee Convertible Debentures occurred to me after reading the winning essay in the 1984-85 contest submitted by Professor Jon Wisman of American University. He suggested that we can accomplish for employee share ownership what the FHA mortgage loan guarantee program accomplished for home ownership, if we use long-term credit guaranteed by the federal government (Wisman, 1988).

With access to such credit guarantees, corporate employees could use the annual interest received on convertible debentures to offset the interest (and eventually the principal) required to purchase a 30-year convertible debenture without any down payment. For example, a $1,000 30-year debenture, carrying a 7 per cent interest rate, would pay $70 per year in interest to the holder. If corporate employees were enabled to buy that debenture through a 30-year government-guaranteed loan at an interest rate of 7 per cent, the employee would have to make annual principal payments of $33.33. Since these annual principal payments would reduce the unpaid balance, the amount of interest that the employee would have to pay would decline from $70 in the first year all the way down to $2.34 in the 30th year. Over that span, the employee would receive interest of $2,100 and would pay out interest of $1,084, leaving the employee with a net interest profit of $1,016, a sum sufficient (before income taxes) to defray the $1,000 principal cost of the debenture.

Use of the leverage created by such a government-guaranteed loan program could enable corporations to offer a very favorable capital acquisition program to their employees. Since these Employee Convertible Debentures (ECDs) could be convertible into the common stock of the corporation during the entire debenture term of 30 years, each employee could profit by converting if the common stock price rose above the original conversion price at any time during the 30-year period. Convertible debentures sold in the securities markets usually have a conversion ratio fixed at about 20 per cent above market, so that if the company's shares are selling for $20 at the time the debenture is issued, the conversion price will be about $25. The ECD legislation creating the government loan guarantees could require the eligible corporations to fix the conversion ratio at the market price at the time of debenture issuance, or it could allow a premium of up to 25 per cent if this proved necessary to make the program sufficiently appealing to the corporations. In either case, each employee would have a continuous day-to-day interest in the company's stock price and the performance that underlies that price. Therefore, ECDs should have all of the motivating factors present in ESOPs with the added incentive that the employee is actually buying the securities with his or her own principal payments and that he or she becomes a debenture holder (and potentially a common stockholder) while active on the job, instead of having to wait for retirement as is the case in ESOP and other post-employment benefit programs.

I see many potential advantages for ECDs. *The employer companies* gain access to a cheap method of financing made possible by long-term government loan guarantees, and at the same time can increase employee motivation and create a new community of interest with the work force. The companies also eliminate the sales commissions (usually 2 to 3 per cent) charged by underwriters who sell debentures to the public. For these reasons, I do not believe that any tax relief for the companies issuing ECDs would be necessary or appropriate. *For employees,* ECDs represent a low-risk method of getting a piece of the action. Over a 40-year work expectancy, each employee could buy as much as $40,000 worth of ECDs on very attractive terms. Many of them would have the opportunity to make substantial capital gains by converting at times of peak common stock prices. *For the nation,* ECDs would represent a method of increasing savings, spurring productivity, and moving toward a community of interest among capital, labor, and government. This is the basic formula for economic renaissance advocated by Jack Kemp, Henry Kissinger, Kevin Philips, and Lester Thurow, among many others.

Type B Ownership: Savings-Based

Type B plans are typified by the IRA (Individual Retirement Account) enacted by Congress in 1982. There is also the Keogh Plan, a form of qualified retirement plan governing self-employed individuals, who may contribute up to 15 per cent of net earnings to a maximum of $7,500 per year on a tax-deductible basis.

Plans to stimulate the purchase of shares through tax relief have some merit but obviously they benefit only those who have savings and so they really represent tax benefits for the sector of our society that is well off compared to those in poverty. Nevertheless, such plans contain some elements which could be worked into the ideal plan for universal capital ownership, especially since we want to stimulate savings, and so we must study them for that purpose.

Type C Ownership: Universal Share Ownership Plans (USOPs)

We now come to the type of expanded ownership which is at once the most difficult and potentially the most rewarding: Universal Share Ownership Plans (or Citizen Share Ownership Plans, as they are known in Great Britain).

The first form of USOP we will examine is one designed by me derived from the writings of Louis Kelso and the ideas of others, including the Joint Economic Committee of Congress. Originally, I called this plan SuperStock. More modestly, I have also called it the Kitty Hawk Plan of universal share ownership in recognition of its primitive nature and in the hope that it will eventually soar like the invention of the Wright brothers. I propose it as one possible starting point in the search for an ideal USOP, rather than as *the* ideal plan itself.

The SuperStock (or Kitty Hawk) Model

Is there anything inherent in capitalism that would prevent us from spreading ownership of the means of production to all of our people? You will search in vain for any such restriction in the Constitution or laws of the U.S. Yet most economists, even liberals, have not opened their minds to such a concept. There is no reason why capitalism cannot function when the means of production are owned by the majority rather than a minority. In fact, if we could find a way to open ownership of the means of production to all citizens, we could make our economic system consistent with our political democracy and our concept of fairness.

One possible way to make capitalism work for everyone is the plan I call SuperStock. Its purpose is to spread ownership of newly formed capital through society, enabling the non-capitalist 94 per cent to derive income from direct participation in capitalism. Because its purpose is to spread newly formed capital, there would be no confiscation of wealth and no need for new taxes.

The Hidden Reservoir

There is a vast hidden reservoir of unowned wealth in this country, in the form of the *new capital* created each year by American business. This hidden reservoir of wealth could be the source of a substantial amount of income for those Americans who presently own little or no capital. (Capital, in this context, does not refer to money, but rather to the plant and equipment that companies build or buy every year.)

This new capital is what financial people call "self-liquidating." It is designed to *pay for itself* out of the increased profits flowing from expanded production. So, for example, the cost of constructing a new automobile factory will be covered by the sale of new cars rolling off the factory's assembly line. In theory, then, anyone could become an owner of this new capital—*if* he or she were extended the necessary credit with which to purchase shares of stock in the companies creating the capital. In practice, however, credit for the purchase of stock or other income-producing capital is available only to those who already have savings or other holdings—those who can provide good collateral for loans.

In 1986, American business invested over $300 billion in the construction and purchase of new plant and equipment. Under our present system, 95 per cent of these new capital expenditures are paid for by a combination of debt (loans or bonds) and internal funds; 5 per cent is financed through the issuance of new common stock. The main vice of this system is that it perpetuates the overconcentration of capital ownership. Billions of dollars are kept bottled up in the corporations for capital expenditures. Wealthy stockholders believe this practice serves their interests, for they would otherwise have to pay income taxes on substantial dividend income. They prefer to have this money remain in corporate coffers where the value of their holdings can increase untaxed.

Even the 5 per cent of capital expenditures that is paid for by the issuance of new stock can be owned only by those who have cash savings or credit. As long as this system remains intact, so too will the process of concentrating ownership of the means of production in the hands of a mere 6 per cent of the population. Expanding employee ownership (Type A) will not reduce this concentration significantly. There is, however, nothing sacred or immutable about this system. It is simply one method—and not necessarily the best method—of financing a modern economy.

Outline of the SuperStock/KHM Plan

SuperStock is one possible way of reversing this overconcentration. It is designed to make stock ownership in America's 2,000 leading corporations available to everyone through a system that would funnel ownership of new capital directly to the 50 million families or households that now own little or no capital. To understand how it would work, let us take as a case in point the fictitious Peerless Pizza Parlors Corporation, which we shall imagine as one of the nation's 2,000 leading corporations. Let us assume that Peerless is building a new $10 million plant to meet increased demand for its new pizza oven. Thus, Peerless is creating $10 million worth of new capital *that is not presently owned by anyone* and that will *pay for itself* over time through the increased production and sale of pizza pies.

Under our present corporate system, Peerless would finance such an expansion primarily through internal funds and debt, which automatically funnels ownership of 95 per cent of the new capital into the hands of the current Peerless shareholders. At the heart of the present system, then, is a mechanism for producing capital ownership that has been employed for centuries by wealthy individuals and businesses: *long-term credit.* At the heart of SuperStock is the same mechanism, but with one key difference: now long-term credit will be extended to the non-capitalists.

Assume you are one of the non-capitalists. Here is how SuperStock would make you a capitalist:

Financing new capital. Under the new federal legislation adopting SuperStock, Peerless will not pay for its new plant through internal funds or debt. Rather, it will be induced or required to finance its capital growth by issuing $10 million worth of a special type of stock to be known as SuperStock shares. This stock will not be available to the 6 per cent of Americans who already own a substantial number of shares. Instead, you and the rest of the non-capitalist 94 per cent will be able to acquire a given number of SuperStock shares.

How do you pay for the SuperStock shares? You do not. A loan will be arranged to provide the money needed to pay Peerless for the stock— and eventually the stock will pay for itself out of its own earnings.

The loan. The SuperStock legislation will establish a government-guaranteed long-term loan program. In effect, *you* will be using the credit power of Peerless to acquire shares of its stock—just as Peerless now uses its credit power to acquire further capital ownership for its present shareholders.

A bank loan of $10 million will be arranged to provide Peerless with the entire cost of the new plant and Peerless will then issue $10 million worth of stock. But the loan will not be owed by you or by Peerless. It will be owed by the SuperStock fund. Until the loan has been repaid, the Peerless shares earmarked for your account will be held in escrow by the bank that made the $10 million loan.

Repayment. The SuperStock legislation requires Peerless and the rest of the 2,000 participating companies to pay out all their earnings as dividends (except those reserves actually needed to run the company). It also exempts Peerless from the federal corporate income taxes on those earnings. Thus, as Peerless begins to realize higher profits from the output of the pizza machines made in the new factory, these profits will be turned into higher dividends that are used to pay for the Super-Stock shares issued to you.

For a number of years, these dividends will be paid directly to the bank until such time as it has recouped its $10 million loan plus interest. Then you become the outright owner of your SuperStock shares and you will receive all future dividends directly. Thus, the new SuperStock system ensures that Peerless's $10 million worth of new capital is owned by those who previously had no real access to capital ownership.

The 2,000 Participating Companies

I have oversimplified SuperStock to give you a bird's-eye view from the standpoint of a single company, Peerless Pizza. Actually, it is designed as a group plan, involving at the start America's 2,000 leading companies, such as General Motors, IBM, ATT, Xerox, and Exxon. These are the companies that every year create most of America's $384 billion of new capital (which I rounded off to $300 billion above to represent the expenditures of these major companies).

To pay for this capital, each company would issue shares of its stock at market value. Each year these shares would be pooled in a sort of mutual fund with each company contributing to the pool the number of shares needed to pay for its new capital expenditures. Shares would be parcelled out to those families and households eligible for the Super-Stock program. Every SuperStockholder would receive a piece of every participating company; there would be no big losers if one of the 2,000 companies did poorly. Eventually, we should be able to include smaller companies in the SuperStock system. But we begin with our 2,000 largest successful companies because we are trying to plug our neediest people into the strongest sector of our economy.

This brief outline of the SuperStock plan leaves many questions unanswered. For example, what is the role of government? Who should the recipients of SuperStock shares be, and what schedule of priorities should govern their choice? Should there be restrictions on voting and transfer of SuperStock shares? What effect would such a program have on the work ethic? How can we arrange for SuperStock shareholders to earn their shares so that this will not be considered a welfare handout? Should the 2,000 corporations be forced to participate or can they be induced to do so voluntarily? All of these questions, together with the possible effects of SuperStock on the economy and various interest groups, are discussed in detail in *The USOP Handbook* (Speiser, 1986, Chapters 3, 4, 6, 7). The economic feasibility of SuperStock is also discussed (Chapter 5), and the findings of a 1977 Brookings Institute Seminar on this subject, as well as articles by Professors Paul Davidson and Robert Lekachman, are reprinted in the Appendix.

These questions and options raised by the outline of the SuperStock plan form the basis for much of the discussion in the following essays. It is interesting to note how the three prize-winning American essays handled some of these questions. (The three essays by Professor David A. Burress, Professor Kenneth B. Taylor, and the Reverend John A. Sedlak are reprinted respectively in Chapters 2, 3, and 4.) Each used Super-Stock/KHM as a starting point and then made major modifications and innovations.

Burress, Taylor, and Sedlak agree that use of the $300 billion reservoir of new corporate capital additions is feasible. They also agree that any USOP program should be implemented gradually, and that eventually it should be used as a substitute for welfare and Social Security. As a concession to attract corporate participation, all three propose that the corporate income tax should be eliminated. They further propose that after the USOP is installed, profits should be allocated between the USOP shareholders and the regular shareholders, and that all earnings except those needed for business operations should be paid out as dividends. Taylor and Sedlak agree that the program should include the 2,000 leading corporations. Taylor adds all regulated utilities and Sedlak adds all publicly-held companies. Burress specifies a voluntary program from which participating companies can elect to exit at any time.

Taylor and Sedlak emphasize performance of public service work to earn USOP shares, with Taylor specifying use of the "Shareholders In America" approach (explained below). Taylor and Sedlak agree that the federal government should guarantee the loans needed to pay for the USOP shares, whereas Burress, believing that such a guarantee would be dangerous, specifies that the banks make their own decisions on such loans. Burress provides some anti-inflation measures that are not mentioned by Taylor or Sedlak. Burress is also concerned with the response of corporate management to the plan. Taylor mentions this concern but feels that it is not feasible at this point to determine that response.

All three authors are concerned with the political attractiveness of the plan. Burress treats this in detail, and Sedlak addresses it indirectly by concentrating on the earning of shares by recipients. Sedlak alone deals with the moral aspects of work and the need for a government-guaranteed-employment opportunity, with the full-time parenting of children below age 19 counting as employment for the purpose of earning USOP shares.

As to voting of USOP shares, Burress and Sedlak say yes, while Taylor says no. On transferability, Sedlak says no, Taylor opts for partial transferability, and Burress does not treat the subject. As to inheritance, Taylor and Sedlak agree that USOP shares should not pass through inheritance, whereas Burress is silent on that point.

In addition to the SuperStock/KHM model, the essay contestants had several other suggested models to work with, all of which were described in *The USOP Handbook* and are summarized below.

The National Mutual Fund

The National Mutual Fund (NMF) was introduced by James S. Albus in *Peoples' Capitalism* (Albus, 1976). Dr. Albus, an internationally recognized authority on industrial robotics with the National Bureau of Standards, proposes creation of NMF as a semi-private in-

vestment company. NMF would use money borrowed from the Federal
Reserve to make stock and bond purchases from private industry. This
increased availability of investment funds would stimulate the economy
and increase productivity. Profits from these investments would be paid
to the general public in the form of dividends, making every adult citizen
a capitalist to that extent. Albus estimates that per capita income from
the NMF could reach $6,000 to $10,000 a year within 25 years, assuming reasonably successful investment of the money available.

The National Dividend Plan

The National Dividend Plan was first proposed by Florida in-
dustrialist John H. Perry, Jr. in his book, *The National Dividend* (Perry,
1964). Perry has refined the plan during the last 20 years and has spent
over $7 million promoting it. The thrust of the plan is to take the col-
lections from the corporate income tax and place them in a National
Dividend Trust Fund. From this fund, a yearly check would be issued
to every registered voter once the federal budget is balanced. These
dividends would be tax-free. Every year that the budget fell out of
balance and into deficit the money in the National Dividend Trust Fund
would be used to reduce the deficit instead of being distributed to the
registered voters. This would give every voter a vested interest in resist-
ing federal deficits—no balanced budget, no national dividend check.

Privatization

Privatization—the sale of government-owned assets and services
that could be owned and operated privately—has come into vogue
throughout the world during the 1980s. This movement was led by the
conservative British government of Margaret Thatcher, which in its first
six years returned 12 major state-owned companies to the private sector, including British Aerospace, Brit Oil, Jaguar cars, and British
Telecom. After France turned out the socialist Mitterand government,
it too privatized many formerly nationalized companies. Other nations
in Europe and Africa have followed suit. Unfortunately, this has been
done by selling shares in the public market, instead of using these nationalized companies as reservoirs for spreading ownership by distributing shares to all citizens. The latter course—using privatization as
a means of creating universal share ownership—is favored by Samuel
Brittan, chief economic commentator for London's *Financial Times*
(Brittan, 1983, 1984, 1985), on the grounds that these companies are

actually owned by all the people, and distributing shares in them is much more equitable than reducing taxes of the wealthy by selling the shares for the account of the national treasury. Under Thatcher's version, privatization serves only the cause of efficiency; under Brittan's, it could serve equity as well. While the United States has no exact counterpart of the British-nationalized companies, it does have "national assets" (public lands, the postal system, etc.) that some American conservatives believe would be better operated by the private sector.

Consumer Stock Ownership Plans (CSOPs)

Louis and Patricia Kelso in their 1986 book, *Democracy and Economic Power: Extending the ESOP Revolution,* proposed that public utilities and other large consumer service organizations should issue shares to all of their customers, as a means of broadening capital ownership and also creating a new source of funding for improvement of service.

Shareholders In America, Inc. (SIA)

I organized Shareholders In America, Inc. as a for-profit Delaware stock corporation for two purposes: to lend a touch of realism to the essay contests, and also to provide a vehicle by which American business could attempt to solve some of our serious economic and social problems without government intervention. In the following discussion, I use SIA merely as a symbol for an unfinished idea. Anyone is free to appropriate all or part of the idea.

SIA would offer share ownership and dividends, in addition to paid employment, as incentives for the unemployed and disadvantaged to work their way out of welfare. All shares of SIA would be owned and voted by its worker-owners; no shares would be held by investors. Shares in SIA would be available only to those who are willing to work at relatively low salaries, doing whatever is needed to improve their own communities and, ultimately, society and the economy. No new government funds would be needed to launch or sustain SIA, although it could draw upon whatever government resources are currently available to all private businesses.

Successful business companies would play a major role by establishing a stream of profits upon which SIA could be built through set-asides, subcontracts, and patronage. For example, without increasing their costs beyond the amounts presently paid for such necessary services, IBM could volunteer to engage SIA for some janitorial and trucking services and Philip Morris could award SIA a contract for a small percentage of its printing and painting requirements. This concept is already working, as evidenced by the $9 *billion* annual patronage organized by the National Minority Supplier Development Council (NMSDC). Business could also lend the services of top management at the outset, giving way to worker-owners of SIA as soon as they are ready to take over.

SIA affords the business community a chance to prove that there is a lot more to capitalism than greed and exploitation. By providing the poorest segment of our society with the opportunity to become working capitalists, business can advance capitalism to a much higher stage of development as a moral, humane, and effective system that does not need to be sustained by the huge doses of welfare transfers that we have been feeding it for the last 50 years. Instead of welfare capitalism, which Harvard economist Joseph Schumpeter described as "capitalism in an oxygen tent," we can move up to universally shared capitalism without government funding.

Set-asides, subcontracts, and patronage by the granting of business opportunities could start SIA's life blood flowing. Eventually, SIA could develop its own captive market to serve the needs of its worker-shareholders and the communities in which they live. This could be done along lines similar to the producer-cooperative and consumer-cooperative movements with the additional bonus of stock ownership for employees. The strong stream of profits flowing from the set-aside and subcontracting programs would furnish a sound basis for successful cooperatives, which often flounder if started without such a foundation.

Further details on SIA will be found in the green supplement to *The USOP Handbook* (Speiser, 1986).

Summary of Potential Reservoirs for USOPs

As we have seen, there are at least half a dozen potential reservoirs which could be tapped to provide universal (Type C) share ownership:

(1) Capital additions of major companies, as featured in the Super-Stock/Kitty Hawk Model of USOP. This is probably the deepest ownership reservoir of an industrial economy.

(2) New stocks and bonds to be issued by American business (as in Albus's National Mutual Fund), which would go into the modernization of business to increase productivity.

(3) Corporate profits, which are the smallest and most difficult reservoir to tap because there are already many claims on them. Perry's National Dividend Plan is an example.

(4) Privatization: government-owned assets and services that could be owned and operated privately.

(5) The credit power of major companies, as used now in leveraged buyouts.

(6) Consumer payments to public utilities, as in Kelso's Consumer Stock Ownership Plan.

(7) Extension of the USOP principle beyond shares of corporate stock to other assets, such as public lands, natural resources, privately owned real estate, and art objects. This is an undeveloped idea which has been proposed by British Nobel Laureate James E. Meade (Meade, 1984).

(8) A requirement for companies to issue new shares without any payment, the shares to be allocated to the new USOP shareholders. This has been suggested in Great Britain, but would not be supported by the American consensus because it requires dilution of present ownership.

These reservoirs could be tested independently, or a program could be designed to test several of them on small scales. For example, we could start with these component parts:

- A limited experimental SuperStock plan, starting with about 5 per cent of the annual $300 billion in business capital additions, on a voluntary basis, with such incentives as credits against the corporate income tax for those companies that volunteer. The goal would be to move up from 5 per cent to 20 per cent of business capital additions within a year or two.

- Testing Shareholders In America (SIA) units for the jobless in five or six cities and experimental integration of SIA shares with USOP shares.

- A 5 per cent experimental version of the Albus National Mutual Fund with controls to test for productivity increases.

- Leveraged buyouts of five or six companies, using the companies' own credit power as collateral for self-liquidating loans, with share ownership to be distributed to disadvantaged citizens who are given the opportunity to earn these shares, preferably by performing public service work. Community organizations could become the conduits for leveraged buyouts that would pass ownership of local business operations to disadvantaged neighborhood families.

- A voluntary experimental program for 1,000 companies of Employee Convertible Debentures to expand worker owner- ship and to apply the FHA financing principle of long-term credit to worker ownership.

- Privatization of government-owned assets on a small test scale, with shares in the privatized companies to be issued to all citizens or to all disadvantaged citizens.

- Testing of Kelso's Consumer Stock Ownership Plan with the customers of 25 public utilities.

- Making ESOP shares convertible into USOP shares on a small test scale.

- Testing the Mondragon cooperative concept with small start- up businesses in several states, both with and without use of SIA shares.

Progress in the difficult area of Type C ownership must be measured now in intellectual terms. We cannot expect real political or material progress until we have done the intellectual spadework required to move ahead from the primitive Kitty Hawk Model of universal share ownership. I believe that these essay contests are providing that intel- lectual spadework and that they will be even more effective as future contestants draw upon the innovations contributed by the earlier es- sayists.

The present plan is to run these contests every two years, allowing the intervening year for study of the papers submitted and publication of succeeding volumes of collected essays. The growth of the USOP concept is reflected by changes in the essay topic. In the 1984-85 com- petition, the topic was the use of broadened ownership as a possible means of reducing tension between the United States and the Soviet Union. The 1986 competitions, which are the subject of this volume, dealt with the simple proposition of spreading capital ownership broad- ly without confiscation or increased taxation. The 1988 competition will go a step further, combining the concepts of work and ownership with the following topic:

How can we use broadened share ownership to alleviate the problems of unemployment, under-employment, and poverty- level wages?

Status of Type C Ownership in the
United States and Great Britain

It appears that the broadening of capital ownership naturally evolves through the three stages of Types A, B, and C. Employee ownership is broadly accepted in the United States, politically as well as theoretically. It has made great strides in the past ten years, largely as the result of tax benefits enacted in the legislation introduced by Senator Russell Long (Democrat, Louisiana), who is truly the father of ESOP. Type B ownership, is also well developed in the United States, largely through the blossoming of the Individual Retirement Account (IRA) during the 1980s. Therefore, the next step is theoretical and political development of Type C—universal or citizen—ownership. So far there has been little or no political interest in Type C ownership, but as evidenced by the essays you are about to read, there is strong academic and intellectual interest.

In Great Britain, because there is a strong socialist movement in the form of the Labour Party (which has actually socialized ownership of important segments of the means of production during its time in power), there is a keen political awareness of the desirability of sharing ownership as broadly as possible. However, since Types A and B (employee and tax-savings) are in relatively early stages of development, the intellectual and academic development of Type C ownership has been lagging, appearing to need Types A and B as a base. In 1984, the leader of the Social Democratic Party, Dr. David Owen, in speaking at the annual party conference, advocated free distribution of shares of the nationalized companies and future distribution of the equity of large private companies to all British citizens. Unfortunately, Dr. Owen found himself in the position of General Patton—making a bold foray but outrunning his supply lines. He appointed a working party to develop a specific program for putting his plan into effect. But after two years of debate, the working party was unable to produce a plan that would merit the party's endorsement, and thus a golden opportunity to inject citizen share ownership into the 1987 election campaign was lost.

In my opinion, this makes the present essay competitions even more important. The political and social need for citizen share ownership has been demonstrated. Now we must develop specific plans which will be worthy of the laudable vision of Dr. Owen and other political leaders in Great Britain. And we must have such plans ready when American political leaders get around to recognizing the importance of citizen share ownership.

Format of This Book

Following this introductory chapter, the book is divided into Part I—The North American Essays (Chapters 2 to 12), and Part II—The British Essays (Chapters 13 to 21).

The prize-winning North American essays will be found in chronological order in Chapters 2, 3, and 4. The next eight chapters (Chapters 5 to 12) each contain a complete essay. Each of these chapters begins with a brief editor's note, followed by an abstract of the essay prepared by its author, and concluding with the full text of the essay.

Notes and references mentioned in each essay will be found at the end of the chapter in which the particular essay appears, although, in some cases, obtaining full bibliographical details was not always possible. (At the very end of the book, there is a bibliography of references on the broadening of capital ownership prepared by me. The references in this first chapter will be found in this general bibliography.) Chapter 12 is a brief summary of other North American essays which contain important ideas.

The three winning British essays are reproduced in full in Chapters 13, 14, and 15. Chapters 16 to 20 each contain the full text of a British essay, using the same format as that described above for the North American essays. And, finally, Chapter 21 contains a round-up of ideas excerpted from other British essays.

The Sponsoring Organizations

The Council on International and Public Affairs (CIPA), organized in 1954, is a non-profit research, educational, and publishing group that promotes the study of problems and affairs of the United States and other nations. To select the three prize-winning essays, CIPA president Ward Morehouse recruited more than a dozen trustees of CIPA to read all of the essays submitted. The final selections were made by a committee of the trustees under Mr. Morehouse's supervision.

The Wider Share Ownership Council (WSOC), organized in 1958, from the outset has worked for extension of share ownership for the people generally, as well as employee share ownership within companies. It enjoys support from all political sectors. Among the leading organizers of the WSOC were Toby Low (now Lord Aldington), Maurice Macmillan of the Conservative Party, and Lord Lever of the Labour Party. Reflecting its impartial character, the WSOC has four deputy chairmen, three of whom are chosen from each of the three major political parties. Selection of the three winning British essays was made by a judging panel consisting of Lord Harris of High Cross, Director of the Institute of Economic Affairs in London; Sir Robert Shone, CBE; and Samuel Brittan, economics correspondent for the *Financial Times*. Harry Ball-Wilson, WSOC's international liaison officer, was of great assistance in arranging WSOC participation.

Part I

The North American Essays

2

THE SPIRIT OF ST. LOUIS MODEL

by

David A. Burress[1]

Editor's Note: *Professor David A. Burress of the Institute for Public Policy and Business Research, University of Kansas was the North American first-prize winner. Professor Burress earned his Ph.D. in economics at the University of Wisconsin in 1985 with distinction in microeconomic theory. As a research economist at the University of Kansas, he serves as the supervisor of the Kansas Dynamic Input/Output Model. His published papers draw heavily on his practical experience in taxation and educational policy matters.*

His essay demonstrates the kind of searching professional analysis of USOP that is needed to bring its blue-sky aspects down to earth. While it gives an important professional endorsement to the theoretical validity of the basic USOP concept, it is also a sobering appraisal of how much hard work remains to be done.

Professor Burress uses the term "KHM" to refer to the Kitty Hawk Model, a term that I used for the SuperStock model in The USOP Handbook. *He calls his plan the "SSLM" for Spirit of St. Louis Model.*

23

ABSTRACT

Stuart Speiser's "Kitty Hawk Model" (KHM) for achieving a Universal Stock Ownership Plan (USOP) is a clever proposal for redistributing wealth in the United States. The present essay is inspired by several valuable insights contained in KHM. The major contribution of KHM is to identify a new form of property, namely, the right to make new investments in an ongoing corporation. KHM proposes a gradual program for socializing this form of property, while widely distributing ownership of the new wealth generated through the exercise of this right. The political strategy of KHM is based on a coalition of the general public with the professional managers of large corporations, in opposition to the shareholders. The rhetorical justification provided for KHM is based on the language of democratic consensus and the idea of the common good.

While whole-heartedly embracing these general features of KHM, the present essay criticizes the details of KHM's execution, especially in relation to the politically potent idea of efficiency which is favored by American conservatives. In particular, the essay argues that the KHM economic program is likely to lead to inflation, to inefficient investment choices, and to reduced government revenues in the short run. Moreover, the KHM political strategy appears to provide inadequate incentives for enlisting the support of corporation managers. The essay then proposes a number of revisions to the KHM machinery in order to address these problems. The essay emphasizes the importance of voluntary participation by corporations in the USOP investment scheme, the need for monetary policy to control inflationary pressures, the need for competitive allocation of USOP investment, and the need for a specific budgeted amount of total USOP investment.

Introduction: The Love of Flight

In his provocative *Handbook* (1986) for this essay contest, Stuart Speiser described his "Kitty Hawk Model" (KHM) for redistributing wealth in advanced capitalist countries. Like the historical effort to achieve powered flight in a heavier-than-air craft, this was a goal worth dreaming about. He proposed a program for a Universal Share Ownership Plan (USOP) which seems to me very creative in some respects, but severely flawed in other respects. These strong but mixed feelings motivate the revised model which I introduce below; consistently with his aeronautical metaphor, I will call it the Spirit of St. Louis Model, or SSLM. The name is intended to imply that SSLM represents (what I hope to be) a real improvement over KHM. In particular, I will argue that the KHM design did not pay sufficiently close and careful attention to the incentives KHM would create for economic and political actors, nor to the important stress points which would be likely to result in practice. SSLM seeks to identify and correct some of these stresses. On the other hand, KHM introduced some important and original design insights, on which SSLM seeks to build.

I will begin my discussion with an assessment of the strengths of KHM. I will then identify the major economic and political tasks which the KHM program must accomplish, and infer some principles for improving the design of KHM. Next, I will apply those principles to the most critical stress points of the design. I conclude with brief comments on several other interesting questions of design.

The Benchmarks Achieved by KHM

KHM is important for four reasons: it reminds us of a fundamentally important policy question; it proposes a new programmatic approach to that question; it suggests a potentially effective political strategy for implementing that program; and it provides an ideological language, or rather a rhetoric, with which to defend the program and advance the strategy. The policy issue motivating KHM consists in the fundamental tension between economic inequality and democratic equality under advanced capitalism. The programmatic innovation of KHM is a new kind of socialization; KHM would not socialize capital itself, as under conventional socialism, but instead proposes to socialize the right to invest new capital in large-scale enterprises. The political strategy of KHM aims to drive a wedge between the professional managerial class and the wealth-holding class, making a mutual alliance of the voters with the managers, at the expense of the shareholders. The rhetorical defense of KHM is rooted in the language of democratic consensus. I will briefly elaborate each of these points.

(1) *Inequality.* Speiser (correctly, I believe) identifies the struggle between the haves and the have nots, often formulated as a conflict between equity and efficiency, as a primary political issue under capitalism. He also points out some of the reverse links, where inequality can lead to inefficiency, for example, by contributing to criminal behavior, unstable business cycles, non-cooperative behavior on the

job, and involuntary unemployment.

(2) *The right to invest.* Speiser's major conceptual contribution is to identify a new form of socializable wealth. In particular, he points out that no clear ownership has been defined for the right to make new investments; he proposes both to define that right and to socialize it. Since the right has not been clearly articulated in the past, Speiser can claim that this act of social expropriation does not constitute either taxation or confiscation. The point is partly rhetorical, but is also concerned both with law and with strategy. With respect to law, Speiser argues that federal socialization of the right to invest is constitutionally permitted. With respect to strategy, Speiser in effect argues that this method of socialization is sufficiently indirect and gradual so as to disarm the potential opposition.

(3) *Suborning the corporate managers.* Speiser's political strategy implicitly recognizes professional managers of corporations as the dominant political group in the U.S. They rule in the name of the stockholders, but they rule. Speiser's plan forces a wedge between the two groups. The stockholders will suffer indirect damage from the scheme, for reasons analyzed below. But the managers may stand to gain an even more secure and favored position in the economy.

(4) *Consensus politics.* Speiser's goal was to design a plan which appealed or could be sold to the vast majority of voters without outraging any well-organized pressure group. In such a conservative society as the U.S., this is the only possible strategy short of violent revolution by which consciously radical social change can be accomplished. Since I accept his goal, I shall generally attempt in this essay to consider the point of view of conservatives. In other words, I shall attempt to disarm the group which is most likely to oppose USOP. In particular, I shall try to make the kinds of arguments which are favored by conservative and pro-free-market economists.[2]

Ground Test: An Economic Deconstruction of KHM

Let us now consider KHM more closely, viewing it as a piece of economic machinery. To succeed on its own terms, KHM, or any similar plan, must accomplish certain irreducible economic tasks. In the following, I will list these general tasks, and also describe and criticize the corresponding design measures employed by KHM.

(1) USOP must provide for the socialization of (some) new investment. KHM accomplished this by requiring or inducing all major cor-

porations to enroll in an investment plan. All new investment under the plan is socialized. I believe that this portion of KHM can work.

(2) USOP must ensure that social saving occurs and is directed to the new investment. In other words, funds which represent some portion of Gross National Product have to be set aside and directed toward investment owned by the USOP mutual fund. KHM was somewhat vague on how this will occur, but seemed to rely mainly on loans from the central bank. In effect, the Federal Reserve Bank would simply print money and direct it to KHM investment. This scheme amounts to a form of forced social saving. KHM provided that the forced saving may be supplemented with voluntary private saving by households. This portion of the plan is also workable.

(3) USOP must ensure that the new money printed for USOP does not lead to inflation. For this function, KHM proper included no definite machinery. In defense of this design (non-)feature, Speiser quoted Lawrence Klein as stating that creation of new credit for USOP stock purchases need not be inflationary, provided that the resulting investment raised productivity. Most economists would agree with this statement. However, Klein's statement does not resolve the problem. A major part of KHM investment would not create new productivity; it would merely replace the depreciation of old productivity. Moreover, there may be an additional problem if the new source of new credit (i.e., central bank loans) duplicates other sources of new credit already embedded in the economy. Speiser does make two suggestions for dealing with inflation: the plan could be implemented gradually, which would spread out the inflationary pressure over time, or a Tax-based Income Policy (TIP) could be adopted. Both of these ideas have some merit. However, TIP is generally opposed by conservatives and will not lead to a consensus. Moreover, these ideas merely contain inflationary pressure (at best) without really removing it. In my opinion, under KHM the price level would take off faster than the rest of the plan.

(4) Closely related to inflation is the problem of taxes and other government revenues. USOP must find some means to replace or do without whatever government resources it displaces. KHM provides for lost revenues directly in the form of corporate tax breaks, and more subtly in the use of central bank funding (more on this below). In the short run, KHM provides for new revenues only in the form of taxes on the increased dividends resulting from the 100 per cent income payout requirement on participating corporations. In my view, this source is insufficient. In the long run, KHM would replace welfare and part of Social Security. I suspect that these funds may be inadequate to pay all

the costs of KHM. Speiser also argues that KHM will revive the economy and lead to an eventual growth dividend. While I have some sympathy with this claim, I doubt that it will persuade conservatives. Indeed, there is a spirit of something-for-nothing running through much of Speiser's argument, which is unpleasantly reminiscent of the arguments Ronald Reagan used to sell his supply-side tax cut in 1981.

(5) USOP must determine a total amount of new investment for participating corporations, and allocate it among corporations. But KHM was silent on the total amount of investment and vague on its allocation. Speiser states that private banks should issue loans to purchase the new USOP shares and this would lead to some kind of private market control over new investment. However, he does not give a blueprint for any specific machinery. If the central bank simply issued loans to cover all investment desired by corporate managers, then according to textbook theories of managerial behavior, the corporations would over-invest. Moreover, since the private banks receive subsidized loans from the central bank, they would have no particular incentive to restrain investment. Unless this essential equipment is designed and installed, I believe that KHM will fall out of the sky in short order.

(6) USOP must provide for the distribution of shares in the USOP mutual fund to individual citizens. KHM was vague about the exact method of distribution. However, Speiser did discuss several possible ways to distribute the shares. In my view, this is primarily a political problem rather than an economic problem; any of the schemes which Speiser discusses could be made to work.

(7) USOP must maintain or replace the incentives which control individual behavior under capitalism and lead people and businesses to be productive. I believe that this is the weakest part of KHM. KHM is very vague as to exactly how bankers will be induced to reject socially inefficient loans in the face of attractive subsidies from the central bank. It does not explain what will prevent corporations from over-investing. KHM provides that the USOP fund should accept a vast amount of non-voting corporate stock, and then fails to explain how corporate managers can be disciplined for their mistakes. KHM says nothing about how the bureaucrats who run the USOP plan are to be managed and controlled. KHM provides that a fat new source of government funds will pass through the financial markets, but says nothing about what part of these funds will be absorbed non-productively by investment bankers and lawyers. KHM seems in many ways like a blueprint for an economy congested by middlemen.

In summary, I believe that the economy would crash soon after

KHM became airborne.

Why KHM Won't Get Off the Ground[3]

Speiser named his plan after Kitty Hawk, where powered flight first began. The comparison is somewhat overblown. Because it is not yet a working model, KHM is not ready to fly. It is not even a blueprint for a model. As I have already suggested, Speiser left many crucial design details unspecified; in many areas he simply raised some questions, or listed some design considerations. (The SSLM model I present below will be similarly underspecified; I cannot accomplish in 5,000 words what Speiser could not accomplish in 50,000. I will, however, attempt to list the most critical areas of the design and then specify them.)

A deeper criticism is that some of Speiser's ideas, even where well specified in economic terms, seem to me unlikely to work politically. First, economic design flaws of the sort I analyzed above cannot be concealed in a project of this magnitude; any existing design flaws are likely to cause substantial opposition to the project. Second, which is my major concern in this section, KHM does not completely accomplish Speiser's twin goals of suborning the managers and creating a rhetorical consensus. That is, KHM will be opposed both by corporate managers and by free-market conservatives.

From the managerial point of view, KHM will seem high in risk and perhaps somewhat low in potential rewards. The most objectionable feature of KHM is that the corporation has no means to escape from the USOP plan if things go sour. (The plan would be even more objectionable to managers if enrollment were made compulsory.) But what could go sour? Well, USOP investment funds might dry up; or the price of investment under the USOP plan might eventually be higher than outside it; or the USOP bureaucrats might find some ways to throw their weight around. The major reward the plan can offer managers is a lower price and increased availability of investment after the plan is adopted than before (see note 8 at the end of this chapter for a definition of the price of investment). A secondary reward might be provided by the built-in stabilizer effect of KHM. In other words, some managers may believe that KHM will smooth out swings in investment and consumption, and thereby make the manager's job easier. Taken as a package deal, KHM will not inspire very intense managerial support. The package needs to be sweetened. One possible sweetener suggested by Speiser would be to design KHM in such a way as to impede corporate take-overs. However, this approach may be socially perverse because it removes an important market discipline on inefficient managers. In SSLM, I will propose voluntarism as the major sweetener.

From the point of view of free-market conservatives, the rhetoric of KHM is unacceptable. It violates the obvious maxim, "There Ain't No Such Thing As a Free Lunch," and it pays no attention to individual incentives and market efficiency. Since most conservatives have no great desire to reduce inequality, there is little chance that they can be enlisted to support the major goal of any USOP plan.[4] However, some conservatives can be convinced to support USOP by arguments based on efficiency. Among these arguments are Milton Friedman's idea that the 100 per cent payout rule would lead to better market discipline on corporate managers; the argument that USOP stabilizes the economy automatically; and the argument that USOP can help reduce crime. Other conservatives cannot be enlisted, but they can be disarmed if the USOP design takes due care not to promote inefficiency. In SSLM, I will try to show how efficiency concerns can be addressed.

Some Recycled Spare Parts from KHM

Despite my criticisms of KHM, many of the features either proposed in KHM or suggested by Speiser without recommendation seem entirely serviceable. In particular, the following provisions have substantial merit and in my opinion should be adopted:

(1) Enrollment of corporations in the USOP plan should be voluntary. This provision is absolutely essential, so as to disarm the potential opposition of current corporate managers to adoption of a USOP plan. It will also tend to reduce the opposition of existing shareholders. Moreover, it is socially desirable since it sets up a market competition between participating and non-participating corporations. If the USOP plan turns out to be either ill-designed or ill-administered, then non-participating corporations have an opportunity to demonstrate their superiority in the marketplace. In other words, socialization of investment rights under any USOP should be subjected to some kind of market discipline. The market can provide an important check and balance against the kind of economic blight we have seen in the Eastern Block countries, which is widely believed to result from their monopolistic socialization of the means of production. Finally, voluntarism is consistent with an experimental and gradual transition to a USOP plan.

(2) The corporate income tax should be completely abolished for participating corporations. This incentive is needed to secure a substantial degree of participation in the plan.

(3) Subsidized private bank credit should be available, but only for participating corporations. Not only is this an incentive for participation but also part of the means of socialization of new investment. Moreover, the use of private bank credit maintains a traditional check on the economic rationality of new investment, provided that the bankers have appropriate incentives to reject unwise loans. (I say more on this subject below.) Finally, the use of private banks is needed to disarm the potential opposition of existing bankers.

(4) New corporate stock should be issued and used as collateral for the bank credit and the loan paid off out of its dividends. The bank exercises all voting rights to the stock, but may not sell the stock without consent of the USOP mutual fund. (The bank may resell the loan note and collateral rights to another bank, however.)

(5) All other means of investment finance should be forbidden for participating corporations. In particular, retained earnings and new private stock subscriptions are forbidden. That is, all operating income of the corporation is paid out as dividends.[5]

(6) Full ownership of the stock should revert to the USOP mutual fund after the loan is amortized. This completes the act of socialization of new investment.

(7) Subsidization of bank loans should be accomplished by means of loans from the Federal Reserve, or government central bank, at a low discount rate. In effect, the government simply prints new money and loans it out. However, the private banks are also free to obtain part or all of their loan funds from private savers. The portion of funds provided by the central bank constitutes a form of forced social saving. I will explain in a later section how this can be accomplished without inflationary consequences.

(8) The USOP fund should never hold more than 49 per cent of the stock of a single participating corporation. The point of this provision is to maintain a substantial degree of private market control over the corporation. This provides some degree of additional protection against bureaucratic excesses by the USOP fund. It also reassures existing shareholders that they will not be forced out of the market. However, this provision also has the effect of insuring that the USOP plan will never hold a majority of the national stock of corporate capital. In the long run, most of the capital stock of participating corporations not held by the USOP fund, will be held by institutional investors (mainly retirement funds). Whether or not this long-run pattern of stock ownership is desirable is a valid subject for future debate, but that debate need not be resolved before a USOP plan has been adopted.

(9) Participation in the USOP plan should be restricted to no more than 75 per cent of the corporations, holding no more than 75 per cent of the public assets, on a first-come, first-served basis. The point of this restriction is to ensure continued competition from non-USOP corporations, as a market check on USOP.

(10) The USOP fund should be specifically precluded from pursuing any extraneous social policy goals (such as pollution abatement, investment in foreign countries, or regional disinvestment), except under the direct orders of outside government agencies. It is the job of Congress, not of USOP, to set the social policy agenda. USOP is not an agency which is well suited to carrying out policy decisions on questions other than the redistribution of capital ownership.

The Spirit of St. Louis Model[6]

In this section, I will propose some of the important new economic machinery that is needed. This essential machinery, plus the recycled parts from KHM, will be referred to as the Spirit of St. Louis Model or SSLM. I necessarily restrict my attention here to only the most critical subsystems of the USOP plan; other subsystems must wait for another essay.

(1) The private banks should be given no default guarantees for SSLM loans. If the income from shares held in collateral proves insufficient to repay the loan, then the cost is borne by the bank. The bank must protect itself against this eventuality by several steps: (a) by holding a balanced portfolio of loans so that occasional losses are simply a normal cost of business to be offset against other gains; (b) by charging a rate of interest which is sufficiently higher than the central bank discount rate so as to provide a margin of reserve against loses; and (c) by purchasing insurance against catastrophic losses. The point of this provision is to maintain the usual incentives for bankers to prudently review the economic wisdom of the investment plans they fund.

(2) The entire income of a participating corporation would be pooled and then distributed to old shareholders and new SSLM-owned shares equally. It is unrealistic to believe that the income from new investment can be cleanly separated from the income from old investment. The attempt to do so would create an accounting and bureaucratic nightmare.[7]

(3) After giving due notice (say, two years), corporations should have the right to exit from the plan, which will greatly increase the attractiveness of participation to the corporation. If things turn sour, the

corporation can get out again without suffering unacceptable damage. The right of exit also creates a strong market control on the SSLM bureaucracy.

(4) The new stock issued to the SSLM plan should have the same voting rights as the old stock. If the voting rights differ, then the market values will also differ, and this, in combination with the provision for exit from the plan, would offer management an opportunity to manipulate the SSLM loans for the advantage of the old shareholders. It is also important to retain voting rights because as a result of the 49 per cent ownership limitation, the SSLM fund sometimes must sell some of its stock on the private market. Finally, the SSLM fund will need to exercise its voting rights in order to prevent management from ignoring its interests (for example, by paying itself too high salaries), just like any other shareholder.

(5) Enrollment in the plan should be available to any widely traded corporation (e.g., any corporation listed on a national stock exchange). Closely held stock does not make good collateral for loans, since it does not have a well-defined market value. Also, a corporation which has exited from the plan should not be allowed to re-enroll for a period of, for example, two years, thus creating an incentive against shuffling in and out of the plan. I am not aware of a need for any other restrictions on enrollment. Indeed, eligibility restrictions should be as few as possible, not only to disarm any opposition from excluded classes of business but also to minimize bureaucratic hassle, as well as to maximize the scope of capital included in the plan. In particular, the plan should not discriminate against small businesses, provided they are widely held.

(6) The U.S. Congress should set an annual budget for net forced social saving—that is, a budget for the amount of new money to be loaned by the central bank for SSLM investments (on top of money to be loaned out of repayments and interest on old loans). This budget item is a fundamental policy variable which has effects throughout the whole economy. These funds amount to a real public expenditure for equalization of wealth. It makes sense to decide on this expenditure in the same democratic fashion that is used for any other public expenditure.

(7) The pot of available central bank loans (from both new and old money) should be allocated competitively between corporations and between private banks by loan brokers in the employ of the SSLM mutual fund. Each broker controls his or her own segment of the pot of central bank funds. The job is to find the best deals for SSLM that can be found. Each deal matches up a corporation that needs a loan with a bank willing to make the loan. The broker seeks the highest ratio of

stock shares to money loaned that can be obtained from the corporation, while also seeking the lowest interest rate from the bank. At the
same time, the broker tries to get the bank to leverage some of its funds
from private savers into the deal to increase the total amount of loans
that can be brokered. He or she is in competition with all other loan
brokers. The effectiveness of each loan broker is evaluated over time,
based on the profits brought in for the SSLM mutual fund. (The loan
brokers might be private market subcontractors.) A three-sided competition between corporations, banks, and brokers is needed, not only
to accomplish a narrowly efficient management of the SSLM fund but
also a broadly efficient management of the whole economy.

(8) The central bank should pursue a policy of inflation management. This is necessary because the practice of financing new investment by printing money will lead to inflation, unless the extra money
is withdrawn from the economy through offsetting transactions of the
central bank. The previous statement needs to be corrected: more
precisely, new money can be printed in proportion to the growth of the
economy without causing any inflation. However, the government is
already doing that, and has been using the new money for other purposes. If we print additional new money to cover SSLM investment,
then we must either raise taxes, or cut government expenditures, or suffer inflation, or "unprint" some other money (i.e., take some offsetting
steps to contract the money supply). Only the last alternative seems to
be allowed under the spirit of this essay contest. That implies that the
central bank must take steps to restrain the supply of money for non-
SSLM purposes.[8]

(9) SSLM, like KHM, proposes no new taxes. However, both
schemes are likely to lead to a substantial erosion of existing sources
of government revenue. The most obvious loss occurs because the corporate income tax is discontinued for participating corporations. A far
larger but less obvious loss results from the practice of printing money
to finance SSLM investment, coupled with restriction of the money
supply. In other words, SSLM is being financed out of the normal
growth of the money stock. But this use of funds displaces prior uses
of the same revenue source by government.[9] That is, this form of
finance does entail a real loss of government revenue. To some extent,
these two losses will be offset by increased tax receipts on the increased
dividends paid to old shareholders of participating corporations.
However, these new taxes cannot cover the entire loss.[10] In the long
run, some funds will be freed up when the SSLM plan begins to replace
welfare and social security expenditures, but this provides no help in

the short run. (An additional long-run new source of revenue might be taxes on the growth dividend that results from adopting SSLM, an argument which will not persuade conservatives.) Under the SSLM design, both short-run and long-run lost revenues will be automatically replaced by additional government debt. (Alternative designs almost necessarily require higher taxes in the short run.)

(10) At the time when the SSLM plan is nearing adoption, all existing stockholders can be expected to suffer a capital loss, experienced as a decline in stock market prices. This loss occurs because SSLM expropriates part of the value which the stock represents, namely, the right to make new investments in successful enterprises.[11] In an ideal design, existing stockholders would be partially compensated for their loss by means of a cash grant proportional to the market value of their holdings as of a certain date. Any such compensation, however, is precluded by the constraint against new taxes. As a consequence, existing private household shareholders can be expected to oppose adoption of SSLM vociferously. But this opposition is diluted by several factors. First, if SSLM is adopted slowly and gradually, then the initial rate of loss will be relatively small. Over time, the more active shareholders will be able to protect themselves against further loss by diversifying their portfolios into real estate, bonds, and foreign stocks. The less active stockholders probably lack the gumption to launch an effective political opposition. Second, the voluntary nature of enrollment in SSLM will tend to disarm opposition; if shareholders do not like the plan, they do not have to participate. Third, the predicted effects on stockholders' wealth depend on indirect (general equilibrium) effects which may be difficult for most stockholders to understand. Fourth, share-holding households do not appear to be an especially well-organized political group. For example, I am able to identify only one powerful lobbying group that represents stockholders, but not business people or professional managers. Fifth, a majority of private stock is held not by households but by institutions; the management of these institutions may have motivations and incentives more similar to corporate managers than to private stockholders.

(11) A second group, which can be expected to suffer from the adoption of the SSLM plan, consists of business people who hope to take their businesses public, i.e., sell stock in their business. This group also should not be compensated for their prospective loss. The political consequences for this group are similar to those for stockholders.

Conclusion: Toward an Air-Worthiness Test

The essay form prohibits a complete specification of SSLM. I have left out some absolutely necessary parts (including machinery for distributing citizen's shares in the SSLM mutual fund) for managing the SSLM portfolio, for controlling the period of gradual transition, for relating SSLM to Social Security and welfare programs, and for defining the citizen's rights to sell or transfer shares. I have not even mentioned such desirable features as the relationship to ESOP plans, the creation of incentives against crime, and the design of explicit machinery to stabilize the economy. I have barely touched on the analysis of the economy under SSLM, and have completely ignored the even more complex transitional period. We are a long way from a flight test. But the society of aeronautical engineers can begin to hold discussions.

Notes

1. Assistant Professor of Economics, Institute for Public Policy and Business Research, University of Kansas.
2. In my view, there are many factual features of the real world that severely restrict the usefulness of the models and arguments favored by conservative economists. In particular, the existence of such phenomena as increasing returns to scale, public goods, bargaining costs, costly information, costly computation and decision making, missing markets in future goods, social norms, love and envy, creativity and stupidity—all conspire to make it very unlikely that markets will generally clear, that perfect competition is perfectly efficient in private markets, that expectations are "economically rational," that government activity is uniformly wasteful, that intersubjective comparisons are impossible, or that the public good is indefinable. However, I do accept the conservative view that we cannot understand the workings of capitalism and other large rationalizing institutions unless we look very closely at the effects of narrow material incentives on individual behavior.
3. From the conservative point of view, the essay contest rules themselves might not fly. That is, from the point of view of a conservative economist who interprets the rules strictly, there is no possible way to spread ownership of capital without taxation or confiscation. For example, the KHM plan requires confiscation of the right

to invest in productive corporations. Under full employment conditions, it also requires one or more of the following: a direct increase in taxes; an expansion of the money supply, which leads to an inflationary tax on holding money; a reduction in government expenditures, which amounts to a confiscation of an expected benefit to some interest group; or an increase in government debt, which amounts to a tax on future generations. Furthermore, from the same point of view, there is no possible way to revive the economy, except perhaps by reducing the size and scope of the government. Finally, the essay form prohibits any satisfactory exploration of the complex economic consequences of any such far-reaching change. Accordingly, I will make use of a somewhat freer interpretation of the contest rules.

4. In particular, I believe that all of the economists cited by Speiser as supporting USOP can be characterized as sympathetic to Keynesian models.

5. Except that there may be some necessary payments on outstanding corporate debt issued prior to enrollment in the USOP plan. It may be desireable to force participating corporations to retire all outstanding debt as rapidly as is practical.

6. The name of the SSLM also refers to some economic literature. The "St. Louis Model" was a macroeconomic model, formulated and used at the St. Louis Federal Reserve Bank in the late 1960s to early 1970s, which was based on conservative economic tenets and methodology. In particular, the St. Louis Model assumed the natural rate hypothesis, and used reduced form equations. The model was influential in monetarists circles, even though a full description of the model was never published (see Anderson and Carlson, 1974 in References). Also, in economics "SLM" refers to yet another model. The SLM model is a particular interpretation of Keynesian economics which is generally used by conservative economists, but has been disavowed by several Keynesian economists.

7. This is essentially equivalent to the problem of measuring true economic depreciation (see Fisher and McGowan, 1983) and citations therein and responses thereto for a discussion of the difficulties. A similar problem arises when one state attempts to tax in-state profits of a corporation which operates in several states. The pro-ration formulas adopted by the states are always rather arbitrary and also are subject to accounting games played by the corporation.

8. Among other consequences, this implies that the discount rate for
    ordinary loans from the central bank will probably be held at a
    higher level than the discount rate for SSLM loans. It also tends to
    imply that the interest rate paid for ordinary private borrowing will
    be held at a higher level than the implied interest rate paid by SSLM
    corporations for new investment. (The implied interest rate from
    the corporate manager's point of view is the internal rate of return
    which equilibrates the amount received for the new stock with the
    expected future stream of dividends to be paid out on the new
    stock.)

9. These subtleties of public finance have recently been emphasized
    by Eisner and Pieper (1984).

10. The proof of this claim is as follows. The extra dividends paid to
    old shareholders are roughly equal to the retained earnings that
    would have resulted without SSLM. But the needed new loans
    from the central bank are also roughly equal to the foregone
    retained earnings. Therefore, since tax rates are much less than 100
    per cent, the extra taxes from the extra dividends are much less
    than the extra dividends or the new loans.

11. More immediately, this loss has several causes. If the stockholders
    allow their corporation to enroll in SSLM, then they will be forced
    to accept rapid payout of their share of earnings, which is subject
    to high ordinary income taxes. If they do not enroll, then the in-
    creased private market interest rates (see previous note 6 and its
    reference) will drive down stock prices by means of two effects.
    First, the cost of new corporate capital will increase, which reduces
    the future stream of earnings available for old capital. Second, this
    future stream of earnings will be discounted at a higher rate of in-
    terest.

References

Anderson, L.C. and K.M. Carlson. "St. Louis Model Revisited," *International Economic Review,* June 1974, pp. 305-27.

Eisner, Robert and Paul J. Peiper. "A New View of the Federal Debt and
Budget Deficits," *American Economic Review,* March 1984, pp.
11-29.

Fisher, Franklin M. and John J. McGowan. "On the Misuse of Accounting Rates of Return to Infer Monopoly Profits," *American
Economic Review,* March 1983, pp. 82-97.

Speiser, Stuart M. *The USOP Handbook: A Guide to Designing Universal Share Ownership Plans for the United States and Great Britain.* New York: Council on International and Public Affairs, 1986.

3

THE COMMON FUND

by

Kenneth B. Taylor

Editor's Note: *Professor Kenneth B. Taylor of Villanova University, the North American second-prize winner, earned his Ph.D. in economics at the State University of New York (Stony Brook) in 1980. He taught at Stony Brook, the University of Connecticut, and Chatham College from 1977 to 1985, and served as Chairman of the Economics Department at Chatham College (1982-1985) before moving to Villanova as Assistant Professor of Economics in 1985. He took a 1987-1988 leave from Villanova to fulfill a Fulbright lecturing-research scholarship at the University of the West Indies. His research papers and conference participations reflect his special skills in computer programming and his grasp of global economic and political policy problems. He served as the compiler and editor of the 1984-85 Speiser essay contest papers, published by the Council on International and Public Affairs.*

ABSTRACT

Increasing economic equity while maintaining existing levels of efficiency form the working criterion for creation of the Common Fund. This proposal not only constitutes a new social policy, incorporating the goals of equity and efficiency, but also the goal of establishing a foundation for elimination of the current, inefficient social welfare apparatus. After the congressional legislation needed to institutionalize the Common Fund concept has been passed, the Common Fund board of directors will begin implementing the initial five-year phase of transforming the participating corporations into Common Fund corporations. These firms will have their financial structures altered, yet the traditional decision-making structure will remain centered around the common shareholders and their elected management. Great effort has been made in the Common Fund proposal to enhance management decision-making flexibility so that historical corporate objectives as well as existing stock markets are unaffected.

Concurrent with this will be the phasing in of the new Common Fund Social Welfare Program. Current welfare recipients will have Common Fund Shareholder Accounts established in their names as they are automatically shifted to the new program. When possible, this program will be tied to the *Shareholders In America* concept and in all cases will stress creating self-reliance based on the strong incentives associated with owning the means of production.

After 18 years of operation, the Common Fund will issue the first universal Common Fund Shareholder Accounts. When the earliest Common Fund Social Welfare Program participants reach retirement age, they will be the first to move into the new Common Fund Social Security Program. This final Common Fund program is designed to be a social welfare rather than a social insurance program. In all, it is envisioned as taking an entire generation to integrate a new comprehensive social policy based on positive incentives into our society and to take apart the incurable social welfare apparatus constructed over the past half century.

Introduction to the Common Fund

In his books, *How to End the Nuclear Nightmare* and *The USOP Handbook,* Stuart Speiser presents persuasive arguments on why America needs a Universal Stock Ownership Plan (USOP).[1] He believes that the principal flaw in the long-term survivability of American capitalism is the increasingly unequal distribution of income and wealth and the defective welfare programs introduced to address this inequality. With this as his working premise, Speiser advocates a new allocation mechanism for the means of production: the Kitty Hawk Model of USOP.[2]

In many ways, the Common Fund is very much like Speiser's Kitty Hawk Model. It is a "fleshed-out" Kitty Hawk Model with particular attention to being at least neutral with regards to existing levels of economic efficiency. Attention also focuses on creating a mechanism serving as a viable substitute for the current welfare/social security apparatus, as well as a constructive tie-in with the Shareholders In America (SIA) concept.[3] Throughout the following essay the term "economic efficiency" will mean the utilization of available resources in such a manner that the maximum amount of output is produced while minimizing waste.

Initially, the Common Fund will be open only to current welfare recipients, yet will become a universal USOP within a generation. In the early years, with limited population participation, the experience gained will provide feedback so that the Common Fund can be so adjusted that it will succeed as it evolves into a universal program. Success will be attained if, and only if, the two underlying principles of desirable public policy are met. Alan Blinder defines these as the principles of efficiency and equity.[4] If a public policy does not result in a more equitable distribution of the social product while maintaining or enhancing the productivity of our economic system, it cannot succeed in meeting long-term public policy objectives.

Once the Common Fund legislation is passed, and the Common Fund institutional apparatus is created, the next step will be to transform the participating firms into Common Fund corporations. As Common Fund stock streams into the central escrow accounts and as accurate forecasts of future stock/dividend flows become available, the phasing in of the welfare recipients' share accounts will commence. After 18 years of operation and fine-tuning, the first set of universal Common Fund Shareholder Accounts will be issued to all individuals born the year the Fund was established. When these early recipients reach retirement age, the modified Social Security Program will begin with the gradual phasing out of the original Social Security Program. By this time, the welfare programs will have been trimmed to their final safety net form and all Americans between 18 and 65 will own Common Fund share accounts. Involuntary poverty will have been eradicated from the American landscape and with everyone participating in the ownership of the means of production, sociopolitical stability will be assured regardless of the nature or pace of future economic growth. It is one thing to imagine such a transformation. It is another to work out the practical details. To these details we now turn.

The Common Fund Apparatus

The board of directors of the Common Fund should be as political-ly neutral as possible, with broad powers to adjust the CF (Common Fund) apparatus in pursuit of efficiency and equity. For this reason,it is proposed that Congress define its working mandate while the executive branch be responsible for appointing each of the seven members.

Beneath the CF board of directors will be the network of CF cor-poration board members. Since CF stock will not be voting stock, the CF board of directors will appoint one person to sit on each of the par-ticipating CF corporate boards to represent the CF shareholders' inter-ests. These appointees will be paid CF personnel, reporting to and supervised by the CF board. The CF administrative structure will work closely with the Securities and Exchange Commission, the Federal Reserve System, the Social Security Administration, and the Depart-ment of Health and Human Services. Design of the CF administrative apparatus should minimize duplication of governmental functions.

Selection and Structure of CF Corporations

Guidelines for selection of specific participating companies require careful consideration.The larger the number of firms participating, the more rapidly the goal of increased equity can be attained. At the same time, the greater the percentage of all firms involved, the greater the probability that any unforeseen systemic errors will lead to deviation from the goal of maintaining economic efficiency. There needs to be a large enough number of firms involved to make the outstanding CF share accounts economically meaningful, and a sufficient number out-side the Fund for maintaining competitive pressure in markets as well as allowing for dynamic entrepreneurship. This balance between par-ticipating and non-participating firms needs to be extensively studied before implementation of any USOP. Nothing is lost in the following discussion by adopting the Kitty Hawk Model assumption of including, by legislative mandate, the 2,000 major American corporations plus all regulated public utilities.[5]

A Participant Review Committee should be formed by the CF board of directors to institutionalize a mechanism for permitting firms not originally included in the Fund to join and those CF corporations which seek to leave the Fund to do so. Strict guidelines need to be established so that any firm that becomes a CF corporation does so for reasons which will not damage economic efficiency. There always exists the possibility that a particular CF corporation in a particular industry will be competitively handicapped by participation in the Fund. Therefore, this committee should also be empowered to permit a CF corporation to leave the Fund, again subject to strict efficiency guidelines.

Once a firm becomes a CF corporation it will be required to modify its existing structure. All existing common stock will remain intact, along with its traditional function, yet issuance of any new common stock will be permitted only for employee stock ownership plans (ESOPs) and only in amounts consistent with the objectives of such plans. Each CF corporation will begin to retire all outstanding short-term debt, long-term debt, and preferred stock, while new financial needs will be met by issuing CF shares. Expansion plans or new acquisitions will be subject to review by the SEC and once approved, the Fund is obligated to accept an issue and provide the required money. Some may argue that having the SEC judge proposed investment projects will lead to an increase in government intervention in the private sector. What is envisioned here is a role for the SEC identical to its historical role. Since CF firms remain ultimately accountable to their common shareholders, there is no reason to presume that unlimited access to investment capital will lead to unreasonable risk-taking. In the same vein, existing antitrust legislation will check unreasonable, anticompetitive growth. Finally, as will be suggested below, excessive expansion will lead to decreasing common shareholder equity as a percentage of total equity and consequently declining earnings per share. Management will find aggressive expansion plans held in check by the effects their plans will have on the traded price of common stock.

An equity account for each CF corporation will be established with each dollar provided by the Fund equal to one CF share. As with common stock, a CF corporation should be allowed to retire some of the CF shares. The exact percentage would be determined by the nature of the industry in which a CF corporation operates. The more stable an industry, the smaller the percentage of CF shares that a CF corporation can retire. This feature of CF shares will permit firms to maintain earnings per share over the course of the industrial/product growth cycles and allow some CF shares to be issued to meet short-term financial needs. In case an emergency financial situation arises, CF corporations should be empowered to issue unapproved CF shares up to a small percentage of CF shares outstanding.

Participating firms should be exempt from paying corporate income taxes to make CF status desirable. With the exception of a small pool of retained earnings necessary for operations, all earnings associated with CF equity will be required to be paid out as a dividend to the Fund. The CF dividend will be determined via the following procedure. First, establish the relative proportions of equity held by the common stockholders and the Fund. Multiply the percentage of total equity attributable to CF stock times total earnings to derive the CF dividend. This amount is transferred to the Fund. The remainder of earnings represents the pool of funds from which the common stockholders receive their dividends. Their dividend will be determined by the existing method and need not exhaust funds available. In years when there is a surplus, these funds should be escrowed with limited usages permitted. Possible uses might include retirement of outstanding common or CF stock, which will boost future earnings per share, or using accumulated monies during lean years to maintain the historical dividend rate. This dividend procedure will help preserve the integrity of existing common stock and thereby minimize stock market price disruptions.

In both of the Speiser books mentioned at the beginning of this essay, it is stated that:

> ... according to reliable projections, American business will create at least $5 trillion worth of new capital over the next 20 or so years. If that figure is divided among the 50 million households who presently own little or no capital, each household would receive $100,000 worth of SuperStock (USOP shares). ... And at the current pre-tax return rate of 20 percent on invested capital, each household could expect to receive about $20,000 (a year) in dividends. ... [6]

Several qualifying comments are in order. First, this statement is based on the assumption of constant economic growth. The author has argued elsewhere that there is good reason to believe that economic growth will slow down in the future.[7] If so, then the creation of $5 trillion dollars of new capital over the next 20 years may be unrealistically high. This would put less CF shares, and consequently dividends, into the hands of those who presently own little or no capital. Second, the current pre-tax return is based on the current financial leveraging practice employed by American business. The author also has suspected that eliminating the use of debt and most retained earnings by the participating corporations may eliminate leverage as a means for magnifying the return on capital. If these suspicions are true, the actual return on capital for CF corporations may well be a fraction of the current pre-tax rate. This means that CF shareholders will likely receive considerably less dividend income than Speiser projects, regardless of the dollar value of the CF shares they own. Another consequence may be to drive private equity investors from CF firms to non-participating firms still enjoying the fruits of financial leverage.

To get a better feel for some of these issues, the author took two prospective CF corporations, General Electric and DuPont, and re-analyzed their financial statements under the assumption that they became CF corporations in 1980.[8] A five-year phase-in was assumed so that both became full-fledged CF corporations in the year 1984. Insights to be gained from this exercise were limited by the small number of firms studied, the short time period involved, and the fact that management was not making decisions as they would if they were a CF corporation. Under these assumptions and the CF framework described earlier, CF equity grew to 94 per cent of total equity for General Electric and 70 per cent of total equity for DuPont by 1985. In the case of General Electric, this was caused in large part by a more than doubling of retained earnings over the period studied. For DuPont the growth in CF equity was fueled by a $6.8 billion increase in debt in 1981 (the year Conoco was acquired). Since these changes were atypical and since there was no provision in the calculations for discretionary retirement of CF shares, these equity results may be unusual. Due to the tremendous drop in General Electric's CF shareholders equity, CF earnings per share on common stock dropped well below the historical levels by 1985 (only 13 per cent of 1985 level). In contrast, CF earnings per share on common stock averaged 50 to 94 per cent *above* historical levels for DuPont. This occurred from the combined effects of an increase in common shareholder equity from the Conoco acquisition and the vigorous debt reduction efforts of DuPont's management after the acquisition (in effect a reduction in CF stock). Finally, given the rapid increase in CF equity (in conjunction with enhanced earnings from elimination of taxes, interest payments, and depreciation charges), dividends flowing back to the Fund over the period more than compensated for *all* the CF shares issued. Again, this may be due solely to factors specific to the companies studied and the lack of management responses to CF status. Despite the limitations, this exercise pointed out several important facts. First, if management is given considerable leeway in controlling the financial structure of the CF corporation, it can be made an attractive short-term investment opportunity for common shareholders. Second, even allowing for considerable variation in managerial response, the debt incurred by the Fund should be paid back in a reasonable period of time. Third, the CF equity created will be considerable and therefore provide the foundation for economically meaningful CF shareholder accounts issued to the public. Fourth, elimination of interest payments, depreciation charges, and taxes permit a higher return to capital and offset to some degree the loss of financial leverage. This is true in the short run, yet no long-term effects can be inferred from this simple experiment. As a final point, the CF model does work up to this point with all the defined components establishing the base for the remaining parts of the model.

The Common Fund Shareholder Accounts

Once CF shares are created by a participating corporation, they will be held in escrow in the central CF trust account until the stream of dividend income pays for the debt instruments issued by the CF to finance the shares. Issuance of new CF debt, as well as retirement of existing CF debt, should be coordinated with the monetary policies of the Federal Reserve so that monetary and capital market disruptions are minimized.

The USOP proposed here would make all American citizens eligible to receive their CF accounts upon attaining the age of 18. The dollar value of an account received will be equal to the average annual value of new capital investments made by the participating corporations over the past 18 years, divided by the average annual national birthrate for the same period. This formula will smooth out the effects of both economic and demographic fluctuations over a long period of time, permitting a more equitable intertemporal distribution of CF shares. Unlike the Speiser plan, which recommends at least a 7-to-15-year phase-in, this current proposal implicitly assumes an 18-year phase-in. Given that economic growth slows down and the dividend payout is not as high as Speiser predicts, it may very well take an average of 18 years for the debt incurred in initially creating CF shares to be paid off.

CF accounts will not carry any voting rights due to their mutual fund nature, yet it is proposed here that CF shareholders be able to sell some or all of the shares they own. Admittedly, if CF shares could be exchanged publicly, it would have a devastating effect on the prices at which the common stock of the 2,000 participating corporations were traded. Still, it is important that the CF shareholder be able to trade in or borrow against the shares they own. The driving force behind entrepreneurship, and thus economic growth in America, is individual innovation and invention. Allowing a person to place his wealth, including CF shares, behind his ideas is an important element in fostering future economic activity. Those people who are willing to take on risk should be encouraged in all ways possible. So that the stock markets are not depressed by an inundation of CF stock, legislation setting up the program should specify that a holder of CF shares may sell his shares back to the CF at their current value and may repurchase them at either their value when they were sold or their current value, whichever is higher. This will allow a holder to liquidate his shares, yet not at the Fund's expense. Returned shares will be treated as new investment, being held in escrow until the stream of dividends pays for the transaction and then redistributed by the formula described above.

For illustrative purposes, let us assume that a CF shareholder wishes to use his CF shares to open his own business. When he was 18, and his account was issued, it contained 100,000 one dollar shares. To calculate its current value, we need to introduce the concept of the core share. The core share value is based on the current market prices of the common stocks of CF corporations with each firm's stock price weighted by its percentage share in the overall CF equity pool. At the time of issuance, let us assume that a core share was valued at $50. This becomes the standard for valuing this individual's 100,000 shares over time. If the core share at the time the CF shareholder desires to tap his account has risen to $55, then each of his CF shares would be worth $1.10.[9] On the other hand, if the core share value had dropped to $45, this person's CF shares would only be worth $.90 apiece.

To determine the quarterly CF dividend for each account, the CF administration will tally up the total amount of dividends paid into the central trust account during the quarter on paid off CF stock, divide this by the total number of CF shares outstanding, and multiply the resultant by the shares in each shareholder's account.

It is also proposed here that CF Shareholders Accounts not be inheritable. Since the CF concept intends to give Americans wealth which they would not have had otherwise, there is no way that this proposal could be construed as being confiscatory. If this suggestion is adopted, it will permit a more equal long-term distribution of this form of ownership. It will take the intergenerational accumulation of CF shares out of the capricious hands of fate and family planning. If a CF shareholder dies ownership rights should be transferred to his or her spouse. If both parents of a minor die, the parents' accounts should be held in trust with invasion of principal allowed to support the child. In any case, when both husband and wife die, or when surviving children receive their accounts, the CF accounts of the deceased should be returned to the Fund for equitable redisbursement. So that people do not cash-out their CF Shareholder Accounts in order to pass its value on to their heirs, provisions should be made in the law to charge a deceased CF shareholder's estate for the value of CF shares withdrawn.

The issue has been raised that if CF share accounts provide substantial income and wealth to CF shareholders that the American work ethic would be seriously undermined. If this were to become true, economic efficiency would be seriously harmed with America strapped with all the imaginable disincentives of a population-wide social welfare program. Due to this contingency, it is proposed that CF share accounts be originally defined as an earned entitlement. By earned entitlement, the author means that every American has the right to receive a CF share account, yet it can be kept only if the recipient works until 62 years of age. Exceptions will be made only in the cases of disability or when a person chooses to do the "work of humanity."[10] It is suggested that CF shareholders be reviewed every five years. Information on which shareholders should be examined would be readily available from the Internal Revenue Service. When a shareholder has voluntarily not worked for the previous five years, his or her account could be reduced by 25%. If this person finds employment or takes on humanitarian work for the ensuing five years, the account should be credited for previously lost shares after the next review. When a shareholder has been involuntarily unemployed for the previous five years, this individual should be shifted automatically to the CF Social Welfare Program (described on the next page). Once enrolled in the CF Welfare Program, the participant's CF Shareholder Account becomes closed with regards to equity transactions and the requirements of this program are imposed and enforced.

The CF Social Security Program

Given that CF Shareholder Accounts have the potential to provide substantial income, the possibility of scaling back and simplifying the Social Security Program exists. Once an individual has a CF Shareholder Account, he or she could automatically move into the new CF Social Security Program. The program would basically work in the following way. In retirement, if the dividend income earned from a retiree's CF Shareholder Account falls below some socially desirable minimum amount, and the retiree meets other income conditions, an additional Social Security transfer will be forthcoming. Over time, as more and more Americans become CF shareholders, the social insurance aspect of Social Security can be passed to the private sector with only the social welfare aspect being administered by the government.[11]

One final suggestion: When an individual retires, he or she should have the option to transfer shares accumulated in an ESOP into an equivalent dollars' worth of CF shares. This may encourage the formation of ESOPs by allowing an individual, upon retirement, to diversify the risk associated with holding stock in only one company.

The CF Social Welfare Program

Welfare recipients at the time the Fund begins operation should immediately be eligible to participate. These individuals should be notified that the current welfare programs will be phased out over the ensuing five years. In their place will be a welfare system based on the CF concept. When a person who had been on welfare signs up for the CF Social Welfare Program, a CF Shareholder Account will be established. Over the next five years equal quarterly amounts of CF shares will be credited to their account until it reaches some predefined amount. The amount must once again produce meaningful dividend income. During the time shares are accumulating and for the ensuing five years, it is proposed that these accounts be closed to CF shareholder exchanges (i.e., no withdrawals). As with the CF Social Security Program, if CF dividend income plus other income falls beneath a socially desirable minimum, a direct welfare transfer from the government will be forthcoming to make up the difference. Dividend income should be based on the average rate of return on CF corporate accounts held by the Fund. Dividends paid in this program should be reimbursed by the government for the initial ten years of a recipient's participation. The idea here is to eventually dismantle the current welfare apparatus by replacing it with one incorporating socially desirable incentives without transferring an excessive funding burden to the earliest universal CF shareholders.

After being in the program for ten years, a participant's status should be changed to that of a universal CF shareholder as outlined earlier. During the first ten years the conditions for being part of the program should be rigorous, with participants being more closely monitored. Conditions should be kept to a minimum and heavily oriented toward creating self-sufficiency. In addition to continuing efforts to find employment in the private sector, a CF welfare recipient should be required to do workfare and/or to participate in a well-managed and designed vocational training program. If a firm set up along the lines of Shareholders In America (SIA) is in the region, benefiting from the CF welfare program may be tied to employment in such an enterprise.[12] Since SIA projects are envisioned as initially emphasizing subsistence salaries and dividends from stock issued to its employees, additional dividend income from CF Shareholder Accounts may help boost worker incentives while these firms are getting started. Tying the two concepts together in this manner should reinforce the success of both programs. As SIA employees gather experience as worker-capitalists and appreciation of how diligent labor can translate into higher income through stock ownership, a broad constituency in support of the Common Fund, as well as employee ownership, will develop in the welfare community.

It was suggested earlier that when upon review it is found that a universal CF shareholder has been involuntarily unemployed for the previous five years that they be automatically shifted to the CF Social Welfare Program. All the same conditions and restrictions just outlined will pertain to these later welfare program participants. The only difference in treatment is that these later participants should not have their CF Shareholder Accounts diluted with new CF shares for participating in the program.

Conclusions

One major disruption that the Common Fund program would cause is a pronounced initial reduction in tax revenue flowing to the federal government. Exempting the largest 2,000 corporations from the corporate income tax may necessitate shifting more tax burden to individuals and non-participating corporations. This would violate our goal of making the Fund at least efficiency-neutral since increased taxation on these other economic agents would create disincentives to work.

It can be argued that in the long term, federal tax revenues will be enhanced by the Common Fund. Once the CF Shareholder Accounts become prevalent in the economy, the taxes paid on CF dividend earnings will gradually rebuild tax revenues. In addition, if the Fund operates as hoped and enhances capital formation, future incomes will rise above what they otherwise would have been, as will federal tax revenues.

This potential tax burden redistribution thus becomes a short-term problem which must be addressed. It was mentioned in the case studies section that for both firms examined, the flow of CF dividends during the six years more than compensated for all debt created by the Fund to finance their shares. If this rapid payback holds true in the aggregate, it may indicate a solution to this tax problem. Legislation setting up the CF Fund could specify an alternative corporate tax levied on the CF dividends to be phased out the year the program issues the first universal shares. This, in conjunction with the government savings enjoyed from the new CF Social Welfare Program, could eliminate the need for increasing taxes elsewhere in the economy. One may argue that this will decrease the value of the early universal CF Shareholder Accounts; yet this is offset to some degree by the benefits these first CF shareholders would receive from the additional income retained by their parents during their childhood.

As far as can be seen, capital, product, factor, and stock markets will not be significantly affected by the Fund's existence. Demand for long-term funds will remain close to what it would have been. The major effect here will be to restructure the market, with the Fund issuing a significant percentage of short-, intermediate-, and long-term debt instruments. Given the diversified nature of the Fund's central trust account, these debt instruments may be perceived as being of lower risk than those of individual corporations. In regard to the stock market, it has been argued that the flexibility of the defined CF corporate structure will permit management to continue pursuing their goal of maximizing return per share for their common shareholders. Pursuit of this goal may slow the CF dividend payout rate, yet this is the price to be paid for maintenance of the traditional corporate decision-making structure.

Although many additional details and questions remain to be delineated or answered, the author is convinced that none of them negate any structural aspects of the Common Fund, as presented in this paper. The weakest point of the Common Fund is the lack of understanding of how the CF corporate management will respond in either the short or long term. Efforts by the author to study this aspect created as many questions as answers. Knowing how CF corporate management will alter their decision making in dealing with the fund over time is essential to defining the desirability of CF corporate status and consequently support for such a program in the business community. However this issue is resolved, there exists enough flexibility in the concept for it to be tuned to work. This being the case, the purpose of the Common Fund will be realized: it can create increased economic equality without diminished economic efficiency.

James Buchanan received the Nobel Prize in 1986 for his work in public choice analysis. Recently he stated that:

> It is time to move beyond the slogan that government is the problem, and to think long, much and hard about the prospects for construc-

tive institutional changes. . . . Let us get on with the task of reconstruction. We have seen through the delusion of Camelot, but let us not be blind to visions of a future that need not suffer from such delusion. It is time to again dream attainable dreams, and to recover the faith that dreams can become realities. It is time to start replacing dystopia with a tempered utopia.[13]

The Common Fund is a tempered, attainable, and socially desirable program. It is a utopian vision in that it negates the notion that efficiency and economic equality are contradictory concepts. That notion is a product of the failure of the Great Society programs. The Reagan era has brought us full circle, to the brink of a new age where constructive institutional change will again be viewed as possible. As six years of experience have shown, the Reagan presidency has not brought constructive reform. Instead, old and failed programs have been weakened without alternatives introduced to take their place. Economic growth has been declared the keystone of the conservative solution, apparently abrogating the need to search for constructive institutional change. Dystopian beliefs have crippled the creative imaginations of our representatives in Washington as well. When the insights of individuals like James Buchanan begin to spark the national imagination, the Common Fund concept will be there to help the nation once more dream about a better future for all its people.

Notes

1. Stuart M. Speiser, *The USOP Handbook: A Guide to Designing Universal Share Ownership Plans for the United States and Great Britain*. New York: Council on International and Public Affairs, 1986.
2. Ibid., pp. 17-49.
3. See Stuart M. Speiser, *Supplement to The USOP Handbook. Shareholders In America, Inc.: A First Step Toward Universal Share Ownership*. New York: Council on International and Public Affairs, June 1986.
4. A. Blinder, "Economic Policy Can Be Hard-Headed—and Soft-Hearted," *Business Week,* August 12, 1985.
5. See discussion concerning public utilities in Speiser, *USOP Handbook,* op. cit., p. 26.
6. Stuart M. Speiser, *How to End the Nuclear Nightmare.* Croton-on-Hudson, New York: North River Press, 1984, p. 142.
7. Kenneth B. Taylor, "The Alpha Proposal" (Entry in the 1984-85

Speiser Essay Contest), Council on International and Public Affairs, New York, 1985.

8. Crucial CF values were calculated by the following formulas:

(a) CF earnings = reported earnings before taxes + reported

depreciation + ($\sum_{i=1}^{5}$ i/5 x reported interest payment from

1980 through 1984; then full interest payment for 1985) +

($\sum_{i=1}^{5}$ i/5 x annual preferred stock dividend from 1980 to

1984; then full preferred stock dividend in 1985).

(b) CF common stockholders equity = recorded equity

$- [(\sum_{i=1980}^{1984}$ 1/5 1979 retained earnings level) + (addi-

tions to retained earnings from previous period)].

(c) CF equity = previous period's CF equity (0 for 1979) + [(1/5 1979 retained earnings level each year from 1980 to 1984) + (additions to retained earnings from previous period)] + [(1/5 1979 total debt each year from 1980 to 1984) + (changes in debt level from previous period)] + [(1/5 total value of preferred stock outstanding in 1979) + (changes in preferred stock outstanding from previous period)].

9. Current CF share value = core share index where:

$$\text{Core Share Index} = \frac{\text{Current Core Share Value}}{\begin{array}{c}\text{Core Share Value at Time}\\ \text{Account Issued}\end{array}}$$

$$= \frac{55}{50} = 1.10$$

10. Speiser, *USOP Handbook,* op. cit., p. 95.
11. See Peter Ferrara, *Social Security Reform,* Washington, D.C.: Heritage Foundation, 1982.
12. Speiser, *Supplement to USOP Handbook,* op. cit.
13. James Buchanan, Speech presented at the Institute for Humane

Studies, George Mason University, Virginia. Excerpts reported in *The Wall Street Journal,* November 14, 1986.

References

Barraclough, Geoffrey. *An Introduction to Contemporary History.* New York: Pelican Books, 1967.

Bell, Daniel. *The Coming of Post-Industrial Society.* New York: Basic Books, 1973.

Davidson, Paul. "Can Effective Demand and the Movement Toward Further Income Equality Be Maintained in the Face of Robotics? An Introduction," *Journal of Post Keynesian Economics,* Vol. 7, No. 3, Spring 1985.

Froman, Creel. *The Two American Political Systems: Society Economics, and Politics.* Englewood Cliffs, New Jersey: Prentice-Hall, 1984.

Galbraith, John Kenneth. *American Capitalism.* Boston: Houghton Mifflin, 1956.

Green, Mark. *Winning Back America.* New York: Bantam Books, 1982.

Harman, Willis W. *An Incomplete Guide to the Future.* New York: W. W. Norton, 1979.

Hawken, Paul. *The Next Economy.* New York: Ballantine Books, 1984.

Heilbroner, Robert L. *An Inquiry Into the Human Prospect.* New York: W.W. Norton, 1980.

_____. *The Limits of American Capitalism.* New York: Harper & Row, 1966.

Jones, Thomas E. *Options for the Future.* New York: Praeger Publishers, 1980.

Kahn, et al., Herman. *The Next 200 Years.* New York: William Morrow, 1976.

Lekachman, Robert. "SuperStock: A Conservative Alternative to the Welfare State," *Journal of Post Keynesian Economics,* Vol. 7, No. 3, Spring 1985.

Leontief, Wassily. *The Future of the World Economy.* Oxford: Oxford University Press, 1977.

Meade, James. "Full Employment, New Technologies and the Distribution of Income," *Journal of Social Policy* (Cambridge University Press, Cambridge), Vol. 13, Part 2, April 1984.

Morehouse, Ward (ed.). *The Handbook of Tools for Community Economic Change.* New York: Intermediate Technology Group of North America, 1983.

Murray, Charles. *Losing Ground.* New York: Basic Books, 1984.

Perry, John. *The National Dividend.* New York: Ivan Obolensky, 1964.

Riech, Robert B. *The Next American Frontier.* New York: Times Books, 1980.

Speiser, Stuart M. *Supplement to The USOP Handbook. Shareholders In America, Inc.: A First Step Toward Universal Share Ownership.* New York: Council on International and Public Affairs, June 1986.

_____. *The USOP Handbook.* New York: Council on International and Public Affairs, 1986.

_____. *How to End the Nuclear Nightmare.* Croton-on-Hudson, New York: North River Press, 1984.

Thurow, Lester. "Building a World Class Economy," *Society,* Vol. 22, No. 1, 1984.

_____. "The Implications of Zero Economic Growth," *Challenge,* March/April, 1977.

_____. *The Zero-Sum Society.* New York: Basic Books, 1980.

Turnbull, C. S. Shann. *Democratising the Wealth of Nations.* Sydney: Company Directors Association of Australia, 1975.

Weitzman, Martin. *The Share Economy: Conquering Stagflation.* Cambridge, Massachusetts: Harvard University Press, 1984.

4

GUARANTEED WORK-OWNERSHIP OPPORTUNITY AS AN ALTERNATIVE TO SOCIAL SECURITY AND CERTAIN OTHER SOCIAL PROGRAMS

by

Reverend John A. Sedlak

Editor's Note: *The North American third-prize winner, the Reverend John A. Sedlak, is a Roman Catholic priest for the diocese of Greensburg, Pennsylvania, where he is a member of the Diocesan Peace and Justice Commission. In 1972, he received a Bachelor of Science degree with major in psychology from the University of Pittsburgh, and a Master of Divinity degree in 1982 from St. Charles Borromeo Seminary, Philadelphia, when he was ordained. He is currently writing a book on nuclear arms control.*

His essay is a forerunner of the 1988 essay competition, which seeks ways of using ownership as a solution for the problems of unemployment, underemployment, and poverty. His concept of government-guaranteed jobs (GGJ) is based on the WPA experience and is similar to the programs proposed by Senator Paul Simon during the 1988 presidential campaign. The difference is that Father Sedlak inserts a

new method of paying for costly public works and government employ-
ment programs: dividends from shares of stock issued under a plan
similar to SuperStock. Another unique feature of the Sedlak paper is
that it establishes four criteria for eligibility to receive USOP shares:
work, education and training for work, incapacity for work, and full-
time parenting of children below age 19.

ABSTRACT

What will be proposed here is a radical four-point restructuring of
certain U.S. social and tax programs intended to bring about universal substantial share ownership of America's productive assets,
without confiscation or increased taxation, and in a way that: (a) alleviates poverty, (b) promotes family stability, (c) makes work the
primary basis for stock ownership awards, (d) guarantees opportunity for work and stock ownership, and (e) revives the economy.
The four main points of this restructuring plan are:

(1) Individual substantial stock ownership, acquired during a
person's workspan years (i.e., 18 to 64 years of age), will gradually replace Social Security (OASDHI) and other mandatory retirement programs (public employee and railroad retirement) as the
basis for income maintenance in retirement, and will provide supplemental income during working years.
(2) Government-guaranteed employment opportunity will substantially supplant certain social programs, such as Aid to Families
with Dependent Children (AFDC), general assistance, food stamps,
Medicaid, unemployment compensation, and subsidized housing.
(3) Revenues formerly expended on social programs reduced by
government-guaranteed employment, and eventually tax revenues
formerly appropriated for Social Security and public employee and
railroad retirement, will be reallocated to fund the government-
guaranteed employment opportunity program.
(4) Using a modified version of Stuart Speiser's "SuperStock" concept, a revolving government stock fund will be established. Stock
from this fund will be awarded to U.S. citizens on the basis of their
work or certain other eligibility criteria in order to replace Social
Security and public employee and railroad retirement programs.

Note: This essay includes an Appendix, which follows immediately after the Notes section.

Introduction

Compelling arguments have been put forward in favor of widespread capital ownership. It has been asserted that when corporate employees also become corporate owners, the right relationship between labor and capital is restored,[1] conflict between labor and management can be reduced,[2] productivity can be bolstered,[3] and the "Keynesian dilemma" of inflation versus full employment can be resolved.[4] It has furthermore been suggested that the current U.S. problem of "speculators' capitalism," due largely to institutional investors collectively owning too much of the nation's public stock, can be remedied by wider, more diversified stock ownership among millions of individual shareholders.[5] In the face of growing numbers of working poor, i.e., people who work full time or part time in low-paying jobs, it is pointed out that awarding shares of ownership on the basis of hours worked may be the best way to supplement wages, reduce poverty, and preserve America's important middle class.[6] And finally, it is argued that if substantial capital ownership can be extended universally, the ideological differences between Marxism and capitalism can be undercut, lessening the possibility of nuclear war.[6]

Even in view of the many benefits predicted for widespread capital ownership, being clear about what one hopes to achieve with it is a requisite that will, to a large extent, determine the design of the plan for its realization. What will be proposed here is a radical four-point restructuring of certain U.S. social and tax programs intended to bring about universal substantial share ownership of America's productive assets, without confiscation or increased taxation, and in a way that: (a) alleviates poverty,[7] (b) promotes family stability,[8] (c) makes work the primary basis for stock ownership awards, (d) guarantees opportunity for work and stock ownership, and (e) revives the economy. The four main points of this restructuring plan are:

(1) Individual substantial stock ownership, acquired during a person's workspan years (i.e., 18 to 64 years of age) will gradually replace Social Security (OASDHI) and other mandatory retirement programs (public employee and railroad retirement) as the basis for income maintenance in retirement, and will provide supplemental income during working years.

(2) Government-guaranteed employment opportunity will substantially supplant certain social programs, such as Aid to Families with Dependent Children (AFDC), general assistance, food stamps, Medicaid, unemployment compensation, and subsidized housing.

(3) Revenues formerly expended on social programs reduced by government-guaranteed employment, and eventually tax revenues formerly appropriated for Social Security and public employee and railroad retirement, will be reallocated to fund the government-guaranteed employment opportunity program.

(4) Using a modified version of Stuart Speiser's "SuperStock" concept, a revolving government stock fund will be established. Stock from this fund will be awarded to U.S. citizens on the basis of their work or certain other eligibility criteria in order to replace Social Security and public employee and railroad retirement programs.

Details of this plan follow.

Replacing Social Security and Other Mandatory Retirement Programs with Substantial Stock Ownership

Aside from employee stock ownership plans (ESOPs), perhaps the most obvious way to broaden stock ownership is by somehow making it an alternative to Social Security and other mandatory retirement programs. That there is some political sympathy for such an idea is evident from the dissatisfaction with Social Security on the part of many in government, and from the proffering of such alternative ideas as that of Delaware Governor Peter du Pont.[9] Du Pont's plan provides that as an optional alternative to Social Security, workers could contribute up to the total of their Social Security taxes to a kind of super individual retirement account (IRA)—referred to as a financial security account (FSA)—and take a credit against their income taxes. Account holders would give up the amount of Social Security benefits proportionate to their FSA contribution. The program would not replace Social Security under du Pont's design; it would be an individual's option that would promise more abundant retirement income and allegedly strengthen Social Security by reducing future outlays. Any worker who preferred to stay in the Social Security system could do so, and current retirees would receive all of their benefits. Until fully implemented, however, du Pont's program would be expected to put greater deficit pressure on Social Security.

If instead of, or along with, having an option to contribute to the FSA, the du Pont plan provided an option to purchase stock, its original objectives would still be accomplished and stock ownership could be broadened. An advantage of the stock purchase option over the FSA option or the Social Security option would be that dividend income from stock ownership would be immediately available to the owner during his/her workspan years, and this could be reinvested or used as the owner sees fit.

Although this concept is attractive, it would not necessarily provide stock ownership opportunity to everyone, nor would it directly provide for alleviation of poverty. Only workers whose income and Social Security taxes were sufficient to purchase stock as an alternative to Social Security would be able to participate in substantial stock ownership via this route. The long-term unemployed and the subemployed, most of whom live below the poverty level, would enjoy few, if any, of its benefits. And herein lies the crux of a dilemma. How can the work-able unemployed person participate in substantial share ownership opportunity?[10] Or again, how can the low-income subemployed person participate in same?

What is proposed here is a program to guarantee substantial stock ownership opportunity on the basis of work, training for work (i.e., education), incapacity for work, and full-time parenting. To assure that the low-income subemployed person can fully participate in the program, hours of work rather than earnings would be the basis for eligibility. Hours of approved volunteer work would also qualify. To provide for the alleviation of poverty and certain other socioeconomic goals within this program, every household would also be given the opportunity to have at least one work-able member employed full time. A government-created full-time job would be provided for any household where no member is otherwise employed full time because such employment opportunity is not available. Details of this are given in the next section.

As an incentive to higher education and to becoming employable, full-time students in college or technical schools would also be eligible for stock ownership awards, as would those persons who are incapacitated for work. To promote family and social stability, either nonemployed parent, who undertakes on a full-time basis the important job of parenting children under 19 years of age, will also fully qualify for the stock ownership opportunity program.

Since stock ownership under this program is eventually to replace Social Security and other mandatory retirement programs as the source of basic retirement income, the amount of stock a person would be eligible to receive during the course of his/her eligible workspan years (i.e., 18 to 64 years of age inclusive) should provide an annual dividend income in retirement comparable to the income that would otherwise be received through Social Security. It is figured that a diversified stock portfolio of about $50,000 would accomplish this. At an annual yield of 10 per cent, it would generate $5,000 per year in basic retirement income.[11] Higher yields, however, could reasonably be expected, but when lower yields generate less than the guaranteed minimum income of $5,000, the shortfall would be made up by way of a direct grant. Persons not qualifying for the maximum amount of stock under the program would have a lower guaranteed minimum retirement income from their portfolio, proportionate to approximately 10 per cent of the portfolio's value midway through a given year.

To acquire the full amount of stock (i.e., $50,000 worth) provided under the program, a person would have to qualify each year, from age 18 to age 64, for the maximum annual stock grant market-valued at about $1,087. He/she would receive a random selection of this amount of diversified stock at the end of each year and would own it until death, when it would return to a revolving government fund for this program. While in the hands of the government, the stock would be non-voting. In the hands of the awardee, it would entitle shareholder voting, but would be non-transferrable. Annual dividend income from the stock would belong to the owner and be immediately usable. Defunct stock would be exchangeable at any time for an amount of current stock proportionate in value to the defunct stock's value at the time it was awarded.

As defined here, as many as 148 million U.S. citizens today,[12] ages 18 to 64, could qualify for annual stock awards. If maximum stock grants are assumed for each eligible person, the program could require as much as $160.6 billion worth of stock annually for stock awards. The fully established revolving stock fund would require about $4.6 trillion worth of stock. Funding for this, without increased taxation or confiscation, will be the subject of a later section. Additional details are provided in Appendices 9 to 11.

Guaranteed Work Opportunity as a Partial Alternative for the Expenditures of Certain Social Welfare Programs and as an Integral Part of the Stock Ownership Opportunity Program

This part of the proposed program rests on the premise that work has a value that goes far beyond financial renumeration—that society depends on work, that an individual has a need and a right to participate in the productive life of society, that he/she can grow in self-discipline and self-esteem from such participation, and that family and social stability are enhanced by it. As a matter of practical consideration, it is also recognized that any plan for broadening capital ownership must posit work as the primary basis for acquiring or awarding stock ownership, if the plan is to garner adequate popular and political support. And it is further recognized that under the proposed program, the alleviation of poverty in the U.S., may only be attainable—or at least may be best attainable—when wages provide the primary basis for income. This program, therefore, endeavors to assure that each U.S. household has the opportunity to have at least one work-able member employed full time. To assure this, it aims to provide a government-guaranteed job (GGJ) for any household with no one otherwise employed full time due to a lack of opportunity.

Appendix 1 shows the eligibility requirements for GGJs. By limiting GGJs to one per household in which no member is otherwise employed full time, only the neediest households would benefit and the number of GGJs would be kept down. Also, a disincentive to marriage that would be inherent in allowing more than one person in a non-family household to hold a GGJ is avoided. By permitting other household members to be employed part time, the economy's market for part-time help would still be served, and by deferring GGJ applicants who qualify for, but refuse, military service or comparable local civilian jobs, GGJs would not create an undue draw for labor from these.

Appendix 3 provides some plausible GGJ specifications. By endeavoring to provide GGJs within the county of the applicant's residence, community stability could be supported, and established government structures close to local concerns would be utilized in the program. Quick placement of eligible job applicants (i.e., within a week of application) would be necessary to avoid the need for interim assistance and the expense of processing applications for such assistance.

The minimum wage pay rate is dictated by the need to make GGJs affordable and to prevent a labor draw from other jobs. At the same time, making GGJs full time with travel allowances, shift differential and medical benefits is necessary to make GGJs more rewarding than "welfare assistance." It could also have the effect of encouraging businesses to meet the same minimum standards for livable income for their employees, in which case fewer GGJs might be needed. Applying medical benefits to, and providing support allowances for, a non-working spouse living in the same household could help to support family stability and promote full-time parenting of any children. Still, the

benefits and allowances would not be so large as to be a disincentive to
the spouse taking on a part-time job and giving up the benefits in exchange for a more lucrative family income. Medical benefits and support allowances for up to four dependent children living in the same
household are also necessary to promote family stability. Allowing dependent children under 19 years of age to take part-time work without
loss of GGJ medical benefits would avoid creating a disincentive for
them to earn money; the GGJ support allowances for dependent
children, which would be given up in such cases, is sufficiently small.

Two weeks paid vacation plus five paid holidays is not only a
humane benefit in support of health and family stability, it is also less
expensive than paying support costs for work during these 15 days. Allowing disability benefits for up to one year is comparable to some
private sector programs, and in cases where the disability becomes permanent, would provide households living on the edge of poverty adequate time to apply for and receive benefits from Social Security
disability.

Support costs for GGJs (i.e., expenditures for materials and administrative personnel) are figured at 100 per cent of the wage rate; the
WPA jobs of the 1930s had a support cost of about 50 per cent of the
wage rate.[13] The 100 per cent figure not only would serve as an estimate
for cost analysis but also as the allowable upper limit for GGJ support
expenditures. The limit would apply to the overall program as well as
to each GGJ project. Since some GGJ projects might have lower support costs and others might even be profitable, the total support cost of
the GGJ program could be lower than, but would not exceed, estimates
based on the 100 per cent support cost figure.

Appendix 4 provides a table showing the expected annual earnings
from a GGJ, along with its medical and support costs, as a function of
the household circumstances of the GGJ holder.

An estimated five million GGJs might be needed to accommodate
all eligible GGJ applicants. At an average annual cost of $17,528 per
GGJ, the gross cost of the guaranteed job program could be about
$88.14 billion per year. Paying for the GGJ program, without increased
taxation or confiscation, will be discussed in the next two sections.

The Reallocation of Monies from Certain Social Programs to Pay for Government-Guaranteed Jobs

Immediate funding for the GGJ program would come by way of re-allocation of monies from certain non-retirement social programs partially replaced by the GGJ program. Households with a member employed on a GGJ would lose their eligibility and need for some of the benefits from these social programs, and the savings realized for them would be immediately reallocated to the GGJ program.

Appendix 6 shows a gross calculation of the amount of savings that might reasonably be expected for social programs partially replaced by GGJs if the kind of GGJ program described here is implemented. Based on this calculation, a range for the net annual cost of providing five million GGJs is given. At worst, it is estimated that the net annual cost would be about the same as the amount of money needed to raise the income level of poor U.S. households above the official poverty level via direct grants, i.e., $46 billion.[14] At best, the annual net cost would be zero and a couple of million dollars saved.

If monies from this reallocation were insufficient to pay for the needed GGJs, and no other revenues were available without a tax increase, the GGJ program could be immediately implemented at some reduced level. Or its implementation could be deferred until other monies, reallocated from Social Security and other mandatory retirement programs (and/or from dividends from surplus stock in the revolving stock fund—see below), become available later. Such monies would become available if the replacement of Social Security and civil service and railroad retirement programs by a stock ownership program could be accomplished in a way that maintains the current tax for these retirement funds and does not require the use of these revenues to purchase stock for the program. Eventually, when these retirement programs are fully replaced by stock ownership, revenues of about $180.5 billion a year would be reallocatable to fund about ten million GGJs or other programs in order to reduce the federal debt, or simply to give back to the taxpayers as a rebate. (Additionally, dividends from surplus stock in the revolving stock fund to be proposed below could be applied for the same purposes. See Appendix 11 and Figure 2.) The key to all of this, however, is to create for the stock ownership program a mammoth $4.6 trillion stock fund without confiscation or increased taxation.

The Application of Stuart Speiser's SuperStock Concept to the Creation of a Stock Fund for Guaranteed Work-Ownership Opportunity

There may be no such thing as a free lunch, but perhaps the nearest thing to it is the capacity of capital to pay for itself, even several times over. An investment in a business may yield several times the original investment in profits. It is this capacity which is at the heart of Stuart Speiser's original SuperStock concept.[15] Under Speiser's proposal, the leading 2,000 U.S. corporations would be required for a time to pay for any new plants or equipment by issuing new corporate stock in exchange for government-guaranteed loans and tax credits. The stock would be held in escrow by the lender until the loan plus interest is paid off by the stock's dividends. It would then go into a government revolving stock fund to be distributed to U.S. households. To speed up this process, corporations would be required to pay out a maximal percentage of their earnings as dividends. Speiser also suggests that government-subsidized low-interest loans be made available for this program for the same purpose.

Since the corporations involved in Speiser's plan are the most solid, very few (if any) loan defaults would be expected. In effect, the revolving stock fund would be created from capital's capacity to reproduce itself. No increased taxation or confiscation of ownership would be involved, even though federal legislation would be needed to permit tax credits and government backing of loans in exchange for new stock, and to require corporate payment of a maximal percentage of earnings as dividends.

The guaranteed work-ownership program proposed here would rely on a modified version of the SuperStock plan to create a revolving stock fund from which would come the stock awards to replace Social Security and other mandatory retirement programs. Along with having all public stock corporations (instead of only the leading 2,000) participate in the program, the main difference between the modified version and the original is that the modified version would require that only half of a corporation's new investments in plants or equipment be funded by the issuance of new stock to the government in exchange for loan guarantees and tax incentives. In connection with this, only those earnings proportionate to the ratio of a corporation's appropriated stock to total stock would be maximally paid out as dividends on the appropriated stock; the remaining portion of earnings could be paid out as usual on the regular stock. Corporate income tax credits would be similarly applied. No corporate income tax would be paid on earnings proportionately tied to appropriated stock, and as an added tax incentive, a tax credit of the same amount would be applied to remaining corporate income taxes. What this amounts to is that when at least one-half of a corporation's total stock is appropriated to the government's revolving fund, that corporation would pay no income taxes. Lesser percentages of appropriated stock would gain proportionally smaller tax reductions.

Under this modified version of Speiser's plan, the amount of stock annually appropriated to the revolving stock fund replacing Social Security, and so forth, would easily be adequate to meet the program's annual requirements for stock awards, and would create at least a temporary surplus whose dividends could be applied to funding GGJs or for other purposes. The modification would also allow for capital gains accruing from the non-stock financing of up to one-half of corporations' capital improvements. For current and future holders of unappropriated stock, this would be an important consideration since their stock investment may rest on the presumption of capital gains in addition to dividend income. This modified version of SuperStock would also permit corporations to have more control over the allocation of earnings since only that portion of earnings tied to appropriated stock would have to be maximally paid out as dividends.

The loss of corporate income tax revenue under the revised tax law would expectedly be offset by increased tax revenues from personal incomes supplemented with stock dividends, and/or from dividends accruing from surplus stock in the revolving fund. Economic revival resulting from lower corporate taxes and more diversified individual purchasing power could also mean more and better jobs and greater tax revenues.

The time frame for the implementation of this program would depend upon a number of factors including corporate earnings and the interest rates on the government-backed loans. These would determine the length of time it would take for corporations to repay the loan, and therefore, the time before the appropriated stock could be awarded to citizens. At best, only about seven years might be needed for this; at worst, up to 30 years could be required.[16] One year beyond this period, all eligible citizens would receive their first stock awards, and in another 25 years, the revolving stock fund would be fully established. The guaranteed work-ownership program would be essentially established in 33 to 56 years.

Closing Comments

By its very nature and size, guaranteed work-ownership opportunity must be a government undertaking. For-profit corporations cannot risk viability in order to artificially bolster employment, and while private initiatives can play a role in the management of job programs, only the government has the public authority to guarantee work opportunity. Similarly, while corporations can help to broaden stock ownership, only the government has the public authority to extend stock ownership opportunity universally to its citizens.

There is, of course, no magical formula for suddenly bringing about guaranteed work-ownership opportunity, but the essential ingredients for a feasible plan that meets the objectives set forth at the beginning of this essay may be clear. Like the building of the U.S. interstate highway system, the magnitude of the universal share ownership goal requires long-range thinking and implementation. That 33 to 56 years may be needed for complete establishment of a plan should not deter the in-depth analysis, refinement, and political support-building needed to make it a reality, especially since its major benefits would be immediately and increasingly tangible.

Notes

1.   Pope John Paul II, *Laborem Exercens (On Human Work)*. Boston: Daughters of St. Paul, 1981, paragraph 4, pp. 34-37.

2.   For example, see Jon Wisman, "Economic Reform for Humanity's Greatest Struggle," Chapter II in Kenneth B. Taylor (ed.), *Capitalism and the 'Evil Empire': Reducing Superpower Conflict Through American Economic Reform*. New York: New Horizons Press, 1988, pp. 25-28.

3.   Ibid.

4.   David Howell, *The New Capitalism: Personal Ownership and Social Progress*. London: Center for Policy Studies, 1986, pp. 5-30.

5.   See John G. Craig, "Crisis in Capitalism" in *The Pittsburgh Post-Gazette,* October 18, 1986, p. 7, in reference to the views of Peter Drucker.

6.   Stuart M. Speiser, *How to End the Nuclear Nightmare*. Croton-on-Hudson, New York: North River Press, 1984.

7.   According to the U.S. government's definition, more than 33 million Americans are poor. This represents about one in every seven persons in the U.S., a rate that is higher than at almost any other

time during the last 20 years.[a] What may be surprising here is that the financial cost for erasing this condition by way of outright public grants is a relatively small $46 billion,[b] or about five per cent of the federal budget. Proponents of widespread capital ownership in the U.S. envision ownership of enormous amounts of capital—as much as $5 trillion in productive assets[c]—being transferred, without confiscation, broadly among the citizenry. Accomplishing this in a way that provides minimum livable income to all Americans would certainly seem to be a plausible objective. And what is more, the resultant diversification of purchasing power would seem to facilitate a healthier economy, more so even than enhancement of concentrated purchasing power.

(a) These figures as quoted in "Economic Justice for All: Catholic Social Teaching and the U.S. Economy." (3rd Draft). Washington, D.C.: National Conference of Catholic Bishops, 1986, p. 47.

(b) See Sar A. Levitan, *Programs in Aid of the Poor.* 5th ed. Baltimore and London: Johns Hopkins University Press, 1985, pp. 52-53.

(c) See Speiser, op. cit., p. 142.

8. As the family goes, so goes society. It seems plain that in the context of family life individuals acquire many social, emotional, and moral ingredients that will ultimately effect the way they shape the society they constitute. When economic conditions or public policy exacerbate the phenomena of single-parent families, unparented kids, and geographic dislocation, they would seem to undermine not only family stability but social stability as well. In developing a plan for widespread share ownership, then, the awarding of or opportunity to acquire capital ownership should not penalize the parent who undertakes, full time, the socially important work of raising children. Nor should it create economic incentive for non-marriage, the splitting up of husbands and wives, or geographic displacement of families. Rather, it should, as much as possible, support community stability, integrated families, and full-time parenting of children.

9. As described by Bandow, Doug, Copley News Service in "Looking at a New Social Security Plan" in *The Greensburg Tribune-Review,* November 30, 1986.

10. The following approaches to guaranteeing substantial stock

ownership opportunity on the basis of work are examined and rejected:

(a) *Trickle-Down Work-Ownership Opportunity.* According to this approach, broad stock ownership among the employed—via the Social Security stock purchase option, employee stock ownership plans (ESOPs) or otherwise—is seen as directly facilitating employment and helping to revive the economy. (For an example of this view, see David Howell, op. cit.) As a result of supplemental dividend income, workers' wage demands expectedly would moderate, making labor more affordable to business. Additionally, dividend income could conceivably enable more self-employment by supplementing otherwise unlivable or unpredictable earnings from such employment. All this could supposedly clear the labor market (i.e., create full employment) and eventuate in universal share ownership.

There is reason, however, to doubt this supposition. Even if business savings from moderating wage demands were applied to adding workers to the payroll, this demand for labor would likely restore upward pressure on wages, counteracting demand for labor. Beyond this, increasing automation and robotics would also tend to reduce demand for labor, and in a workplace that is ever more service-oriented and technologically sophisticated, the unskilled or otherwise marginally employable person will probably be unable to find work, even in a boom economy.

Nor is a transition to self-employment likely to take up enough slack to clear the labor market. This is because not everyone is suited to self-employment, perhaps least of all those unskilled or otherwise marginally employable who are not likely to find gainful work under almost any foreseeable circumstances or scenarios.

It would be a mistake, then, to suppose that stock ownership among the employed will eventuate in full employment and universal stock ownership. Such a view clearly represents an economic approach to this matter whose anticipated "trickle-down" benefits would not accomplish the objective of guaranteeing opportunity for gainful work and substantial capital ownership.

(b) *Enhancement of Work Incentive via Ownership Opportunity.* It has been suggested that awarding capital ownership on the basis of work or training for work (i.e. becoming employable) will provide an incentive that will eventuate in full employment and universal capital ownership. This supposition rests on the notion that for able-bodied people who desire gainful employment enough jobs are available or could be generated via self-employment if these people were sufficiently motivated to accept them, to train for them, or to create them. It is furthermore supposed that even part-time and full-time jobs with low pay and few benefits would attract plenty of takers since the share ownership these jobs would provide could generate substantial supplemental income.

What is overlooked, however, is that there is already substantial incentive for people to work, train for work, or create gainful work for themselves, even to accept part-time and full-time jobs with low pay and few benefits. Yet it has not produced gainful employment for all the able-bodied persons who desire it. Similar to the Great Depression era in the U.S., when so many desperate people willing to accept any work could not find it, today's unemployment clearly has more to do with an insufficiency of gainful employment opportunities, especially for the unskilled or marginally employable, than with a lack of incentive to accept work, train for work, or create self-employment. In fact, studies have demonstrated that even when training is provided for the structurally unemployed and their motivation is high, the majority often remain unemployed because of a lack of job opportunity. (As cited in Leonard Goodwin, *Causes and Cures of Welfare*. Lexington, Massachusetts: Lexington Books, 1983, pp. 135-38.)

Even when taken together with the suppositions found in the first approach it would seem to be untenable to suppose that awarding capital ownership on the basis of work or training for work will provide a work incentive that will eventuate in full employment and universal capital ownership. Such an approach to guaranteeing work and substantial ownership opportunity, then, would clearly be inadequate.

(c) *Work/Workfare/Volunteer Work-Ownership Opportunity.* This approach to guaranteeing opportunity for work and share ownership would provide that those persons unable to secure payroll employment or to succeed at self-employment could still participate in share ownership opportunity through other kinds of work, namely, workfare or volunteer work. It has been suggested that much of society's necessary but unfunded work could be done by persons such as these who would thus earn share ownership.

The problem with this kind of approach is twofold. In the first place, it seems that opportunities for workfare or volunteer work are very limited, mostly due to the substantial support costs for these and, in the case of volunteer work, because not every unemployed person is suitable. While the majority of welfare recipients not participating in workfare are mothers with young children, other reasons given for the reluctance of most states and counties to implement workfare include (i) the cost to governments of choosing jobs, channeling people to them, and providing supervision; and (ii) the lack of transportation available to most welfare clients. Similar factors would limit the opportunities for volunteer work, but another factor here would be that volunteer work usually demands people with considerable skills and personal qualities. Anyone who has ever applied for volunteer work with the Peace Corps, VISTA, or any other humanitarian or religious organization knows well the high qualifications that are usually required for acceptance.

And even if the volunteer work were to be done independently rather than for an organization, the same and other considerations would apply, namely, support and verification costs and competency.

The second problem with this approach is that it is not geared to alleviating poverty. Even with supplemental income derived from capital ownership, the income of people who would depend on workfare for extended periods of time probably would not be sufficient to raise them out of poverty until perhaps later in life. And also, as income derived from accumulating capital grew, cutbacks in welfare assistance would probably offset any gains. All that has been said here concerning workfare applies equivalently to volunteer work which would carry with it no regular income.

(d) *Work/Lack of Work-Ownership Opportunity.*   Unlike the above approach which would require workfare or volunteer work to earn capital ownership when no other employment opportunities were available, this approach would award capital ownership on the basis of payroll employment, self-employment, and the lack of local opportunities for these, without requiring workfare or volunteer work. An advantage of this approach would be that work opportunity would not be a limiting factor in ownership opportunity, and costs to support workfare would not be incurred. Its inadequacies, however, would be at least threefold: (i) the individual and social benefits of work would not obtain for that segment of the population which remains without employment; (ii) poverty among the unemployed population would either not be alleviated or would not be alleviated in a timely manner; and (iii) the awarding of capital ownership without the work-able person earning it via work would probably be popularly unacceptable. While this approach may have some attractiveness, then, it is not adequate for meeting the proposed objectives.

11. The average annual Social Security retirement benefit per retired worker for 1985 was $5,734 (data from the Social Security Administration, Greensburg, Pennsylvania).
12. U.S. Census Bureau, 1985 statistics.
13. This figure comes from dividing the difference between the WPA monthly cost per man of $82 (Arthur M. Schlesinger, Jr., *The Age of Roosevelt: The Politics of Upheaval.* Boston: Houghton Mifflin, 1960, p. 349) and the WPA monthly pay of $55 (Robert S. McElvaine, *The Great Depression: America 1929-41.* New York: Times Books, 1984, p. 266) by the WPA monthly pay.
14. Levitan, op. cit.
15. Speiser, op. cit.
16. Ibid., p. 140.
17. Basil Rauch, *The History of the New Deal* [1944]. 2nd ed. New York: Octogan Books, 1980, p. 164.
18. The average Medicaid annual payment of $1,500 per eligible person is figured from the following 1985 statistics from the U.S. Health Care Financing Administration: Actual Beneficiaries— 21,808,305; Estimated Number of Eligibles—16.2% more than beneficiaries; State and Federal Benefits—$37,507,639,305. The $1,500 per year cost is divided by 2,000 annual work hours to arrive at the $0.75 hourly cost.

19. Bureau of Labor Statistics, third quarter data, 1986.

20. Ibid.

21. Medicaid 1985 statistics from U.S. Health Care Financing Administration. All other data (except for unemployment insurance) based on that from *National Data Book and Guide to Sources: Statistical Abstract of the U.S.* 105th ed. Washington, D.C.: U.S. Interior Department, Bureau of the Census, 1985, Table No. 593, p. 357 (1983 figures adjusted to project 1985 estimates). Unemployment insurance figures from Table No. 596, p. 359 (1982 figures adjusted to project 1985 estimates).

22. Social Security 1985 data from Social Security Administration, Greensburg, Pennsylvania. Public employee and railroad retirement data from *National Data Book and Guide to Sources,* op. cit., Table No. 596 (1981 data adjusted to project 1985 estimates).

23. In 1985, corporations paid $68 billion in taxes on earnings (data from *The Economic and Budget Outlook: Fiscal Years 1987-1991.* Washington, D.C.: Congressional Budget Office, February 1986, Table C-2, p. 134).

Appendices

(Reference numbers within text refer to foregoing Notes section.)

Appendix 1: Government-Guaranteed Job (GGJ) Eligibility

To be eligible for a GGJ, a person must:

(1) be a U.S. citizen,

(2) be 18 to 64 years of age,

(3) not be in a government prison or detention center,

(4) not be ineligible due to having been duly dismissed two times from GGJs for reasons of misconduct, negligence, or gross incompetence,

(5) be the only person holding a GGJ in his/her household, *with no other member of the household otherwise employed full time,*

(6) if a military service job was offered and refused, wait at least two years from the date of the first offer and refusal to begin the GGJ, and

(7) if a civilian job with wages and benefits comparable to a GGJ was offered and refused, wait at least one year from the date of the latest offer and refusal to begin the GGJ.

Appendix 2: Possible Government-Guaranteed Jobs (GGJs)

(1) *Types of Jobs Yesterday*—examples from a small, random selection of WPA accomplishments during its first two years.[17]

3,300 storage dams, 103 golf courses, 5,800 traveling libraries established, 1,654 medical and dental clinics established, 36,000 miles of new rural roads, 128,000,000 school lunches served, 2,000,000 home visits by nurses, 1,500 theatrical productions, 134 fish hatcheries, 1,100,000 Braille pages transcribed, and 17,000 literacy classes conducted per month.

(2) *Types of Jobs Today*—a few examples of the many possibilities.

(1) construction and maintenance of public housing; (2) low-cost home repair for low-income families; (3) additional construction and maintenance of public parks, roads, bridges, rail lines, and depots; (4) services not otherwise provided to homebound or handicapped persons; (5) teachers' aides; (6) environmental reclamation, beautification, and protection; (7) humanitarian services to developing countries; (8) supplemental federal, state, and local civil services; and (9) operation of some manufacturing plants, or other businesses or utilities in the public interest (e.g., the manufacturing of products for which there are no other U.S. producers).

Appendix 3: Government-Guaranteed Job (GGJ) Specifications

(1) *Location:* within the county of residence
(2) *Placement Period:* within one week of application
(3) *Hours:*
  (a) maximum of 8 hours per day, any day of the week
  (b) 40 hours per week, no overtime
  (c) 1,960 hours per year
(4) *Pay and Benefits:*
  (a) base rate of $3.35 per hour or the prevailing minimum wage
  (b) travel allowance according to the following schedule:
    Zone 1 (0-5 miles one way to job site)....................$0.00/hr.
    Zone 2 (5.1-10 miles one way to job site)..............$0.10/hr.
    Zone 3 (10.1-15 miles one way to job site)............$0.20/hr.
    Zone 4 (15.1-20 miles one way to job site)............$0.30/hr.
    Zone 5 (20.1-25 miles one way to job site)............$0.40/hr.
    Zone 6 (25.1 miles or more one way to job site) ...$0.50/hr.
  (c) family support allowance according to the following schedule:
    non-employed married spouse living
    in same household ....$0.75/hr.
    each of up to four non-employed children
    (under 18) living in same household......................$0.25/hr.
  (d) shift differential according to the following schedule:
    shift 1 (8 a.m.-4 p.m.)..$0.00/hr.
    shift 2 (4 p.m.-midnight) ....$0.10/hr.
    shift 3 (midnight-8 a.m.)..$0.20/hr.
  (e) medical benefits value/cost:[18]
    GGJ worker...$0.75/hr.
    non-employed married spouse living
    in same household ....$0.75/hr.
    each of up to four children (under 18) not
    employed full time, living in same household ....$0.75/hr.
  (f) temporary disability: up to one year at base wage rate and medical benefits
  (g) vacation: one hour paid vacation per 25 work hours; five holidays at base rate with medical benefits
(5) *Employment Support Cost:* 100 per cent of base wage rate for hours of actual work

Appendix 4: Government-Guaranteed Jobs (GGJs)
—A Table of Illustrative Wages, Benefits and Support Costs
as a Function of Holder Circumstances (in Dollars)

	Zone 1	Zone 2	Zone 3	Zone 4	Zone 5	Zone 6	
Single	6,968	7,168	7,368	7,568	7,768	7,968	Wages
	8,528	8,728	8,928	9,128	9,328	9,528	+Med. Ben.
	15,128	15,328	15,528	15,728	15,928	16,128	+Sup. Cost
shift 2	7,168	7,368	7,568	7,768	7,968	8,168	Wages
	8,728	8,928	9,128	9,328	9,528	9,728	+Med. Ben.
	15,328	15,528	15,728	15,928	16,128	16,328	+Sup. Cost
shift 3	7,368	7,568	7,768	7,968	8,168	8,368	Wages
	8,928	9,128	9,328	9,528	9,728	9,928	+Med. Ben.
	15,528	15,728	15,928	16,128	16,328	16,528	+Sup. Cost
+Spouse	8,468	8,668	8,868	9,068	9,268	9,468	Wages
(unem-	10,028	10,228	10,428	10,628	10,828	11,028	+Med. Ben.
ployed)	16,628	16,828	17,028	17,228	17,428	17,628	+Sup. Cost
shift 2	8,668	8,868	9,068	9,268	9,468	9,668	Wages
	10,228	10,428	10,628	10,828	11,028	11,228	+Med. Ben.
	16,828	17,028	17,228	17,428	17,828	17,828	+Sup. Cost
shift 3	8,868	9,068	9,268	9,468	9,668	9,868	Wages
	10,428	10,628	10,828	11,028	11,228	11,428	+Med. Ben.
	17,028	17,228	17,428	17,628	17,828	17,928	+Sup. Cost
+1 Child	8,968	9,168	9,368	9,568	9,768	9,968	Wages
(under 19,	10,628	10,828	11,028	11,228	11,428	11,628	+Med. Ben.
unem-)	17,228	17,428	17,628	17,828	17,928	18,128	+Sup. Cost
ployed)							
shift 2	9,169	9,368	9,568	9,768	9,968	10,068	Wages
	10,828	11,028	11,228	11,428	11,628	11,828	+Med. Ben.
	17,428	17,628	17,828	17,928	18,128	18,328	+Sup. Cost
shift 3	9,368	9,568	9,768	9,968	10,068	10,268	Wages
	11,028	11,228	11,428	11,628	11,828	12,028	+Med. Ben.
	17,628	17,828	17,928	18,128	18,328	18,528	+Sup. Cost
+2 Children	9,468	9,668	9,868	10,068	10,268	10,468	Wages
(under 19,	11,128	11,328	11,528	11,728	11,928	12,128	+Med. Ben.
unem-	17,728	17,928	18,128	18,328	18,528	18,728	+Sup. Cost
ployed)							

Appendix 4 (cont.)

	Zone 1	Zone 2	Zone 3	Zone 4	Zone 5	Zone 6	
shift 2	9,668	9,868	10,068	10,268	10,468	10,668	Wages
	11,328	11,528	11,728	11,928	12,128	12,328	+Med. Ben.
	17,928	18,128	18,328	18,528	18,728	18,928	+Sup. Cost
shift 3	9,868	10,068	10,268	10,468	10,668	10,868	Wages
	11,528	11,728	11,928	12,128	12,328	12,528	+Med. Ben.
	18,128	18,328	18,528	18,728	18,928	19,128	+Sup. Cost
+3 Children (under 19, unemployed)	9,968	10,168	10,368	10,568	10,768	10,968	Wages
	11,628	11,868	12,068	12,268	12,468	12,668	+Med. Ben.
	18,228	18,428	18,628	18,828	19,028	19,228	+Sup. Cost
shift 2	10,168	10,368	10,568	10,768	10,968	11,168	Wages
	11,868	12,068	12,268	12,468	12,668	12,868	+Med. Ben.
	18,428	18,628	18,828	19,028	19,228	19,428	+Sup. Cost
shift 3	10,368	10,568	10,768	10,968	11,168	11,368	Wages
	12,068	12,268	12,468	12,668	12,868	13,068	+Med. Ben.
	18,628	18,828	19,028	19,228	19,428	19,628	+Sup. Cost
+4 Children (under 19, unemployed)	10,468	10,668	10,868	11,168	11,268	11,468	Wages
	12,168	12,368	12,568	12,768	12,968	13,169	+Med. Ben.
	18,728	18,928	19,128	19,328	19,528	19,728	+Sup. Cost
shift 2	10,668	10,868	11,068	11,268	11,468	11,668	Wages
	12,368	12,568	12,768	12,968	13,168	13,368	+Med. Ben.
	18,928	19,128	19,328	19,528	19,728	19,928	+Sup. Cost
shift 3	10,868	11,068	11,268	11,468	11,668	11,868	Wages
	12,568	12,768	12,968	13,168	13,368	13,568	+Med. Ben.
	19,128	19,328	19,528	19,728	19,928	20,128	+Sup. Cost

Note: For single-parent families or families with a spouse employed part time for any part of the year, GGJ wages, medical benefits, and support cost totals are determined by subtracting the following allowances from the appropriate figures for the number of dependent, unemployed children in the family:

FROM WAGES, SUBTRACT 1,500;
FROM WAGES PLUS MEDICAL BENEFITS VALUE/COST, SUBRACT 1,500;
FROM WAGES PLUS MEDICAL BENEFITS VALUE/COST PLUS SUPPORT COSTS, SUBTRACT 3,000.

Appendix 5: Estimated Number and Gross Cost of Government-Guaranteed Jobs

(1) Number of eligible family households
(i.e., families with no member employed
full time and at least one member seeking
employment)...2,250,000[19]

(2) Number of eligible non-family households:

    (a) Non-family households with householder
        seeking employment...793,000[20]

    (b) LESS the number of non-family households
        with at least one member employed full time
        and the householder seeking employment........ (− unknown)

    (c) PLUS the number of non-family households
        with householder employed part time, no
        other member employed full time, and at
        least one member seeking employment............(+ unknown)

(3) Number of known family and non-family
households eligible for a GGJ......................................3,043,000

(4) Estimated number of households not showing
up in the above statistics that might be eligible
for a GGJ...1,957,000

(5) TOTAL NUMBER OF ELIGIBLE
HOUSEHOLDS..5,000,000

(6) Minimum annual cost for a GGJ
(i.e., single person, zone 1, shift 1).................................$15,128

(7) Maximum annual cost for a GGJ
(i.e., GGJ worker has a non-employed spouse,
4 children under 18 years of age, non-employed
full time, zone 6, shift 3)..$20,128

(8) ANNUAL COST FOR AN AVERAGE GGJ...................$17,628

(9) TOTAL ANNUAL GROSS COST FOR
GGJ PROGRAM...$88.140
(billion)

Appendix 6: Immediate Financing for Government-Guaranteed Jobs (GGJs)—the Reallocation of Monies from Some Partially Replaced Non-retirement Social Programs

(1) Estimates of Savings to Certain Non-retirement Social Programs Partially Replaced by GGJs:

Non-Retirement Programs	Cost Without [21] GGJ Program	*Savings Reallocatable to GGJ Program*	
		Estimated Minimum	Estimated Maximum
Medicaid	37,508	18,754 at 50%	33,757 at 90%
A.F.D.C.	16,508	8,254 at 50%	14,857 at 90%
General assistance	2,264	1,132 at 50%	2,038 at 90%
Earned income tax credit	1,935	967 at 50%	1,742 at 90%
Food stamps	14,245	7,123 at 50%	12,821 at 90%
Women, infants and children	1,245	622 at 50%	1,121 at 90%
Low-income housing assistance (Section 8)	5,360	1,340 at 25%	4,020 at 75%
Low-rent public housing	3,440	860 at 25%	2,580 at 75%
Low-income energy assistance	2,037	1,018 at 50%	1,833 at 90%
Employment and training services	1,887	1,887 at 100%	1,887 at 100%
Job corps	662	662 at 100%	662 at 100%
Work incentive programs	323	323 at 100%	323 at 100%
State/railroad unemployment insurance	25,262	0 at 0%	12,631 at 50%*
NON-RETIREMENT PROGRAMS TOTALS	112,676	42,942 at 39%	90,272 at 81%

* via reduction of eligibility period from 6 months to 3 months

(2) Net Cost of GGJ Program with Reallocation of Savings from Certain Non-retirement Social Programs Partially Replaced by GGJs:

    (a) Annual gross cost of 5 million GGJs ....$88.140 billion
    (b) Estimated minimum reallocated savings ....$42.942 billion
    (c) Estimated maximum reallocatable savings.............................$90.272 billion
    (d) MAXIMUM NET COST FOR 5 MILLION GGJs ....$45.198 billion
    (e) MINIMUM NET COST FOR 5 MILLION GGJs....................-$2.132 billion

**Appendix 7: Long-Term Financing for Government-
Guaranteed Jobs (GGJs)—the Reallocation of Monies from
Social Security and Other Mandatory Retirement Programs
Replaced by Stock Ownership (and/or from Dividends from
Surplus Stock in Revolving Fund)***

(1) Annual expenditures of social retirement programs:[22]

    (a) Social Security..$128.832 billion

    (b) Public employee retirement
        (federal civil service, other federal
        employees, state and local government)........$47.441 billion

    (c) Railroad retirement...$4.146 billion

    TOTAL RETIREMENT
    PROGRAM EXPENDITURES..................$180.491 billion

(2) Portion of retirement program expenditures
reallocatable to GGJ program each year
after stock ownership awards begin.....................1/46 or 2.174%

    (a) Amount...$3.922 billion

    (b) Fundable GGJs at $17,628 per GGJ 222,504

(3) Retirement program monies annually
reallocatable after stock ownership fund
has been fully established...................................$180.491 billion

    Fundable GGJs at $17,628 per GGJ 10,238,881

*Dividends accruing from temporary surplus of appropriated stock in
revolving fund (see Figure 2).

Appendix 8: Overall Financing Strategy for the GGJ Program

(1) The GGJ program could be implemented as soon as its operating procedures and personnel were in place, and if needed, supplemental monies were available.

(2) Initially, for each GGJ established, a fixed amount of money from each of the non-retirement social programs then benefiting the job applicant and the members of his household would be reallocated to pay for the GGJ. If additional money were needed, appropriated supplemental funds would be applied.

(3) Supplemental funding may be necessary for about 8-31 years until monies from Social Security and other retirement programs can be reallocated to the GGJ program. If additional GGJs beyond the estimated five million were needed, these could be established only when reallocated monies from the retirement programs, or from surplus stock in the revolving stock fund, rose above the level at which they superseded supplemental funding. Eventually, about 10-15 million GGJs would be funded via the reallocation of monies from certain non-retirement and retirement programs and from surplus stock dividends. If this number were not needed, the extra monies could be applied to other needs, such as reducing the federal debt.

Appendix 9: Stock Ownership Awards Eligibility

To be eligible for annual stock ownership awards valued at $1,080-$1,095, a person must:

(1) be a U.S. citizen,

(2) be 18 to 64 years of age,

(3) not be in a government prison or detention center, and

(4) have worked at least 1,920 hours in that year in one or any combination of the following types of work (lesser hours will entitle proportionally smaller stock ownership awards):

    (a) regular payroll civilian employment,

    (b) self-employment which generated a gross income of at least $5,000,

    (c) military service,

    (d) a GGJ, or

    (e) approved volunteer service, or

(5) be a non-employed parent with a dependent child under 18 years of age living in the same household, or

(6) be matriculated as a full-time student in a college, professional, or technical school.

Appendix 10: Estimated Number of Eligible Persons, Gross Cost of Stock Ownership Awards and Total Revolving Stock Fund

(1) Total Annual Cost of Stock Awards $160,591,200

    (a) U.S. population age 18 to 64 years (1985).........147,738,000

    (b) Maximum number of persons
(18 to 64 years of age) eligible for
stock ownership awards......................................147,738,000

    (c) Maximum annual stock award per
eligible person...$1,087

    (d) Total annual cost equals (b) and (c).

(2) Total Revolving Stock Fund.......................................$4.6 trillion

    (a) Eligible persons 18 to 64 years of age times
median value of stock portfolio ($25,000)
for persons 18 to 64 years of age.........................$3.2 trillion

    (b) Persons over 64 years of age (28 million) times
value of maximum stock portfolio ($50,000) .....$1.4 trillion

    (c) Total revolving stock fund equals (a) plus (b).

Appendix 11: Financing the Stock Ownership Awards Program via a Modified Version of Stuart Speiser's SuperStock Plan

(1)   With the initiation of the stock ownership awards program, every U.S.-based public stock corporation will be required to issue (for appropriation by the U.S. government agency handling the stock awards program) new stock in order to finance not less than 50 per cent of its capital improvements or expansion. Not less than 75 per cent of the earnings proportional to the amount of appropriated stock to total stock will be paid out as dividends on the appropriated stock. This stock will be non-voting while in government hands. It will become voting but non-transferable when awarded to an eligible U.S. citizen. When the stock awardee dies, his/her stock portfolio will return to the government's revolving stock fund.

(2)   In exchange for the appropriated stock, the U.S. government will guarantee repayment of the privately arranged loans to cover the stock if (a) the U.S.-based corporation issuing the stock is among the 2,000 leading U.S. corporations, or (b) had a profit of at least $1 million the previous year, or (c) is a new corporation in the making. Otherwise, such loan will not be guaranteed.

(3)   Also, in exchange for the appropriated stock, federal, state and local corporate income taxes will be reduced by twice the percentage of a corporation's total stock that has been appropriated. Thus, when half its total stock has been appropriated, the corporation will pay no income taxes. Until then, it will pay proportionally less in income taxes as the percentage of appropriated stock to total stock increases to a maximum of 50 per cent.

(4)   The above stipulations should (a) produce up to $192.2 billion worth of appropriated stock annually (this is one-half of the amount of new capital American business was to require in 1985) and (b) stimulate business growth as a result of the corporate income tax incentives. Dilution of stock values should not be a problem since dividends (and therefore demand for the stock) would be unaffected or improved, while non-stock financing of up to 50 per cent of capital improvements should insure gains in its value.

(5) The appropriated stock should pay for itself in 7-30 years, after which it would be awarded to eligible U.S. citizens on the basis of work, training for work, incapacity for work, and full-time parenting up to approximately $1,087 annually.

(6) This pool of (up to) $192.2 billion worth of annually appropriated stock would meet the requirements for the (up to) $160.5 billion worth of stock needed for stock awards each year. It would also provide for the establishment of the revolving stock fund of $4.6 trillion in about 25 years. During this period, annual appropriations to the stock fund would exceed annual stock awards, creating a surplus from which dividends could be applied to GGJs, or toward subsidizing government-backed loans, reducing the federal debt, or supporting other programs (see Figure 2). Any stock appropriated after this would be used to keep up with population increases or to replace defunct stock.

(7) Loss of corporate income tax revenues[23] would be offset by greater personal income tax revenues accruing from dividend income and the fruits of a more vigorous economy spurred on by corporate income tax reductions.

Figure 1

ILLUSTRATIVE HOUSEHOLD INCOME UNDER
GUARANTEED WORK-OWNERSHIP OPPORTUNITY

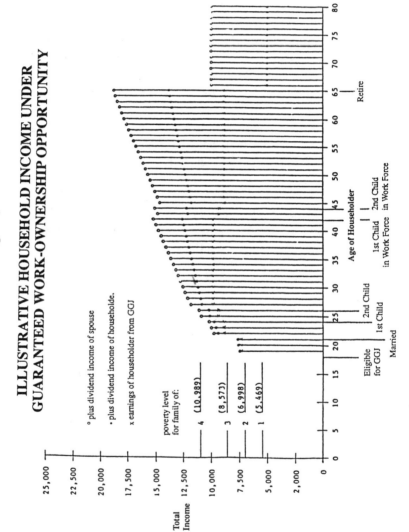

Figure 2

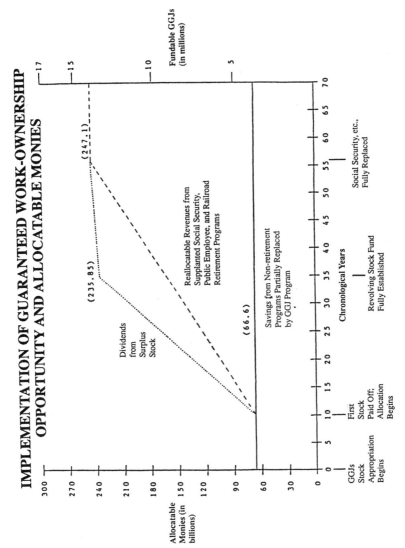

IMPLEMENTATION OF GUARANTEED WORK-OWNERSHIP OPPORTUNITY AND ALLOCATABLE MONIES

5

THE GOLDEN AGE THAT COULD BE

by

James S. Albus

Editor's Note: *Dr. James S. Albus is Chief of the Robot Systems Division, National Bureau of Standards, Department of Commerce, Washington, D.C.* He is internationally recognized as a leading authority on robotics. In this essay, Dr. Albus updates his National Mutual Fund Plan, which he first announced in his book,* Peoples' Capitalism: The Economics of the Robot Revolution *(Kensington, Maryland: New World Books, 1976).*

ABSTRACT

Real economic growth depends upon productivity growth, which in turn is directly caused by investment in education, technology, and new production facilities. America's investment rate is about 10 per cent of GNP, whereas in Japan the rate is 30 per cent of GNP.

---

* The views expressed in this essay are those of the author alone and do not necessarily reflect the policy of the National Bureau of Standards or the Department of Commerce.

If we raised our investment rate to the Japanese level of 30 per cent of GNP, the rate of productivity growth, and hence real GNP growth, would rise to 9 per cent per year, against the current level of 2 to 3 per cent per year.

The National Mutual Fund is proposed as a method of increasing our investment rate and sharing the benefits with all Americans. The National Mutual Fund (NMF) would be a semi-private investment company. It would use money borrowed from the federal reserve to make stock and bond purchases from private industry. This increased availability of investment funds would stimulate the economy and increase productivity. Profits from these investments would be paid to the general public in the form of dividends, making every adult citizen a capitalist to that extent, as each adult citizen would receive one share of NMF stock.

Per capita income from the NMF could reach $6,000-$10,000 a year within 16 years, assuming reasonably successful investment of sufficient capital. At a dividend rate of 15 per cent per year on invested capital, a total investment of about $9 trillion would be needed. In order to accumulate this amount within 16 years, the NMF would have to invest enough to raise the United States investment rate to a level comparable with that of Japan (30 per cent of GNP, which is about $900 billion per year).

The NMF could ramp up its investment rate to $600 billion per year over a period of seven years, and then continue to invest at about 20 per cent of GNP thereafter. The resulting investment rate would produce productivity growth of about 9 per cent per year. The accumulative effect would produce the required total investment of $9 trillion within 16 years.

If the NMF were to raise investment by $600 billion per year through borrowing a loan, it would create strong inflationary pressures due to growth and the money supply. To counteract this, a "demand regulation policy" would be used, and savings from consumers would be temporarily withheld in order to prevent disposable income from rising before productivity gains from NMF were actually realized. This mandatory savings plan would be designed so that low-income people would be less affected, and they would earn interest in excess of current inflation. Savings withheld from consumer income would go into Industrial Development Bonds to be used by the National Mutual Fund for investment. This

is in addition to the funding by direct loans from the Federal
Reserve Bank.

America is in an era of decline. We have just gone from being the
world's largest creditor nation to the world's largest debtor. Last year
the U.S. trade deficit exceeded $170 billion and the federal budget
deficit was even larger. Despite extensive efforts over the past decade
to cut the federal budget, we as a nation currently live so far beyond our
means that in order to meet current operating expenses our government
must borrow almost $1,000 per year for every man, woman, and child
in the country. Interest payments on the national debt constitute the
fastest growing item in the federal budget. Fourteen per cent of all tax
revenues now go for debt servicing.

Consumer debt is also dangerously large. Americans owe about
$2,000 per capita for consumer loans and about twice that amount for
home mortgages. The U.S. farm economy is in a state of depression.
Bank failures are numerous and growing rapidly. Basic industries such
as steel, automobiles, electronics, textiles, mining, lumber, and oil are
under severe pressure from foreign competition. Political demands for
import trade restrictions build with each election. Economists such as
John Kenneth Galbraith see parallels between today's and 1929's stock
markets.

The decline of U.S. economic strength can no longer be denied. The
only real question is whether the decline can be arrested or reversed
before it is too late.

The Basic Problem

Unfortunately, the decline of the American economy does not represent a temporary downturn, but is the result of a fundamental structural deficiency. We have a chronic lack of adequate savings and
investment. For four decades, America has had the lowest savings and
investment rate of all the industrially advanced countries in the world.
The fact that we have been able to maintain our high standard of living
for so long with so little investment in the future is remarkable, but the
time of reckoning is now here. The bill for a long string of free lunches
has finally come due.

The seeds of the current trouble were sown in the late 1940s, 1950s,
and early 1960s. The United States came out of World War II with unprecedented and unparalleled productivity capacity. At that time, we

should have implemented saving and investment policies that would have preserved and renewed our enormous productive resources forever. Instead, we embarked on an economic policy of self-indulgence. We promoted consumption, stimulated spending, discouraged saving, and took productivity growth for granted.

For two decades between 1946 and 1966, Americans lived in a period of unprecedented luxury. The American dream of two cars and a house in the suburbs became reality for millions. "Made in the U.S.A." was a mark of excellence. Brimming with self-confidence, we accepted new responsibilities as farmers, manufacturers, bankers, policemen, and philanthropists to the world.

In the late 1960s, the folly of our economic self-indulgence was compounded by the military disaster in Southeast Asia. Because the Vietnam war was unpopular, neither the administration nor the Congress had the courage to face taxpayers with the real cost of the conflict. By 1968, an irresponsible policy of "guns and butter" had kindled the fires of inflation. For the next decade, the Johnson, Nixon, and Ford administrations were preoccupied with short-term, politically painless measures to contain inflation. Temporary cuts were made in federal investment spending for such items as education, research, and development. Those "temporary" cuts have never been restored.

To the average citizen, the first visible evidence of the serious nature of the problem came with the 1973-74 OPEC oil embargo. By that time, the economy had grown too weak to absorb the oil price shocks. The dollar had to be devalued, and despite wage-price controls, inflation raged out of control.

During the early 1970s, economic incentives for individuals to save and invest were almost totally wiped out. The rate of inflation rose well above either the interest paid on savings or the returns which could be realized from capital investments. As a result, what little private savings and investment there was virtually disappeared.

Later in the 1970s and the early 1980s, as inflation soared to unprecedented heights, restrictive monetary policy was applied, and interest rates rose even higher than inflation. This at least began to encourage savings, but the high cost of borrowing made only the shortest term business investments viable. Virtually the only borrower that could afford the cost of interest was the government itself.

In the past six years, the national debt has tripled. The rate of government borrowing for current operating expenses has kept interest rates well above the point at which money can be reasonably invested in industrial plants and equipment. Government borrowing and consumer credit have absorbed most of the available savings, as well as huge amounts of foreign investment capital, and for the first time, the United States has become a debtor nation.

In this environment, long-term investment is unprofitable. Business accounting methods have been forced to focus increasingly on short-term profit and loss. Plants have been allowed to decay and machines to become obsolete. We have mortgaged our future to finance current consumption in ways that will inhibit economic growth for generations to come.

Overseas, where interest rates have been lower for decades, investment in new plants, equipment, and production technology has far exceeded investment in the United States. The inevitable result is that productivity growth in the U.S., which already was among the slowest in the industrialized world even during the 1950s and 1960s, fell even further relative to the international competition. Thus were laid the foundations of today's massive trade deficits.

Yet, despite the leveling off of productivity growth caused by underinvestment, we consumers have managed to stave off significant declines in our living standard. We have increased family income by adding more wage earners to the work force. The number of families with two wage earners has grown rapidly. Many of our young are postponing marriage, living in smaller homes, and having smaller families. But most of all, we are living on borrowed money. Consumer credit is a major industry. The largest single item in the unbalanced federal budget is direct payments to individuals. These constitute 42 per cent of the budget, as opposed to 29 per cent for defense, 14 per cent interest, 10 per cent grants to states and localities, and 5 per cent for all other federal operations.

The economic recovery of the past four years and the resulting illusion of prosperity has been maintained almost entirely on borrowed money. The debt we have accumulated numbs the mind, yet we have little to show for it. Most of the money we have borrowed has gone directly into the pockets of consumers who have spent it on current consumption. We have literally been "eating our seed corn," and it is now almost gone.

Competitiveness, Productivity, and Investment

Secretary of Commerce Baldridge recently said, "We are going to become competitive in the world. There is no question about it. The only question is, 'Will we become competitive by lowering our standard of living, or by increasing productivity?'"

In the long term, real economic growth is almost entirely due to productivity growth. Productivity growth is what creates the increased wealth that makes a rising standard of living possible. Rapid productivity growth is our only hope for maintaining, or raising, our standard of living.

Productivity growth, in turn, is directly caused by investment—in education, technology, and new production facilities and equipment. The graph in Figure 1 shows a direct relationship between the investment rate and the productivity growth rate. This relationship can also be expressed by the formula:

Productivity growth rate = 1/3 x Investment rate − Depreciation

The investment rate is measured as a percentage of the gross national product. The multiplier of 1/3 is empirically determined from economic data comparing productivity growth to the rate of capital investment for a number of industrialized countries from 1960 to 1978.

Depreciation is caused by wearing out of machines, decay of plants, and the loss of human knowledge and skills through accidents, aging, and death.

Figure 1 at the end of this essay graphically illustrates how our problems of slow economic growth and lack of international competitiveness are caused by our low rate of capital investment. It suggests that until we drastically raise our savings and investment rate, we can never again be prosperous and competitive in the world marketplace.

The data plotted in Figure 1 also indicate that the problem is so large and so long in the making that it will not be easy to correct. For example, in order to retain our current competitive posture vis-a-vis the Japanese, we need to raise our investment rate from about 10 per cent to almost 30 per cent of GNP. This is an increase of 200 per cent! (The average Japanese family saves about 20 per cent of its income—four times the rate of saving for the average American family.) In order to increase our world market share against the European Community, we need to raise our investment rate to 15 per cent of GNP, an increase of 50 per cent over the current rate.

The Political Problem

Unfortunately, under current economic policies, there is no hope of making such massive increases in our savings and investment rate. Out current methods of financing investment rely almost entirely on wealthy individuals and institutions, such as pension funds and insurance companies to finance capital investment. There is no politically acceptable way that these sources could be given sufficient incentives to voluntarily increase their investment rate by even 50 per cent, not to mention 200 per cent.

In light of the fact that the average American family saves only 5 per cent of its income, there exists a considerable margin for additional savings. Yet there are few incentives for increased savings by individuals. In fact, the recent reform of the tax laws has actually reduced incentives for individual savings by phasing out preferential treatment for capital gains and individual retirement savings accounts.

Our first priority must be to balance the federal budget so that government borrowing does not consume such a large fraction of the nation's savings. Even this will be extremely difficult, however, because there exists such a strong political coalition against tax increases. Recent elections have demonstrated that candidates frank enough to face the deficit problem stand small chance of being elected.

To go beyond the tax increases needed to deal with the deficit, to generate the enormous increase in savings needed to finance the investments necessary to regain a position of leadership in productivity and industrial competitiveness, will require some radical new departures. We cannot expect to reverse the downward trend of the past 30 years without some fundamental changes in the way we conduct our economic affairs.

A New Economic Policy

Wise economic policy is built on hard work, saving, and investment. A shift from our current profligate, self-indulgent economic policies to a course of wisdom, leading to prosperity, will require that we reverse our long-term habit (since 1945) of subsidizing consumption and ignoring production. It will require us to pay our bills as they come due and stop our irresponsible practice of living high on borrowed money. It will mean doing a hundred different things to improve productivity, reduce waste, and shift attention and effort away from instant gratification and toward future rewards. On the bottom line, it will take increasing savings and investment. Insufficient saving and investment is our underlying economic problem. We will not see our economic fortunes turn around until we increase investment and save more for the future.

Coming to terms with reality, balancing our budget, and increasing our savings rate will require a great deal of belt tightening. If the discomfort of that effort is not perceived to be shared fairly, it can never happen in a democratic society.

Therefore, the first element in the formulation of a wise new economic policy must be to devise a method for sharing fairly in the pain of paying as we go and saving for the future.

The experience of the past six years indicates that the only hope for balancing the budget is by raising taxes. Therefore, we should phase in a tax policy designed to eliminate the deficit.

Even more important, however, is to increase the national level of savings and investment to an internationally competitive level, which is a very large amount. We therefore should also introduce a program of mandatory savings, administered through the internal revenue system, to withhold from everyone's income a savings tax. This savings tax would be *invested* in industrial plants and equipment—not simply added into the general revenues to pay for current expenses.

This brings us to the second element in the formulation of a wise new economic policy: the creation of a mechanism for sharing fairly, both in the near-term profits of increased investment and in the future prosperity which will result from increased productivity. In order to accomplish this, a National Mutual Fund should be established to invest the funds generated by the savings tax. The National Mutual Fund would invest in stocks and bonds, and would pay dividends to the general public on profits from the money invested.

Through the National Mutual Fund, every adult citizen would share equally and directly in the benefits of increased savings and investment. This would happen in two ways. First, everyone would receive interest on their money withheld by the savings tax. This interest would be indexed to 4 per cent above the current rate of inflation. Second, every adult would receive dividends from profits made on National Mutual Fund investments. Profits earned by the National Mutual Fund would be declared dividends, and distributed equally to every citizen above the age of 21.

The operation of the mandatory savings policy and the National Mutual Fund is illustrated in Figure 2. Savings withheld from consumer income would go into Industrial Development Bonds to be used by the National Mutual Fund for investment. Additional Funding for the National Mutual Fund would be obtained through loans from the Federal Reserve Bank. The amount obtained from the Federal Reserve Bank would be determined by the Federal Reserve Board. These loans would become a new mechanism by which the Federal Reserve System controls the nation's money supply.

The savings tax, in addition to providing a source of investment capital, could also serve as a mechanism for controlling inflation. If the amount of savings withheld through the savings tax were made to depend on the consumer price index, then the savings tax would act as a "servo feedback governor" on the amount of consumer spending power in the marketplace. For example, if prices were rising, the savings rate would rise to reduce consumer demand and force prices down. If prices were falling, the savings rate would fall so as to stimulate consumer demand and cause prices to rise. The result is that prices could be stabilized under all economic conditions.

An important result of this would be that under conditions of low inflation, the savings tax would be small and National Mutual Fund investment would derive almost entirely from funds borrowed from the Federal Reserve. Only when growth in the money supply caused inflationary pressures to build would the savings tax significantly reduce consumer spending power. Thus, the savings tax would impose a significant burden on consumers only during periods of high inflationary pressure caused by rapid expansion of investment borrowing. These would also be periods when the demand for labor was high and salaries were rising rapidly. Hence, high savings tax rates would tend to coincide with periods of rapid growth in consumer income. The result is that the proposed savings tax would impose the heaviest burden precisely during those times when consumers were in the best economic position to afford the additional savings tax.

It is also important to note that National Mutual Fund borrowing from the Federal Reserve would provide a powerful new mechanism for achieving whatever investment rate is required to produce any desired rate of economic growth. This investment mechanism would be independent of interest rates and the rate of inflation. Thus, a healthy rate of investment could always be maintained, and real economic growth could be made both rapidly and steadily under all economic conditions.

The Issue of Control

A National Mutual Fund to make investments for the public, and a mandatory savings policy administered through a tax, are new (some might say revolutionary) ideas. They certainly raise many questions as to how saving and investment policy would be formulated and executed, and what would be the likely results. The formulation of investment policy and strategy, and the selection of types of enterprises to be targeted for investment are both economic and political decisions. These types of decisions should be made by corporate officials democratically elected by the stockholders (the American people), and charged with the responsibility of maximizing the long-term return on the stockholder's investments. The National Mutual Fund would thus operate as any for-profit corporation, the only difference being that every adult citizen would own one, and only one, share of stock. It would be controlled by a Board of Governors consisting of nine members, who would be elected for six-year terms; two each from four regions of the country and one at large who would serve as Chairman of the Board.

The formulation of legislation controlling the savings tax would be the prerogative of Congress.

Expected Results

The effect of the economic policies proposed above would be dramatic. Figure 3 shows the predictions of a computer model of the economy if the rate of investment were raised from its current rate of 10 per cent of GNP to a desired rate of 30 per cent. The rate of productivity growth, and hence real GNP growth, would rise to 9 per cent per year.

The 9 per cent growth rate would be stimulated by National Mutual Fund investments financed by the savings tax and Federal Reserve Bank loans. A savings tax based on the inflation rate would stabilize prices even in the face of 9 per cent real economic growth.

The impact on the average citizen would be profound. Figure 3 shows that 9 per cent real economic growth would cause the average per capita salary to rise from its current level of about $15,000 per year to $25,000 by 1996. This would grow to more than $35,000 by the turn of the century. In addition to these salary increases, dividends from the National Mutual Fund would reach $5,000 per capita per year by 1999, and $10,000 by 2004.

Over a longer period, the effects would be even more spectacular. Figure 4 shows that by the year 2015, average per capita salary would rise above $150,000 per year, and by 2025 would reach $500,000. National Mutual Fund dividends would contribute an additional $100,000 to every adult citizen's income by 2025. In 2035, National Mutual Fund dividends would exceed $200,000 per year, over and above salary and other income. All dollar figures are in constant 1987 dollars.

It should be noted that the year 2035 is within the expected lifetime of about half of Americans living today. It will come before retirement for those under age 15.

Is Nine Per Cent Growth Sustainable?

Many economists would argue that a 9 per cent growth scenario is simply not possible. The historical average for the United States is 3 per cent , and has averaged less than 2 per cent for over two decades. Yet it is a historical fact that the Japanese economy has grown at almost 9 per cent per year for the last 30 years, and has done so despite a severe shortage of natural resources. Japan has few mineral resources, no domestic energy supplies, and extremely limited space for food production. The Japanese have demonstrated that 9 per cent growth is possible in spite of major disadvantages. Surely, similar growth is possible in the United States under much more favorable conditions.

There are many good reasons to believe that the technology exists to support 9 per cent economic growth. The pernicious notion that rapid economic progress cannot be achieved because of fundamental "limits to growth" is rapidly being dispelled. It is now widely recognized that economic growth is limited mainly by productivity growth, and productivity growth is limited mainly by technological knowledge.

Knowledge is by far the most important resource, for new technological knowledge makes it possible to substitute new materials for old and to create new resources from materials that were previously not usable. Knowledge is not used up, nor does it wear out; instead, it increases exponentially with use. The more that is known, the easier it is to discover new things and there is no limit to what there is to know. Knowledge is limited only by our commitment to invest in the pursuit of it. Investment in education, research, and development accelerates the growth of technological knowledge, and investment in new plants and equipment speeds the transfer of new knowledge into industrial production.

Recently, there have arisen fundamentally new technologies of computer integrated manufacturing, robotics, materials science, and genetic engineering. These have the potential to increase industrial productivity by hundreds, even thousands of per cent. We are, in fact, on the verge of a new industrial revolution (Toffler calls it the Third Wave) which will change the world as profoundly as the invention of agriculture, the development of the steam engine, and the discovery of electricity.

Computer-integrated manufacturing and robotics will create new industries that will produce goods and services without significant amounts of human labor. Eventually, factories will reproduce themselves at exponentially declining costs. What the significance of such self-reproduction might be can be understood by looking at what has happened over the past 30 years in the computer industry, where computers are routinely used to make other computers. In 1955, a large computer cost on the order of $3,000,000. Today a computer with comparable capabilities can be purchased for about $3,000. If similar reductions in manufacturing costs had been realized in the automobile industry, a luxury car comparable to that sold in 1955 for $3,500 could be purchased today for $3.50.

In the future, robotics will make it possible to mine the sea bed and farm the oceans for food and non-polluting fuel. Robotic construction techniques will make customized homes of wood, stone, and synthetic materials inexpensive and available anywhere on earth. Robots will eventually provide care for the sick and aged and function as household servants.

Genetic engineering will enable us to produce drugs to eradicate many types of disease and make food plentiful and inexpensive everywhere. Materials science will create new building materials which will lead to new types of buildings and transportation facilities.

Working together, these new productive technologies will bring huge improvements in productivity. The only questions are, "When?" and "Where?" Will it be within the next 20 years, the next 50, or the next 200? Will the countries leading the revolution in production technology be in Asia, Europe, North America, or elsewhere?

The limits to growth are not in resources or technology. The limits are set by the percentage of income a society is willing to save and invest in the future. The secret of 9 per cent sustained real growth is an investment rate of 30 per cent of GNP coupled with a savings rate high enough to support that rate of investment without inflation.

Implications for the Future

This means that if America were to pursue wise saving and investment policies, we could reverse our current decline and lead the world into a new industrial revolution. If this were done, we could create an age of unprecedented prosperity. The key is to make available the investment capital that is necessary to commercially exploit these technologies. If the United States were wise enough to invest adequately in the future—in education, research, technology development, and social welfare—we could yet create a golden age of mankind.

Our generation has the power to choose from a wide spectrum of possible futures. The alternatives range from continued economic decline to great prosperity.

If we continue our current economic policies of self-indulgence, it is virtually certain that we will increasingly be reduced to a nation of debtors. Economic growth will stagnate due to lack of investment, inflation will rise as the dollar depreciates, and unemployment will grow worse as more and more industries succumb to foreign competition.

On the other hand, if we have the wisdom and discipline to change our ways—to save our money and invest in the technology of the future—we could create a golden age for ourselves, our children, and our grandchildren. We have the opportunity to lead the next industrial revolution and enjoy the prosperity it will generate.

The future is ours to make. Which future will we choose?

Figure 1

RELATIONSHIP BETWEEN PRODUCTIVITY GROWTH AND
CAPITAL INVESTMENT IN SIX INDUSTRIALIZED
COUNTRIES OVER THE PERIOD 1960-1978

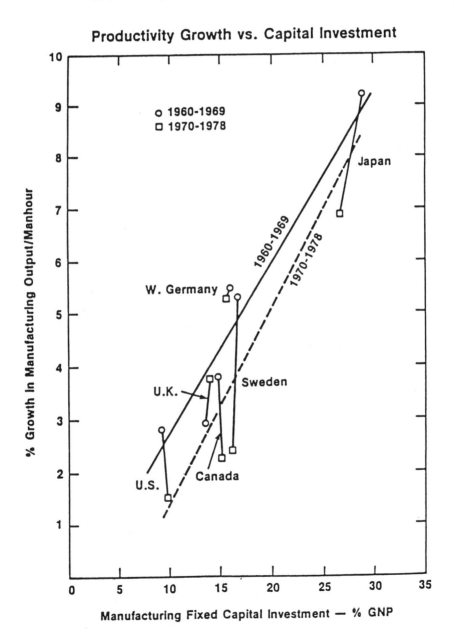

Figure 2

RELATIONSHIP OF NATIONAL MUTUAL FUND (NMF)
AND MANDATORY SAVINGS POLICY (INDUSTRIAL
DEVELOPMENT BONDS) TO THE FEDERAL
RESERVE AND PRIVATE INDUSTRY

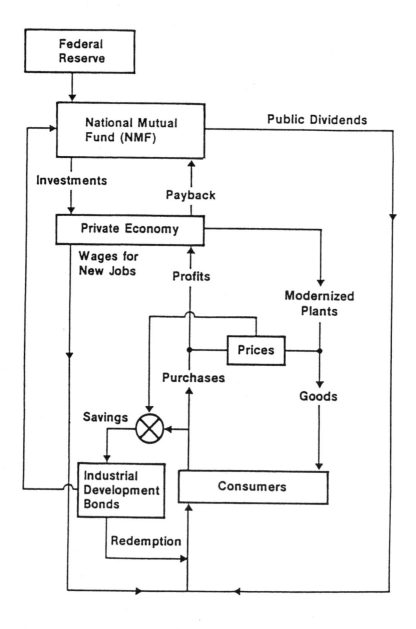

Note: NMF investments are financed by a combination of Federal Reserve loans and mandatory consumer savings. Profits from NMF investments are distributed directly to consumers as public dividends. Mandatory savings are withheld as a surcharge on income tax based on the inflation rate. This provides investment capital and stabilizes prices during rapid economic growth.

Figure 3

EFFECTS OF IMPLEMENTING THE NATIONAL MUTUAL FUND AND A SAVINGS TAX

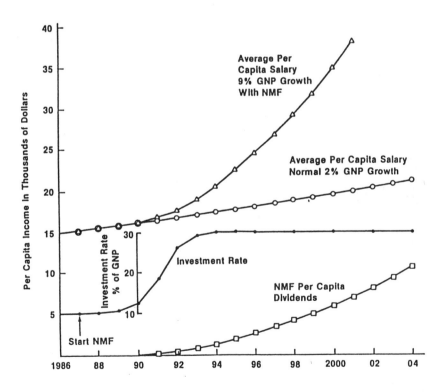

Note: From 1988 to 1994, the investment rate rises from 10 to 30 per cent of GNP. This produces 9 per cent real economic growth. Per capita NMF dividends grow to $1,000 per year by 1994, and to 10,000 by 2004.

Figure 4

LONG-TERM EFFECTS OF THE NATIONAL MUTUAL FUND AND MANDATORY SAVINGS PROGRAM

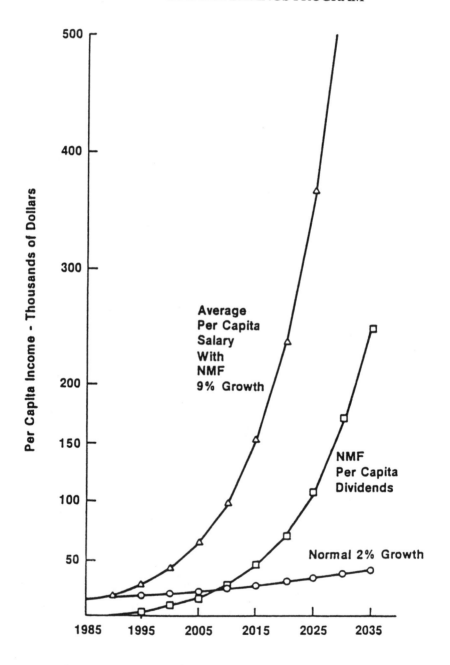

6

ANOTHER AMERICA

by

C.S. Shann Turnbull

Editor's Note: *Shann Turnbull of Sydney, Australia, is a business, financial, and management consultant who holds an M.B.A. degree from Harvard. His 1975 book,* Democratising the Wealth of Nations, *is one of the earliest sources of specific plans for creating universal share ownership.*

Turnbull's use of the term "stakeholder" in the following essay found a reflection in the $300,000 "Stakeholder Essay Competition for Students" sponsored by the National Cash Register Company in 1988. NCR defines its stakeholders as its customers, employees, suppliers, shareholders, and all of the people in the communities in which it operates.

ABSTRACT

The current rules for owning productive assets can provide investors with profits in excess of the incentive which they require to make their investment. Such profits are described as "surplus profits" and their existence is inconsistent with the rationale for a market economy to be either efficient or equitable. To reduce this defect, dynamic rules of corporate ownership are proposed. These dynamic rules of tenure would automatically transfer the ownership of productive assets with the passage of time so that surplus profits could be shared by other enterprise stakeholders.

Stakeholders are those people who are most affected by the activities of the enterprise. They include the stockholders, employees, suppliers, customers and the host community. Thus, while stakeholder tenure would make productive assets more broadly held, it would also tend to localize their ownership and control around the community where they were located. This would empower communities to manage and/or modify productive assets in such a manner that they may best sustain the local environment and quality of life—a result which will need to be achieved on a global basis if humanity is to be sustained on this planet after the next century.

The incentive for existing corporate stockholders to vote a change in the by-laws of their corporations to adopt dynamic ownership arrangements could be provided by elected politicians at all levels of government. The most universal incentive would be a two-level Federal enterprise tax. The concessional level would only be available to enterprises which adopted dynamic tenure. This lower level would make it more profitable for stockholders to give up, say, 5 per cent of their interest in the enterprise each year. By this means, all ownership and control would be transferred from stockholders to other stakeholders over a 20-year period.

Stakeholder ownership and control provides a powerful grass roots basis for obtaining a political mandate through all levels of elected governments for adopting dynamic rules for owning and controlling not only corporations but urban land and shelter. The process of introducing dynamic tenure would be greatly reinforced by allowing elected officials at the lowest practical level of government to define who would be eligible to be classed as a stakeholder in their community. The formation of Community Land Banks in each local government area would ensure that every citizen would obtain an ownership interest in the land and shelter with a basic income distributed from the rents obtained from the productive assets located in their precinct.

To make it profitable for stockholders to give up, say, 5 per cent ownership each year, corporate taxes would need to be reduced by around 15 cents in the dollar. This could be part of a process to transfer the tax base from corporations to stakeholders. By this means, all levels of government could reduce their welfare expenditures as local citizens and/or their local hospitals, schools, pension plans, etc., obtained a share in the profits of productive assets located in the community. In effect, the proposal provides a technique to privatize and localize the tax and welfare system of government. It would also sensitize the distribution and creation of wealth to local needs and priorities.

Dynamic tenure would also increase the tax base since both stockholders and stakeholders would want their corporations to distribute all their profits each year, rather than the corporation retaining some to invest tax free each year. Business growth would be financed by stockholder/stakeholder reinvestment in corporate "offspring." This reinvestment process would create a boom in the securities business and make the capital markets much more efficient, as it would allow market forces to allocate the reinvestment of corporate profits. It would also facilitate changes in management to individuals sensitized to local concerns. Dynamic tenure creates an Ownership Transfer Corporation.

Stakeholder ownership would create the basis for making enterprises self-governing and so reduce the need for government laws, regulations, control, supervision, and associated bureaucracies. The various classes of stakeholders with their different vested interests provide a basis for building internal checks and balances into the governance structure of an enterprise. The Mondragon cooperatives in Spain illustrate in a limited manner the potential of this approach.

The size and cost of government would be reduced by both privatizing the tax/welfare system and through corporations becoming self-governing. The economic power of the nation would be democratized and so localized to empower communities to act locally to sustain the planet globally.

. . . devise a plan for spreading ownership of America's productive assets broadly among the people, and reviving the economy, without confiscation or increased taxation.

The Vision

The need to spread broadly the ownership of productive assets is not just to revive the economy, but also to create a more efficient, equitable, satisfying, and sustainable economic system. This new type of system is described as *Social Capitalism.*[1]

Social Capitalism would introduce:

(1) A two-income economy as described by Kelso[2] to provide a universal minimum income for all citizens. The revenues distributed by the broad ownership of income-producing assets would create an alternative to government welfare. This would provide a long-term basis for stimulating the economy by eliminating the need to finance welfare by taxation and/or debt.

(2) The elimination of taxation on enterprise profits to provide a major incentive for reviving the economy. The process of eliminating enterprise taxation would create the incentive for changing the rules for owning assets so as to broaden their ownership without confiscation. The introduction of Social Capitalism is not dependent upon the techniques proposed by Kelso, Speiser,[3] and others—which are complementary—but upon the adoption of new rules for owning property—which are described as "dynamic tenure." These rules change the ownership of property with the passage of time.

(3) A highly decentralized and diverse economy which could adapt its power structures and so its technology, patterns of consumption, and production to those most compatible with the local bioregion. This would nurture the biosphere to give humanity a chance of being sustained on our planet in perpetuity.

(4) A common goal for developing the current forms of socialism, capitalism, and other types of economic organization. This would remove the need to defend diverse political ideologies by warfare that could exterminate humanity from our planet.

There cannot be a vision of any future for humanity unless the current level of environmental degradation and the possibility of catastrophic nuclear warfare is avoided. Social Capitalism provides a basis for making a direct contribution in both regards.

The introduction of Social Capitalism is dependent upon evolutionary rather than revolutionary changes. Because it creates a highly decentralized social order with great diversity, it can only be achieved on a piece-by-piece basis. It requires top-down and bottom-up initiatives. The process by which such diverse initiatives can reinforce each other and introduce a new mind set or paradigm is illustrated by the "green movement."

The green, peace, alternative energy, health, and other movements are the cutting edge of current social change. The spontaneous coordination of their diverse decentralized initiatives is achieved by the sharing of common values and vision. These are shared by Social Capitalism, which provides the means for not only embedding them into social institutions but making the institutional structure reflect the values and vision of the alternative movements.

The motives and mind-set for the spontaneous adoption of the principles of Social Capitalism already exist in the alternative movements. What is lacking is a widespread sharing of the insights set out in the *Handbook of Tools for Community Economic Change*,[4] which describes how Social Capitalism can be introduced on an economically and politically attractive basis.

While the disparate alternative movements seek to save humanity by altering the patterns of consumption, production, and their associated technology, they do not focus on changing the power structure of society that determines these issues. Social power is determined by the ownership and control of land, enterprise, and banking which roughly equate to what economists call "factors of production." Social Capitalism would transform their current centralized pattern of ownership and control to a decentralized one.

However, the pattern of decentralization would not be random. The ownership and control of resources would be concentrated on the local community where they were located. Enterprises would be owned by their "stakeholders." Stakeholders are all those people who are significantly affected by the operations of an enterprise. They would include its stockholders, employees, suppliers, customers, and host community. By this means, local self-governance could be introduced to allow the slogan of the alternative movement to "think globally, act locally" to become a reality.

Social Capitalism is different from Universal Capitalism as described by Kelso,[5] and Peoples' Capitalism proposed by Albus,[6] because it corrects the mechanisms by which ownership is concentrated. It does this for both income- and non-income-producing assets in localizing the ownership and control of both. The decentralization of economic power occurs not just from broadening the ownership of productive assets, but by also providing a basis for decentralizing power within the institutions that own either productive assets or community infrastructure.

Universal Share Ownership Plans

A basic political and economic building block of Social Capitalism is the Community Land Bank (CLB). A CLB would represent the lowest level of local government. It would own all the land and community infrastructure within its precincts but not any private buildings. Dynamic tenure would ensure that every voting citizen in the CLB precinct would obtain an equity interest in the land and shelter they occupied. In this way, every citizen could be assured of obtaining a basic income from CLB dividends generated by the rental income obtained by the CLB from productive assets in its precinct. The stakeholders in a CLB precinct would provide a focus for the ownership and control of the productive assets so that their ownership and control was localized. This would allow the productive assets in the CLB to be managed in the best way to nurture the bioregion.

It is not intended that a CLB would own any assets that were directly involved in productive activities. For operational and governance reasons explained later, it is intended that ownership and control of all productive assets be held by their stakeholders. The CLB obtains income from the productive assets in the form of rents and/or royalties. In return, the CLB provides community infrastructure and services. This arrangement will be found in the town of Letchworth, 30 miles north of London.[7]

The concern of this essay is to devise a plan for spreading ownership of America's productive assets. CLBs are an adjunct; they spread the income of productive assets but not their ownership. The plan proposed in this essay does not require the creation of CLBs or the development of other aspects of Social Capitalism, such as decentralized banking arrangements, and so they will not be developed further here. The techniques for introducing CLBs and decentralized banking on a voluntary basis are set out in the *Handbook*[8] referred to above and other writings.[9] These complementary aspects of Social Capitalism are mentioned to indicate how they interact and reinforce each other to achieve the objectives cited above.

All physical productive assets made by mankind have a limited life. They all wear out. The government recognizes this by providing tax deductions (called depreciation and depletion allowances) to allow pre-tax dollars to be used to replace assets as they wear out or are depleted. These deductions allow stockholders, who are a minority of all citizens and who are typically already rich, to get richer. These deductions could and should be made conditional upon the introduction of dynamic tenure "for spreading the ownership of America's productive assets broadly among the people."

However, because the rich are currently entitled to such tax deductions for maintaining and pyramiding their wealth, the denying of these deductions may be considered to be confiscation. There are, however, many alternative approaches for introducing dynamic tenure on a voluntary basis to expand broadly the ownership of productive assets. One approach would be to reduce the level of enterprise tax or provide other incentives for corporations that voluntarily adopt dynamic tenure arrangements. As these arrangements distribute ownership with its associated income, the need for the government to finance welfare and so raise taxes would decrease.

This approach would meet the requirement for "spreading the ownership of America's productive assets broadly among the people," and would also "revive the economy, without confiscation or increased taxation."

The specific arrangements would require stockholders to introduce dynamic tenure provisions in their corporate by-laws. There are various ways in which this could be achieved. One way would be to divide all common stock into two categories called, for example, venture capital common stock and stakeholder common stock. The stakeholder common stock would have no rights until the first dividend was paid.

The total rights of the issued stakeholder stock to capital, reserves, earnings, dividends, and votes would increase after the first dividend was paid at the ownership transfer rate specified of, say, 5 per cent per year. The total rights of the venture capital common stock on issue would decrease at a corresponding rate. It would not matter how many shares were issued in each category, and this arrangement would allow additional stakeholder shares to be issued from time to time. A corporation with by-laws that achieved a 100 per cent ownership transfer over a specified period will be referred to as an Ownership Transfer Corporation (OTC). The principle could be utilized in such unincorporated enterprises as partnerships, joint ventures, and trusts. For brevity, only corporations will be mentioned in the following discussion.

The incentive for stockholders to change their by-laws to create an OTC would be that the corporation would obtain sufficient tax concessions and/or other benefits to provide a more attractive return for stockholders who vote for the fade-out by-laws. To provide stockholders with an equivalent after-tax return with a 5 per cent per year fade-out, the corporate tax rate would need to be reduced by around 15 cents in the dollar. Thus, if the tax rate for those corporations that provide perpetual claims to their wealth was 34 per cent, the OTC rate would be 19 per cent.

The tax concessions for OTCs would be lost in the event stakeholder stock was not issued to the appropriate parties. It is recommended that the legislation providing the OTC concessions delegate to lower levels of government some or all of the power to decide how stakeholders and their interests would be determined. Such delegations could be made conditional upon welfare and other costs to the level of government providing the incentive being reduced by the value of the benefit foregone.

Ownership Transfer Corporations

Many people will find the concept of limited life direct investment alien to their instincts. This is so even though all man-made physical productive assets wear out. Limiting property rights to an investment through dynamic tenure does not mean that the time period of the operations are limited or that the wealth of the original stockholders is lost. It only means that the ownership and control of the operations change.

While the original stockholders lose ownership and control, they do not lose their wealth. On the contrary, they should increase their wealth, as they will be obtaining a more attractive alternative. This is analyzed further below. During the fade-out period, the dividends received by the stockholders should not only pay back the cost of the original investment but provide a more attractive return than if the investment were not to fade out. This would be achieved by the original stockholders recycling their wealth into new ventures.

Dynamic tenure would introduce a profound change into corporate financing. Because the equity of the original stockholders would be fading out each year by, say, 5 per cent, the corporation would be under very strong pressure to pay out all its earnings each year as a dividend. Corporations typically retain over 50 per cent of their earnings so that dividends are less than half of earnings. Unless an OTC had growth prospects well in excess of its transfer rate, it could be expected to pay out all its earnings each year as a dividend. This would typically more than double the dividend payment made to its stockholders.

The tax or other concessions provided to form OTCs should be sufficient to create a transfer rate which would encourage most, if not all, earnings to be paid out each year as a dividend. This would produce a number of beneficial effects on the efficiency of corporate management and the capital markets generally.

If corporations distributed all their earnings each year, then management would need to go to the capital markets to finance growth. The need to raise funds from the highly sensitive and competitive capital markets instead of retaining earnings would keep management on their toes. The capital markets would become far more active and important in allocating funds throughout the economy. OTCs would create a boom in the securities industry.

Enterprise growth would be financed through OTCs giving birth to corporate "offspring" in which the dynamic tenure provisions would not be triggered until they paid their first dividend. The corporate children could acquire all or part of their parents' activities and be formed by the stockholders and stakeholders of the parent corporation having pro-rata rights to take up stock in the corporate progeny. This process would magnify the value of the transactions exposed to the capital markets.

The corporate offspring might also acquire some or all of their parents' management. This would not only keep management on their toes but provide an opportunity to introduce new management and/or a different corporate culture. As ownership and control localized, management sensitive to local needs would develop. Through these processes, corporations would be "humanized." They would become smaller and subject to change on a continuous basis to emulate nature.

Stakeholder Ownership and Governance

Ideally, elected officials at the lowest practical level of government should decide who is entitled to become a stakeholder. Candidates for elected positions would seek office on the policies they would adopt in deciding how stakeholder stockholdings would be allocated. This would lead to a great diversity in ownership patterns focused on the community within the area of local governance. Some communities may include institutional stakeholders as a way to fund local hospitals, schools, and welfare agencies. Others may not. But to ensure operational integrity, it would always make good sense to include those individuals with the greatest direct vested interests, like the employees, customers, and suppliers.

This would be achieved by the corporation forming associations of employees, customers, and suppliers. Membership of each association would be identified through the corporate records. To encourage support for the corporation, stakeholder stock entitlements could be distributed in proportion to each member's economic contribution to the enterprise, that is, in proportion to employee remuneration, customer purchases, and the value of goods and services supplied. Democratic principles would require that each stakeholder stockholder would have one vote.

While not essential for the objective of broadening ownership, the creation of various stakeholder associations would provide the basis to introduce corporate self-governance. The most advanced and successful example of self-governance is found in the Mondragon cooperatives in Spain. Not one of these cooperatives has failed in its first five years, whereas over 85 per cent of conventional enterprises fail within this period. In addition, these cooperatives are more productive than conventional enterprises, where capital employs labor rather than labor employing capital.

While Mondragon cooperatives are self-managing, they are not completely self-governing. Their level of self-governance would be improved by incorporating all stakeholders into their innovative governance structure. Self-governance would minimize the need for government regulatory agencies to intervene in the affairs of corporations, as all the people who were significantly affected by the behavior of the corporation would have a say in its management by being a stakeholder.

The broad spread development of corporate self-governance would have profound implications on the structure of government. Many government functions could be eliminated or attenuated. It would allow reduction of the size and cost of government at all levels.

There are also a host of operational benefits which could arise by having stakeholders participating in the governance structure of a corporation. Customer associations could provide information on the quality, functionality, and design of the goods and services produced directly to management. They may even contribute to product development, as has recently been achieved by some computer user associations. Modern manufacturing techniques of zero-defect quality control depend upon making the production employees directly responsible to the customers. Stakeholder participation would institutionalize this approach. New techniques for minimizing inventory levels by "just in time" delivery from suppliers is another procedure which could be facilitated by a supplier association being involved in the governance structure of the enterprise.

USOP Incentives

The conversion of corporations and other forms of enterprises to dynamic tenure principles could be encouraged at all levels of government on a unilateral basis. To indicate the value of the incentive required to encourage stockholders to vote for the OTC form, let us consider an example in which a number of simplifications have been made.

The first simplifying assumption is that the corporation pays a constant dividend of $1.00 per year per stock unit forever. The next is that stockholders can reinvest the dividends received to earn 10 per cent per year. This means that the value of receiving a $1.00 dividend in one year's time is equivalent to having 90.9¢ today. This is because 90.9¢ invested today at 10 per cent per annum would accumulate to $1.00 over the year. Similarly, because 15¢ will accumulate to $1.00 over 20 years when earning interest at 10 per cent, the value today of receiving $1.00 in 20 years' time is 15¢. If we add up the value today of receiving a $1.00 dividend each year, the total value only accumulates to $10.00! It reduces to $5.00 if the stockholder can reinvest the dividends to earn 20 per cent per annum rather than 10 per cent per annum.

The stockholder will obtain 90 per cent of the total possible value of $10.00, $6.67, or $5.00 in 24, 16, or 13 years, if during this time the stockholder can reinvest the proceeds at respectively 10 per cent, 15 per cent, or 20 per cent per annum. To make up for the stockholder not receiving any returns after 24, 16, or 13 years, compensation would only need to be equivalent to 10 per cent of the value today of all payments. This would be $1.00, $0.67, or $0.50 respectively. The compensation needed to terminate the stockholders' return would not be greater than the dividend payment for the first year. In practice, it would be much less since due to uncertainty, equity investment analysts rarely consider future returns after ten years.

The point of this example is that a relatively small benefit can provide the incentive to introduce dynamic tenure without confiscation. The benefit required could well be within the means of state or local governments. The cost of providing the benefits could be more than offset by the advantages that accrue from capturing what is described below as "surplus profits."

Correcting Private Property Rights

Property rights to all real and intangible assets in the world are limited by the life of the owner or the property, except those relating to land and corporations. This represents another fundamental defect of modern market economies, as it exacerbates the emergence of "windfall" and "surplus" profits. Windfall profits are those created for landowners by the non-owners. Surplus profits are those which are in excess of the incentive required to bring forth an investment in productive assets.

Both types of profit make the economic system inefficient and unequitable. They are inconsistent with the rationale for a market economy where competition is supposed to limit profit. Property rights to land and corporations with dynamic tenure would improve the equity and efficiency of a market economy by limiting the emergence of windfall and surplus profits. CLBs capture windfall profits for the community that creates them rather than let them be acquired by individuals. OTCs distribute surplus profits to the individuals who contribute to their creation by being a stakeholder through supplying goods, services, custom, or infrastructure.

Because businessmen cannot predict the future, they do not rely on receiving income from an equity investment after 10 to 15 years. The investment may last longer and/or be replaced from the tax savings created by depreciation or depletion allowances. However, only guesses can be made about future competition, market share, product and production obsolescence, and operating costs. Even if an analyst makes estimates of revenues and costs for 20 years, the decision makers will require that the return on investment be calculated over a shorter period. The point in time up to which income is recognized in investment analysis is called the time horizon.

The more uncertainty and risk perceived in an investment, the shorter the time horizon used. While time horizons for domestic investments may extend out to 15 years in periods of economic stability, the risks perceived in foreign investment may result in a time horizon being used as short as three or four years. Within this period, the investment will need to pay itself off and provide a competitive return with domestic investments. Investments made with such short time horizons could well pay for themselves many times over.

All returns received after the investment time horizon are surplus profits since they are in excess of incentive needed to produce the investment. Foreigners who invest in the U.S., and obtain returns after their time horizon, are capturing surplus profits. From a national point of view, the U.S. is giving away more than it needs to for attracting the investment. This is a bad deal and inconsistent with the rationale for a market economy where competition is supposed to limit excessive profits. It is also a bad deal for the state and the community economy where the productive assets are situated. It means that they are exporting more earnings than they need to attract resources to their state or community.

With foreign investment, it is in the interest of the nation, host state, and host community to make a better bargain. The same can be said for the host state and host community when the investor is not foreign but located interstate. A better bargain can be struck by providing an incentive for the investor to adopt dynamic tenure arrangements. From the above considerations it should be evident that the cost of the incentive could pay for itself many times over, especially as the value of the future income transferred from the investment to the community for the purposes of consumption are not discounted. If inflation is ignored, the value or use of a dollar received 10 or 20 years in the future for food, shelter, health, education, and so forth is the same as a dollar today.

Many people may find it difficult to accept that business analysts would discount future dollars to such an extent that OTC would be feasible. It may help to give them confidence to consider the billions of dollars that are invested in projects with a limited life, such as mining projects and films. These may yield revenues for only four or five years, yet pay back all their original investment and produce a very attractive return. There may not, of course, be any residual values for stakeholders to acquire, but by vesting the residual rights in the stakeholders, the investment could well produce values which might not otherwise appear for the venture capitalists. This is especially so in mining where the employees and host community would have an incentive to husband the reserves. They would also have the incentive to husband their environment.

The stakeholder concept allows qualitative considerations to be introduced into productive activities to nurture and sustain the environment. It does this by vesting control of the productive assets with those people who have the biggest stake in their operations, and people who have the most knowledge about them and the environment in which they are situated. It also creates the opportunity for local self-governance of enterprises and local communities.

Dynamic tenure and the stakeholder concept would create a new type of political economy which would (1) facilitate economic change on a self-correcting, equitable, and sustaining basis; (2) maintain a dispersion of economic and political power at a grassroots level; and (3) encourage enterprise development to improve the quality of life and the environment.

The OTCs created by dynamic tenure would be simpler to establish than Employee Stock Ownership Plans (ESOPs), Consumer Stock Ownership Plans (CSOPs), and similar arrangements proposed by Kelso. The Kelso proposals are complementary in broadening ownership, but they do not cure one of the root causes of why the rich get richer: surplus profits which concentrate the ownership of productive assets. In a similar manner, Kelso's proposal for a Government Capital Diffusion Insurance Corporation (CDIC) to guarantee loans to finance ESOPs and others is also complementary. But like ESOPs, it does not cure the root cause created by a government-controlled currency system. The economies of scale of a centralized financial system are such that it favors the rich getting richer.

Even the most market-orientated societies are based on centralized, hierarchical social structures. Markets depend upon there being a choice. Choice can only exist with diversity. Diversity is restricted with centralized institutions. A rich diversity in the quality and type of lifestyle at the community and local government level would be dependent upon bottom-up initiatives from individuals and grassroots organizations that share the vision of Social Capitalism. The federal government could nurture and facilitate bottom-up initiatives by providing incentives in the tax system to create OTCs and delegating arrangements for the structuring of OTCs to lower levels of government.

The initiatives suggested would be a further step in "spreading the ownership of America's productive assets broadly among the people, and reviving the economy, without confiscation or increased taxation." It would also be a first step for introducing Social Capitalism, a cause which will attract the energy of the current most effective social activists and the votes of the majority who own the minority of productive assets.

Notes

1.   C. S. Shann Turnbull, *Democratising the Wealth of Nations*. Sydney: Company Directors Association of Australia, 1975. This book was written to introduce the ideas of Louis Kelso to Australia for his 1975 visit, and is dedicated to him. It is the manifesto of "Social Capitalism," a term Kelso later used.
2.   Louis O. Kelso and Patricia Hetter, *Two-Factor Theory: The Economics of Reality*. New York: Random House, 1967.
3.   Stuart M. Speiser, *SuperStock*. New York: Everest House, 1982.

4. Ward Morehouse (ed.), *Handbook of Tools for Community Economic Change.* New York: Intermediate Technology Development Group of North America, 1983.
5. Kelso and Hetter, op. cit.
6. James S. Albus, *Peoples' Capitalism: The Economics of the Robot Revolution.* Kensington, Maryland: New World Books, 1976.
7. Letchworth was founded in 1905 to reflect the ideas of Sir Ebenezer Howard, who wrote *Garden Cities of Tomorrow: A Peaceful Path to Real Reform.* London: S. Sonnenschein, 1901.
8. Morehouse (ed.), op. cit.
9. Details of the Community Land Bank (CLB) will be found in:

Scott Solowoway and Thomas Johnson, "The Use of Co-operative Land Banks and Other Alternative Forms of Public Finance to Promote Community Economic Development." Unpublished thesis for a Masters Degree at the Massachusetts Institute of Technology, Cambridge, for Professor James Carras, Spring 1986.

Ward Morehouse (ed.), *Handbook of Tools,* op. cit.

C. S. Shann Turnbull, "Community Land Bank: The Way Forward," *Town & Country Planning Journal* (Town & Country Planning Association, London), Vol. 55, No. 9, September 1986, p. 237.

_____. "Co-operative Land Banks" in Paul Ekins (ed.), *The Living Economy: A New Economics in the Making.* London: Routlege & Kegan Paul, London, 1986, pp. 181-89.

_____. Co-operative Land Banks for Low Income Housing" in Angel, Archer, Tanphiphat, Weggelin (eds.), *Land for Housing the Poor.* Singapore: Select Books, 1983, p. 512.

_____. "Back-to-Front Thinking on Land Costs," *RYDGE's Business Journal* (Sydney), Vol. LII, No. 1, February 1979, p. 22.

_____. "Land Leases Without Landlords." Unpublished paper presented at the United Nations Habitat Forum, Vancouver, June 8, 1978.

_____. "Beyond Federalism: Self-Financing Local Government." Paper presented to the 15th Biennial Congress of the International Institute of Planners, Sydney, September

26, 1977. Published by the Royal Australian Planning Institute, Sydney, 1978.

_____. "Landbank: A Way Out of the Land Price Spiral," *Real Estate Journal* (Real Estate Institute of New South Wales), Vol. 27, No. 3, August 1977, p. 81.

_____. "New Modes of Land Tenure." Transcript of Proceedings: Australian Government Commission of Enquiry into Land Tenures, July 23, 1973, pp. 598-617 and 602-22.

7

TOWARD A MORE EQUITABLE AMERICA: A UNIVERSAL SHARE OWNERSHIP PLAN

by

Neysa C. Chouteau

Editor's Note: *Neysa C. Chouteau of Kirkwood, Missouri, recently retired as senior editor of textbooks for McGraw-Hill Book Company. She is now the editor of* Loretto *magazine, published by the Roman Catholic Order of the Sisters of Loretto. She is the author or co-author of some 15 books, many on mathematics. She has drawn upon several of the models mentioned in* The USOP Handbook, *and developed her own set of five criteria for viable USOPs. Her Consumer Equity Plan breaks new ground in consumer stock ownership.*

ABSTRACT

In this essay, I suggest certain guidelines, which any Universal Share Ownership Plan should meet, and conclude that no one plan could meet all guidelines. Proposed, therefore, is a three-part plan.

The three parts consist of the Shareholders In America, Inc. plan, as discussed in Speiser's *Supplement to The USOP Handbook* (with slight modifications); a modified version of the Perry National Dividend Plan, called the Citizen Mutual Fund Plan; and a plan for corporations voluntarily to share part of their profits with their customers, the Consumer Equity Plan.

I then suggest ways of implementing the three-part plan, beginning with inviting essayists to purchase stock in Shareholders In America, Inc., and moving to suggestions for implementing the Consumer Equity Plan and the Citizen Mutual Fund Plan.

> In 5,000 words or less, devise a plan for spreading ownership of America's productive assets broadly among the people, and reviving the economy, without confiscation or increased taxation.

My response to the challenge above is based upon the ideas discussed in Stuart M. Speiser's *The USOP Handbook*[1] and his *Supplement to The USOP Handbook.*[2]

The essay topic offers only two rules: no confiscation and no increased taxation. However, the plans proposed by Speiser, Wisman, Perry, and others, along with Speiser's discussions of the limitations and advantages of each plan, suggest certain guidelines for a USOP beyond those mentioned in the essay topic. Following are the guidelines that I found important.

(1) The plan should be voluntary. A voluntary plan does not have to wait on government action, and it is less restrictive of individual or corporate freedoms.

(2) The plan should have a lasting effect. It should enable people to accumulate capital over a period of time, rather than offering a periodic bonus which may nor may not be saved.

(3) The plan should benefit the have-nots more than the haves.

(4) The plan should be simple to explain and to maintain.

(5) Benefits of the plan should be earned.

No plan discussed in *The USOP Handbook* or the *Supplement* meets all of the guidelines above. Perhaps it is unrealistic to assume that any one plan could. For that reason, a three-part plan is proposed. Not only are at least three parts needed in order to meet all the guidelines, but if the three parts are pursued independently, we have three chances of success rather than one.

The Three Parts

The three parts proposed include the Shareholders In America plan, a modification of the Perry National Dividend Plan, and a segment that might be called the Consumer Equity Plan.

Shareholders In America, Inc. (SIA)

Of all the plans discussed in *The USOP Handbook* and the *Supplement,* Shareholders In America, Inc., or SIA, comes closest to meeting the guidelines above. It is voluntary. If successful, it will have a lasting effect. It will benefit the have-nots more than the haves, and participants will earn the benefits. However, it does not meet guideline (4) in that it is not simple to explain, and it will certainly not be simple to maintain.

There is also some danger that it will fail to meet guideline (2), that of having a lasting effect. As discussed in the *Supplement to the USOP Handbook,* the plan requires a stream of income from corporate patronage (*Supplement,* page 1) and the donation of high-caliber management services (*Supplement,* page 14) in order to get off the ground. The projects that do get off the ground will be new businesses, and new businesses historically have had a high failure rate. Ideally, many of these new businesses will engage in work that does not offer high profit potential, such as slum clearance and geriatric social work (*Supplement,* page 8). Further, these new businesses should be run by the worker-owners (*Supplement,* pages 14-16). Even with the support of high-caliber management services, developing self-sustaining management skills will take time.

However, potential problems are far outweighed by potential gains. As Speiser makes clear, SIA is not a replacement for other USOP plans (*Supplement,* pages 19-21). Rather, it can be a trailblazer and a supplement to other Universal Share Ownership Plans and it can be pursued independently of other plans. A number of models from which we can learn already exist, such as the Campaign for Human Development and the Local Initiatives Support Corporation (*Supplement,* pages 8-10). For these reasons, Shareholders In America, Inc. should be an important part of any Universal Share Ownership Plan.

Modification of the Perry National Dividend Plan: Citizen Mutual Fund (CMA)

The Perry National Dividend Plan meets only guideline (4) in that it is simple to explain and to maintain. However, it could be modified to have a more lasting effect and to benefit the have-nots more than the haves.

The Perry National Dividend Plan is explained in *The USOP Handbook:*

> The thrust of the plan is to take the collections from the corporate income tax and place them in a National Dividend Trust Fund. From this fund, a yearly check would be issued to every registered voter, once the federal budget is balanced. These dividends would be tax-free. Every year that the budget fell out of balance and into deficit, the money in the National Dividend Trust Fund would be used to reduce the deficit instead of being distributed to the registered voters (page 111).

I propose a modified plan, the Citizen Mutual Fund (CMA). In this plan, government would allocate a portion of the collections from the corporate income tax to the Citizen Mutual Fund. This fund would be invested in shares of all the stocks in the Wilshire 5,000 equity (or comparable) index.

Shares in the Citizen Mutual Fund would in turn be issued on a non-transferable basis to all citizens 18 years of age or older who are not incarcerated. Shares would be issued in proportion to gross income, with the largest block of shares going to the working poor, and only nominal numbers of shares going to higher income citizens. Dividends earned from the fund shares would be taxable.

Since a balanced budget is not one of our objectives—our only concern being the more equitable distribution of ownership of productive assets—the balanced budget provision of the Perry National Dividend Plan is ignored. I ignore as well the registered voter requirement for the same reason. The reasoning behind these modifications follows.

In the modified version of the Perry plan, only a portion of the corporate income tax proceeds would go to the Fund. With the huge national deficit, Congress would find it almost impossible to give up all the corporate income tax revenues, so it would be much easier to gain legislative approval for a small share of the tax than for all of it. Shareholders in the Citizen Mutual Fund would pay tax on their dividends for much the same reason: the plan should disrupt the existing tax system as little as possible.

One more explanation is needed. I have suggested a fund index, such as the Wilshire 5,000 equity index, rather than using the 2,000 leading corporations, as proposed by Speiser for the Kitty Hawk Model (*Handbook,* page 23). He points out that beginning with the 2,000 leading corporations could represent a potential threat to small business (*Handbook,* page 74). Expanding the group to 5,000 makes that threat smaller. Using an index eliminates the need to "establish guidelines for selection of specific companies" or to "design safeguards" (*Handbook,* page 26). The only safeguard needed would be to design an orderly buying program so that purchases for the new mutual fund do not disrupt the normal working of the market (if the market can be called normal in these days of program trading), and to make sure that the fund does not acquire too many shares of the smaller companies.

In the modification of the Perry plan, proceeds from the corporate income tax go into purchase of shares of stock, with non-transferable shares of the resulting mutual fund going to participants rather than lump-sum payments being made directly to them. The reason for this modification is to meet guideline (2): the plan should have a lasting effect, enabling people to accumulate capital over a period of time.

The distribution of funds would be modified in that not every eligible citizen would receive the same number of shares. Instead, shares would be distributed according to gross income, with the largest number of shares going to the working poor. This modification is to meet guideline (3): the plan should benefit the have-nots more than the haves. By channeling the largest distribution to the poor who are working, the modification also partially meets guideline (5): benefits of the plan should be earned.

A major drawback of this plan, just as with the Perry National Dividend Plan, is that it requires legislation. As Speiser points out in discussing the Kitty Hawk plan, it is "unlikely that politicians are going to push for such a change" (*Supplement,* page 2).

However, as we are unlikely to achieve *universal* share ownership unless the government does intervene, I include this Citizen Mutual Fund Plan. This plan is suggested rather than the Kitty Hawk Model because it comes closer to meeting guideline (4): simple to explain and maintain.

The Consumer Equity Plan (CEP)

My phone company and my credit card companies regularly advise me on how many discount dollars I have been earned. My electric company lets me contribute to a charity each month, and my favorite department store issues trading stamps. If I so choose, I can put those trading stamps in a book and when the book is filled, I can turn it in for cash or for tickets that can be applied to purchases of merchandise.

If all of these companies can offer these services so readily, could they not let us earn shares of their stock almost as readily? The third part of my three-part plan is for companies to issue shares of stock to the people who buy their products.

The big drawback of this part of the plan is that it fails to meet guideline (3): it does not benefit the have-nots more than the haves. However, even the have-nots buy food and many pay their own utility bills. Furthermore, according to a study from the Survey Research Center of the University of Michigan, 90 per cent of the American people have little or no net worth. If we take away home equity, a non-income-producing asset, the capital-ownership picture becomes even bleaker. Even middle income families tend to be have-nots in the area of capital ownership.

If significant numbers of utilities, grocery chains, food companies, and manufacturers of cars, appliances, and other retail goods could be persuaded to channel part of their advertising and public relations budgets into stock distribution plans for those who buy their products, many Americans could accumulate shares of stock in a variety of companies. The earnings that they spend now for daily living would also help them build their future.

How the Three Parts Work Together

As discussed earlier, all of the three parts described above meet the requirements of the contest (no confiscation or added taxes) and none of the three parts completely meets all of the additional guidelines proposed. Taken together, however, the three parts do meet the guidelines, as shown in the following table.

	Guideline	SIA	CMF	CEP
1.	Voluntary	yes	no	yes
2.	Lasting effect	probably	yes	yes
3.	Benefit have-nots more	yes	yes	no
4.	Simple to explain and maintain	no	yes	yes
5.	Benefits earned	yes	partially	indirectly

Ideally, we can implement all three of these plans, or similar plans which achieve the same goals. Even if only one of the plans can be implemented, it moves us closer to our goal of universal share ownership. How then might we go about implementation of each plan? Some suggestions are given below.

IMPLEMENTING THE THREE PLANS

Implementing Shareholders In America, Inc.

Since Shareholders In America, Inc. exists, that is where we should begin. As the first step, I suggest that all of the essay contributors be invited to purchase stock in SIA. (Other interested persons could also participate, but the essayists are suggested because we are obviously interested and readily accessible.) If 200 essayists each purchased $100 worth of stock, we would have a $200,000 kitty. I agree with Speiser's idea that SIA shares should be owned only by employees. Among the essayists, there probably are those who would like to remain involved with the quest for universal share ownership. If they could become involved, they would retain their shares. If they could not function as employees in some way, they would sell their shares back to SIA at the end of a certain period of time, perhaps three years.

Step Two: With the money raised from essayists (and others), we hire fundraisers to recruit business sponsors, obtain grants from foundations, and develop working relationships with religious organizations where appropriate.

Step Three: The business and religious people recruited in step two formulate a business operating plan and select SIA pilot projects, as discussed in the *Supplement to The USOP Handbook* (page 14). Through the money that the fundraisers have procured, the SIA group helps the pilot projects get started with financial and/or managerial assistance.

Step Four: The pilot projects in turn set up their own corporations,

becoming local SIAs which are independent of the parent SIA.
However, each local SIA is required to provide for dividend-paying
shares of stock to be issued to employees, plus a small percentage of
shares to go to the parent SIA. As a local SIA becomes successful, it
repays the parent SIA all or part of the start-up fund. These repaid funds
plus the dividends from the local SIA stock are used by the parent SIA
for three purposes. The great bulk of the money, perhaps 80 per cent,
goes toward locating and providing start-up support for more local SIA
projects. About 10 per cent goes for dividends to employees of the
parent SIA. Another 10 per cent of the money is used for researching
and promoting other plans for achieving universal share ownership,
such as the Consumer Equity Plan, the Citizen Mutual Fund Plan, or
the Kitty Hawk Model.

Implementing the Consumer Equity Plan

The Consumer Equity Plan seems the most logical area to develop
after SIA is under way and some money is being returned. In order to
implement the Consumer Equity Plan, we must persuade a number of
corporations that it is in their best interest to allocate some of their current advertising and public relations budgets for issuing stock to their
customers. We will already have contacted some of those corporations
in our work with SIA, and it may be possible that we will have already
identified some corporations who want to launch a consumer equity
program.

One of the best corporate areas to target might be utilities. I suggest utilities because of their special status as regulated monopolies
which must take into account the public good. For a utility to operate
in a favorable regulatory climate, both the public service commission
and the consumers must perceive it as a responsible civic citizen. If individual customers (not businesses) were to receive a fractional share
of stock for every dollar they paid on their utility bills, they would be
more likely to be well-disposed toward the utility, more likely to choose
electric over gas, or vice versa, and perhaps even less likely to protest
rate increases. Such a stock distribution plan might also give the utility
more room for flexibility when negotiating with the public service commission over rates.

Furthermore, the utilities are probably the corporations who most
regularly collect money from the least affluent of our society, and their
bills are regular enough and high enough for even a small rebate to build
into a share of stock within a reasonable length of time—especially

since utility shares tend to be relatively low-priced.

Since a large portion of the income of poor families goes into food purchases, food companies would be another good industry to target. These companies are already deeply into rebate programs through offering cents-off coupons and encouraging customers to send in proof of purchase for cash rebates. They could build even stronger customer loyalty by encouraging customers to save such documents over a long enough period of time to earn a share of stock.

Makers of large and small appliances, grocery store chains, department store chains, and others could also participate. Somewhere out there is a company that is ripe to become the first Consumer Equity participant.

Implementing the Citizen Mutual Fund Plan

Implementing the Citizen Mutual Fund Plan should be third on our list of priorities for several reasons. A successful SIA launch is needed to generate funds for promoting the other plans. The SIA and Consumer Equity plans have higher chances for success because they do not require the passage of legislation. Success with SIA and Consumer Equity will help create a favorable climate for extending share ownership even further.

To implement the Citizen Mutual Fund Plan, we must persuade legislators to sponsor it. One way of persuading the legislators is to build grassroots support among voters, who would in turn pressure their representatives to enact such a measure. Another way is to demonstrate good results from SIA and Consumer Equity.

Perhaps we should also consider trying to establish the Citizen Mutual Fund Plan by beginning at the state level. The state could set aside part of the tax it receives from corporations to set up a mutual fund which buys shares of companies that operate in the state. This would give the state an attractive lure to seeking new businesses. Its purchases of shares in state corporations would help such companies keep up the market value of their shares, and since many citizens would be shareholders via the state mutual fund, these companies could expect the citizens of the state to have a stronger than usual interest in their welfare.

The state might also use such a fund to reduce the welfare tax burden. If it so chose, the state could reduce welfare payments to match part or all of the dividends that a person on welfare received from the state mutual fund.

We could select from one to three states to target, states that have relatively small and readily accessible populations and that have and use initiative and referendum. We could work to build enough grassroots support in those states, either to obtain legislative action or to win support for an initiative.

If the Citizen Mutual Fund Plan is adopted and works in one state, others will soon adopt similar plans, and eventually the federal government will follow. After all, 15 states granted voting rights to women before the federal government did.

Summary

I strongly support the idea of universal share ownership and of achieving that widespread ownership without violating any of our individual rights. I am awed by the time and energy and intellectual power that have gone into the various plans discussed in *The USOP Handbook* and the *Supplement to The USOP Handbook*. I found something that I like in nearly all of them, but a completely satisfying answer in none of them. For that reason, the plan proposed really consists of three plans— to begin with Shareholders In America, Inc., helping people build and share in their own companies; to proceed to the Consumer Equity Plan, where corporations voluntarily share part of their profits with the consumers who buy their products; and then to move to the Citizen Mutual Fund Plan, where every adult citizen receives an equity in America's corporations. I further propose that all of the essayists be invited to invest seed money in the existing corporation, Shareholders In America, Inc., not only because seed money is needed—but also because I want to change the world and have to begin where I am.

Notes

1. Stuart M. Speiser, *The USOP Handbook: A Guide to Designing Universal Share Ownership Plans for the United States and Great Britain.* New York: Council on International and Public Affairs, 1986.
2. Stuart M. Speiser, *Supplement to The USOP Handbook. Shareholders in America, Inc.: A First Step Toward Universal Share Ownership.* New York: Council on International and Public Affairs, June 1986.

8

THE CORNERSTONE OF AMERICAN LIBERTY: HOW CAN A MORE EQUITABLE DISTRIBUTION OF PROPERTY BE ACHIEVED?

by

Paul Derrick

Editor's Note: *Paul Derrick of London, England, is a world authority on the cooperative movement and common ownership. Over the past 40 years, he has published two books and more than 80 papers on this subject. He served as research officer for the International Co-operative Alliance and as secretary of the Co-operative Productive Federation. His essay brings us a global vision of USOP, drawing on his experience of common ownership in other nations as well as the United States. Although he is British, his essay was submitted in the North American competition.*

ABSTRACT

Stuart Speiser argues in *The USOP Handbook* that the way to achieve the more equitable distribution of private property favored by many Americans would be to change the plumbing system to ensure that the benefits of the growth of the 2,000 biggest American corporations accrue to those most in need rather than to existing shareholders. It is suggested that a huge investment corporation should be created to spread risks and that special USOP bonus shares should be issued to those in need, with the collaboration of such banks as may survive into the 21st century.

This essay suggests that a simpler way of achieving this objective of a more equitable distribution of property would be to set a permanent limit on the return, as well as the liability of existing shareholders of these huge corporations, and to arrange for the distribution of the bonus shares—non-voting redeemable preference shares—not only to those in need, but also to people employed by the corporations concerned and to customers, suppliers, and others (even though some of them may live in countries other than the United States).

During the 1980 U.S. election campaign, the Republican Party platform declared that "the widespread distribution of private property is the cornerstone of American liberty." The widespread distribution of private property has indeed been an American ideal since the time of Thomas Jefferson, and such measures as the Homestead Acts have helped many to achieve economic independence through ownership. Nevertheless, the growth of industry in the U.S. has led to greater inequality because capital accumulation within industry has been highly concentrated in a few hands. Thus, Robert Hamrin calculated in 1976 for the Joint Economic Committee of Congress that 0.5 per cent of the population owned 50 per cent of the corporate stock. And in a paper for "The Other Economic Summit" (TOES) in London in June 1984, Ward Morehouse of the Council on Public and International Affairs noted that around 6 per cent of the people of the U.S. owned around 95 per cent of its productive assets.

What can be done about this concentration of ownership in the hands of the few, which is so contrary to the hopes of the founding fathers of the Republic? Stuart Speiser of the Center for the Study of Expanded Capital Ownership has done much work on this problem and has asked others to contribute their ideas. He asks for ways of achieving this goal in a manner that will revive the economy, but without confiscation or increased taxation. I have been writing about means of achieving a more equitable distribution of property for 40 years. My principal work on the subject, *Lost Property,* was published in 1947.

Distributism

I was much influenced by the ideas of G. K. Chesterton and Hilaire Belloc, who developed their Distributist ideas in the 1920s and 1930s as an alternative to the state socialist ideas of the Labour Party in Britain, and to the willingness of Conservatives to accept a continued concentration of property in the hands of the few. They emphasized the value of small-scale production by people owning their own businesses, small holdings owned by those working them, and the role of small shopkeepers. Their ideas had some impact on Elliott Dodds and the Liberal Party, who were campaigning in the 1940s for "Ownership for All" through some form of co-ownership. But in the years since the Second World War, the Conservative Party has won votes by calling for "a nationwide property-owning democracy," while the Labour Party insists upon the need for a more equitable distribution of wealth and income (which would seem to be something not so very different from a more equitable distribution of property). Perhaps we are all Distributists now. At the 1984 Annual General Meeting of the Chesterton Society, I suggested that the world was likely to move in a Distributist direction, involving an extension of cooperative production with more people *owning* the productive resources with which they work.

In his *USOP Handbook,* Stuart Speiser rejects confiscation as a means of "spreading the ownership of productive assets broadly among the people," advocating a gradual approach. But more direct approaches such as the Russian revolution have sometimes helped to bring about a more equitable distribution of property. Hilaire Belloc argued in his preface to the 1926 edition of *The Servile State* that the Russian revolution had resulted in a more equitable distribution of property rather than in collectivization as prescribed by state socialist theorists. But this was in the years of the New Economic Policy and before wholesale collectivization. Sixty years later, in November 1986, the Soviet government announced that it intends to legitimize small-scale private enterprise and workers' cooperatives, and since then has begun to move cautiously in a libertarian or Distributist or cooperative direction in the way pioneered by the Hungarians and the Chinese. But since confiscation presupposes such acute inequality as to provoke a revolution, Speiser is completely right to rule out confiscation as a way of achieving a more equitable distribution of property. The problem is how to achieve a more equitable distribution of property through democratic and constitutional procedures.

Taxation

It is a little more surprising that Speiser should rule out "increased taxation" as a means of achieving a more equitable distribution of property. Like Hilaire Belloc in *The Servile State,* he has his doubts about "welfare capitalism," which taxes the rich to help meet the needs of the poor. It is not altogether clear whether Speiser rejects *any* kind of tax changes to help achieve a more equitable distribution of property, or rejects only an overall increase in taxation in relation to the national income or gross domestic product. He commends the Tax Reduction Act of 1975, the Expanded Ownership Act of 1981, and the use of tax changes to promote Employee Stock Ownership Plans. He proposes substantial cuts in corporation tax, which would presumably involve some increases in other taxes if the same level of government services were to be maintained.

Wealth taxes are used in some countries to help achieve a more equitable distribution of property, and in Britain, special levies on investment incomes in 1948 and 1968 had the same purpose. In my view, the separate taxation of personal earned and investment incomes (as in Britain between 1907 and 1920) could help to achieve a more equitable distribution of property.

Speiser proposes arrangements to ensure that the growth of large companies would lead to more and more people in need becoming owners instead of further concentration in the hands of existing owners through increased value of their shares. Turning more and more people into shareholders in this kind of way is, however, just as much redistributive as would be taxation of the growing incomes of existing owners combined with the distribution of welfare benefits to those in need. The latter can be described as "welfare capitalism," and perhaps Speiser is right in arguing that redistribution through taxation and welfare payments should be excluded from a consideration of ways of achieving a more equitable economic system.

Ownership and Shareholding

Speiser opens his *USOP Handbook* by discussing employee shareholdership as a foundation for universal share ownership, but argues that employee share ownership cannot lead directly to universal share ownership. He recognizes that employee share ownership can increase incentive, but notes that some employees may be cautious about putting too many eggs in one basket through employee share ownership. While recognizing that around ten million U.S. employees participate in Employee Stock Ownership Plans (ESOPs), Speiser criticizes tax concessions to encourage employee shareholding, pointing out that such employees generally have steady jobs in profitable companies and are thus a more fortunate minority than many others who are jobless or hold low-wage, often insecure jobs, frequently in very small enterprises. He is critical of "pension fund socialism" and of Swedish Wage Earners' Funds, although these can be regarded as forms of indirect wider share ownership. But an important question is whether wider share ownership, or even universal share ownership, is sufficient to achieve the "spreading of ownership of productive assets broadly among the people," let alone the widespread distribution of private property which is said to be the cornerstone of American liberty.

People value economic independence and like to be owners of the productive resources with which they work, exercising some control over their working lives. Real ownership means more than shareholdings in a wide variety of companies, such as the 2,000 largest American companies. It means owning one's own land and hearth and homestead, not merely holding shares in vast remote corporations over which one can exercise no real control at all. Therefore, wider (and indeed universal share ownership) can be regarded as only one among a number of means of achieving a widespread distribution of property. And the promotion of universal share ownership by the Kitty Hawk method proposed by Speiser might result in rather more bureaucracy and centralization than many advocates of widely distributed property would like to see.

Kitty Hawk

As a master plumber, Stuart Speiser notes that the 2,000 largest U.S. companies undertake new investment from retained earnings and through borrowing, and that their common shares increase in value with the increase in value of the assets of the company. Speiser thinks it unfair that these gains from new investment should accrue mainly to the relatively wealthy existing shareholders and proposes to arrange that they should instead accrue to the much larger number of people owning relatively few shares and little other property. The existing shares in the companies concerned would stop growing in value, and with the help of the banks and the public authorities, new USOP shares would be issued to those most in need.

This new plumbing system would be imposed by federal legislation, even though some of those whose shares were prevented from increasing in value might object to such a stop as an intolerable and socialistic intervention by government in the economy. The controlling shareholders in these 2,000 giant corporations would presumably be *required* to accept the imposition of a curb or ceiling on the value of their shares in the name of wider share ownership. A huge unit trust (mutual fund) or investment corporation would be created to hold the new USOP shares issued by these big companies, and would itself issue USOP shares to be held ultimately by the needy.

Speiser thinks that one of the more controversial aspects of this Kitty Hawk plan would be deciding just who should be lucky enough to receive these new USOP shares. He also suggests that some people might argue that the USOP program would lead to extensive government economic planning and possibly to a "command economy," as in socialist countries. The federal government would be deeply involved in providing guarantees; and Speiser suggests that the needy receiving the USOP shares should not get common or ordinary shares, which might appreciate in value, but instead non-voting, non-cumulative preference shares. Like the wealthier holders of existing shares, their new USOP shares might not appreciate in value, and they would not be marketable.

Speiser recognizes that the managements of some large U.S. corporations might not like being *required* to distribute a substantially higher proportion of earnings as dividends, even though this would be accompanied by reductions in or elimination of corporate taxes. He also acknowledges that existing shares would not increase in value with the growth of the company, but might even *decline* in value. After all, the market value of shares reflects the expectation that they will increase in value along with the growth in the value of the assets of the company. When it became clear that the object of the new legislation was to prevent economic growth from leading to increases in the value of existing shares, their values would be likely to fall.

Speiser also recognizes that wider share ownership through USOP shares under the Kitty Hawk Model might reduce incentive and productivity. While ESOPs in theory help to increase incentive and productivity because employee shareholders benefit from the success of their companies through increased value of their shares, Speiser is less than enthusiastic about ESOPs since he wants to achieve a more equitable distribution of property through wider share ownership. Many people of limited resources working for smaller enterprises would receive shares in the 2,000 largest companies in the U.S. for nothing. Although these shares might be non-voting, non-cumulative preference shares, they would in time provide these persons with substantial income from dividends and, in some cases, might reduce their incentive to increase their earnings by hard work. A full spread of *real* ownership, making more and more people owners of the enterprises for which they work, should help to increase incentive and productivity.

Alternative Possibilities

The Kitty Hawk Model is clearly important pioneering, but there are, as Speiser recognizes, other ways of achieving a more equitable distribution of property. He mentions Martin Weitzman's proposals in *The Share Economy* for increasing profit-related pay, in which the British Chancellor Nigel Lawson has been taking an active interest, and Professor James Meade, whose recent writings develop ideas about "labor-capital partnerships." He also discusses the Loi Monory in France, the Mondragon cooperatives in Spain, the John Lewis Partnership in Great Britain, Karl Marx's views on the socialization of the limited company, and the implications of the constitution of the British Labour Party.

The basic problem is that when successful companies grow they increase to an unlimited extent the fortunes of the limited number of people who have provided the original risk capital. It is reasonable that these people should receive a generous return when they have risked their savings. But should they receive an *unlimited* return when their liability is limited? Speiser says that it should not, and that the benefits of the growth of large U.S. companies—many of them multinationals—should go to those most in need in such a way as to achieve a more widespread distribution of property. Professor J. K. Galbraith declared in his Reith Lecture in 1966 that "no grant of feudal privilege in British history has ever equalled for effortless return that of the American grandparent who endowed his descendants with a thousand shares in General Motors or IBM."

But if we want to prevent the common shares of the 2,000 largest American corporations from increasing indefinitely in value, is Speiser's SuperStock method with its many steps already discussed the simplest way of accomplishing this goal? It seems a most extraordinarily complicated way of achieving a more equitable distribution of property. Would it not be much simpler to deal with the problem directly by telling the shareholders of the 2,000 giant corporations that their returns, unlike their liability, would no longer be unlimited and that the time had come that at least some of the gains from the growth of their corporations would be distributed in a more equitable way.

Limited Liability

In the 19th century in Britain, America, and elsewhere, it was found that limited liability was a necessary condition for raising the capital needed for large-scale industrial development. There was considerable argument, as in Britain in the 1840s, about the morality of generalizing limited liability that had previously only been authorized by Parliamentary action. But the collapse of a bank in Glasgow in the 1840s and the ruin of many small investors resulted in the legalization of the limited liability company in Britain. Since that time, many people have taken it for granted that it is part of the natural order of things for the return of the company shareholder to be unlimited, even though his liability is limited. But there have been some who have questioned it.

The Christian Socialists did so in the 1850s when they were promoting cooperative producer societies in which the return as well as the liability of their shareholders was limited. These societies were less successful than contemporary companies, partly because the return on share capital was not only limited but too low to raise needed capital. The issue of limited liability was addressed by Archbishop William Temple in his 1941 book, *Christianity and the Social Order,* in which he declared that both the return and the liability of the company shareholder should be limited by law. The issue was also raised by W. S. Gilbert 50 years earlier in *Utopia Limited* in this poetic passage:

They then proceed to trade with all who'll trust them,
Quite irrespective of their capital,
It's shady but it's sanctified by custom,
Bank, railway loan or Panama Canal,
You can't embark on trading too tremendous,
It's strictly fair and based on common sense.
If you succeed your profits are stupendous,
And if you fail: pop goes your eighteen pence....

If you come to grief and creditors are craving
—For nothing that is planned by mortal head,
Is certain in this Vale of Sorrow saving
That your liability is limited—
Do you suppose that signifies perdition?

If so you're but a monetary dunce,
You merely file a winding up petition,
And start another company at once.

Though a Rothschild you may be in your own capacity,
As a company you've come to utter sorrow
But the liquidators say: Never mind, you needn't pay,
And you start another company to-morrow.

At about the same time, Cardinal Manning was helping Pope Leo XIII to produce the major Papal Encyclical *Rerum Novarum,* attacking state socialist ideas and calling for a more equitable distribution of property. It inspired Hilaire Belloc to produce *The Servile State* 20 years later, but it did not explore in detail the implications for company law of the concept of an equitable distribution of property in an industrial age. Nor did the Guild Socialists who were critical of state socialism in the early 1920s, although A. J. Penty discussed the evolution of company law in his book, *A Guildsman's Interpretation of History.*

The Guild Socialists used cooperative law for their building guilds and some Guild Socialists, such as Maurice Reckitt, were also active Distributists in the 1920s. R. H. Tawney called for a limitation on return as well as liability of the shareholder in *The Acquisitive Society* in 1920, as did Wickham Steed in *A Way to Social Peace* in 1932. Berle and Means declared in *The Modern Corporation & Private Property* in the same year that it was completely illogical for the shareholders of large companies to be paid more than a limited return. As power in such companies passes from shareholders to management, there was no point in paying more than was needed to ensure an adequate supply of capital. Similarly, J. M. Keynes argued in 1926 in *The End of Laissez Faire* that there was no need for shareholders to be paid more than a conventionally adequate dividend.

In 1919, the American Catholic Bishops' Program of Social Reconstruction argued that the principle of paying a fair average return on investment should be applied not only to public service monopolies but also to private companies generally. In 1950, James Callaghan told the Labour Party Conference that it was quite immoral for company shareholders whose liability was limited to be paid more than a limited return, and in 1952, Austen Albu, M.P. and John Strachey, M.P. expressed the same view in the *New Fabian Essays* In February 1967, Douglas Jay, M.P. (then President of the Board of Trade) told the House of Commons that the time had come to re-examine the whole theory and purpose of the limited company. And in 1969, the Labour Party statement, *Agenda for a Generation,* asked why shareholders should be entitled to increased incomes as capital accumulation in industry proceeds, and proposed that various plans for the limitation of dividends should be examined.

In order to help stabilize costs and prices in an expanding economy, Labour and Conservative governments in Britain have appealed at various times for restraint in wage claims and in the distribution of dividends since 1945. Temporary legislation for the limitation of dividends was introduced by a Labour government in 1966 and again in 1968, and by a Conservative government in 1972. It is odd that a 1974 Labour Party report on company law had nothing to say about dividends.

If the U.S. government were to enact legislation to set a permanent limit on the return as well as on the liability of the shareholders of the 2,000 largest U.S. companies, would this not be as acceptable to U.S. industry as elaborate changes in the economic system designed to ensure that the gains of growth . accrue to those in need rather than to existing shareholders? Such a relatively simple measure might in fact be welcomed by management—at least in private—because it would help to protect management from merger mania and such corporate raiders as T. Boone Pickens, who sends shivers of apprehension through boardrooms across America.

Pickens and his associates made $760 million from an unsuccessful bid for Gulf Oil. Ted Turner, Carl Icahn, and Ivan Boesky have made millions in the same game. Australians, such as Alan Bond, Rupert Murdoch, John Elliott, and Robert Holmes a Court, have been happy to join in, and there has been a major increase in take-over bids in Britain as well. People who have built up successful businesses by good management and have allowed substantial gaps to develop between share values and asset values through prudence in the distribution of earnings have found themselves liable to be thrown out by financial speculators. One reason for the considerable growth of Employee Stock Ownership Plans in the U.S. in the last ten years is that they can provide some protection against corporate raiders. But the legal limitation on the return as well as on the liability of the shareholder would provide greater protection.

Although U.S. corporations are incorporated under state rather than federal law, it would presumably be possible for federal legislation to require the 2,000 largest corporations to set a limit on the return and the liability of their shareholders. Such a change should be attractive to management because it would provide protection against raiders. But it could be made even more attractive if the corporations concerned were exempt from corporation tax or allowed to pay at a substantially reduced rate. This would probably make it necessary for the maximum return to be set rather lower than it otherwise might have been. Stuart Speiser has pointed out that such an exemption would mean the collection of more revenue from personal taxation, but it would be important to ensure that it did not result in an undue increase in the remuneration of management.

The Gains of Growth

Suppose the U. S. Congress were to decide that it had been a mistake to allow the dividends of company shareholders to be unlimited when their liability was limited. What should happen to the benefits of the growth that established companies are able to make without much in the way of share capital? Speiser takes the view that they should accrue to those members of the community most in need in order to achieve a more equitable distribution of private property, the cornerstone of American liberty. But a considerable number of people argue that the surplus earnings of enterprises should accrue to those working for them, so that they become *owners* of the productive resources with which they work. This, after all, was the purpose of the Homestead Acts and has been one of the objectives of Employee Stock Ownership Plans in the U.S. in recent years. They help to end the division in industry between "us" and "them," creating a sense of common purpose and increasing incentives for workers.

In Britain, in 1929, John Spedan Lewis inherited the John Lewis department stores, founded in 1864, and decided to form the John Lewis Partnership Ltd. so that the stores were owned by all those working in them. The return paid on share capital held by individuals was limited and surplus earnings went to employees in proportion to the value of work contributed, partly in cash but largely in the form of non-voting preference shares carrying a limited return. The Partnership prospered and over the next 40 years grew to employ some 25,000 people, owners of the enterprise for which they worked.

At the 1946 Conservative Party Conference, Winston Churchill declared that Conservatives should "seek as far as possible to make the status of the wage earner that of a partner rather than that of an irresponsible employee," and since that time Conservatives in Britain have often spoken about the need for a spirit of partnership in industry and a nation-wide property-owning democracy. Pope Pius XI expressed a similar view when he called in *Quadragesimo Anno* in 1931 for the wage contract to be modified by a contract of partnership, a view that was further discussed by Pope John Paul II 50 years later in *Laborem Exercens,* and in a 1986 statement by the U.S. Catholic Bishops.

At the same time, the Liberal Party in Britain has been calling for profit sharing, co-partnership, and employee shareholding since the publication of the Liberal Yellow Book in 1928. And the Labour Party is committed by its constitution to securing for workers the full fruits of their industry and the most equitable distribution thereof that may be possible upon a basis of "common ownership." In its 1986 statement on *Social Ownership,* the Labour Party made no proposals for further nationalization, but placed much emphasis on the value of a major extension of employee shareholding and of cooperative development. All the parties in Britain say that they want to encourage cooperatives in which workers are owners of the enterprises for which they work, and more than 1,300 of these have been formed in Britain in the last ten years.

There would seem to be considerable support in Britain for a move toward some form of social ownership, whether it be partnership in industry, or co-ownership, or the cooperative form of common ownership. But the argument here is that the surplus earnings of enterprises should no longer go exclusively to existing owners of shares, but to a greater or lesser extent to the *workers,* so as to make them at least to some extent *owners* of the productive resources with which they work. On the other hand, while Speiser agrees about the limitation on existing owners, he argues in *The USOP Handbook* that the gains of growth in large American and British companies should go primarily to those members of the community most in need to help bring about a more equitable economic system. But why should not the gains of growth go both to those working for a company and also to those members of the community most in need?

The Scott Bader Commonwealth

The Scott Bader company set an example in dividing surplus earnings in such a way in Britain in 1951. It was a family business owned by Ernest Bader and members of his family, which had been engaged for 30 years in the production of polyesters and other chemicals. Bader was a Christian and was persuaded that it would be a good idea to transfer the shares of the company to a company limited by guarantee without a share capital, of which the employees would be members. This company was called the Scott Bader Commonwealth and the shares were transferred over a period of years, mainly as a gift. Although a high proportion of the earnings of the company continued to be invested, a complicated constitution required that any surplus earnings should be distributed equally to the worker-members of the Commonwealth company, and that an equivalent amount should be allocated to good causes and social purposes of benefit to the larger community. For example, old people in the village of Wollaston in Northamptonshire were among the beneficiaries, and a wide variety of projects and good causes have been supported by the Commonwealth over the years.

If the 2,000 largest companies in the U.S. were to be required to set a limit on the dividends paid to existing shareholders, they could also be required to issue bonus shares both to employees *and* to people in need. Since share values reflect anticipated increases in dividends (and Speiser's aim is to prevent further increases in the value of existing shares rather than to cause a decline in their value), the limit on dividends would not necessarily need to be an immediate freeze on dividends.

Legislation for the limitation on return and liability of shareholders might apply to middle-sized as well as to large companies. But the companies would need to be large enough to ensure an adequate supply of capital. If the maximum return were linked to asset values, after a few years it might still be very generous, even though capped with a ceiling. Cooperative productive societies have had rather limited success over the last 150 years, perhaps in part because the return paid on capital has not only been limited but too low to attract needed capital. The Mondragon cooperatives in the Basque Provinces of Spain have been more successful than others. This may be partly to their having their own bank—the Caja Laboral Popular—and also because the worker-members share in the growth of assets when earnings are ploughed back through a system of capital credits.

The worker-members of the Mondragon cooperatives invest $3,000 to $5,000 in the shares of their own cooperatives. But they and other local people also invest their savings in the Caja Laboral Popular, and the bank in turn provides a large part of the capital required by the cooperatives. Risks are spread in this way so that workers do not need to put too many eggs in one basket or risk too large a proportion of their savings in their own cooperatives. Local Enterprise Boards in Britain have helped to finance the development of workers' cooperatives in a similar manner, and it may be that the risks of investment could be reduced by people investing their savings in such local Enterprise Boards or Community Banks, instead of wholly in their own enterprises. Wage Earners' Funds in Sweden might develop a similar role.

Local Community Banks or social funds might also develop a role in allocating some part of the surplus earnings of successful companies to those most in need. If bonus shares, reflecting the growth of successful companies, were allocated to some extent to such Community Banks or social funds, they in turn could allocate something rather like USOP shares to those most in need. To some, this would simply provide needed income; others might find whatever they received would help them establish small enterprises of their own and become *owners* of the productive resources with which they worked.

Spread of Ownership

The imposition of a limit on the return as well as on the liability of the shareholders of large companies would prevent the unlimited appreciation of the value of such shares and help the development of a more equitable economic system. It would also help to stabilize costs and prices in an expanding economy, as companies would be run in the interests of their employees and the surrounding community. Trade unionists would therefore be more likely to exercise restraint in wage claims than when companies are run for the profit of wealthy investors and speculators. Such bonus shares issued to employees would, as suggested by Speiser, be non-voting, non-cumulative preference shares, and until the maximum dividend was reached, could be linked to increases in dividends in such a way as to give employees a legal claim on a share of retained earnings.

While organized on a conventional basis, many large American companies make generous donations to good causes. Such authorities on the modern corporation as R. H. Tawney and Berle and Means argue that if a limit is set on the return and liability of the shareholder, then those in need and the community as a whole, as well as employees, should be beneficiaries of the gains of growth. But there are very many people in need, and not only in the industrialized countries in which most large corporations are headquartered. With multinational companies, it might be quite a complicated business to arrange for the return paid on share capital to be limited both for the parent company and for its subsidiaries.

The possibility of applying the basic cooperative principle of a limited return on capital to multinational companies was discussed in 1967 in a report from the International Co-operative Alliance, *Co-operatives and Monopolies in Contemporary Economic Systems,* in another 1972 report entitled, *Multinational Corporations and the International Co-operative Movement,* and in a 1981 paper for the United Nations Commission on Transnational Corporations. The Commission has been developing a code for transnational corporations since 1974 with a view, as its then Director Dr. Klaus Sahlgren put it in 1978, toward "harnessing their immense energies and capacities for the good of mankind." If this objective is to be achieved, the help of legislators is needed to prevent these energies and capacities being used for the benefit of financial speculators and corporate raiders. The simplest way of doing this is to set a limit on the return as well as the liability of their shareholders.

Wider share ownership is an admirable objective, but if the return of the shareholder is unlimited while his liability is limited, the result is likely to be an extension of the casino economy rather than a nation-wide property-owning democracy. When Mrs. Thatcher sells the family silver by privatizing British Telecom and British Gas, she enables substantial numbers of people with surplus savings to make speculative gains like T. Boone Pickens. This is not helping those most in need or enabling more people to become owners of the productive resources with which they work. If on the other hand, a limit were set on the return as well as on the liability of the shareholders of the 2,000 largest American corporations, the fruits of their growth might not only accrue to less fortunate Americans but also to employees and suppliers and customers in developing countries, thus bringing about a more equitable distribution of property between both countries and individuals. This would be good for trade and stimulate demand by putting more money in the pockets of people in need of the goods produced and not mainly in the pockets of people wishing to reinvest.

Common Ground?

A great deal of confusion has been caused by the way in which the Communist Manifesto in 1848 called for the "abolition of private property," immediately after saying that the distinguishing feature of communism was *not* the abolition of property generally but the abolition of "the exploitation of the many by the few." At the time, "socialism" was not identified with state ownership but with cooperative ownership (as pioneered by Robert Owen), and in 1864, Marx declared that the value of the great social experiments in cooperative production "cannot be overestimated" and that they "should be fostered by national means." The British Labour Party's constitutional commitment to "common ownership," quoted by Stuart Speiser, is broad enough to cover cooperative ownership as well as state ownership, and the Party in recent years has been inclined to place increasing emphasis on cooperative ownership since the further extension of state ownership is not popular with voters.

Although cooperative ownership is generally regarded as a form of "common ownership" or "social ownership," it is also a form of *private* ownership in that cooperatives are independent of the state. Indeed, Chambers' Dictionary has defined "socialism" as "any one of various schemes for regenerating society by a more equal distribution of property," while Webster's Dictionary has termed it "a system of social reform which contemplates a more just and equitable distribution of property." In calling for a more equitable distribution of property, Speiser might be fairly labelled a socialist, according to these definitions, but that would not make him a state socialist. The chairman of the New Lanark Association is also the Conservative Party's prospective parliamentary candidate for Lanark. He may be happy enough to call himself an Owenite, but he does not describe himself as a "socialist"—a word widely associated with state ownership.

There would seem to be a certain amount of common ground underlying what some Conservatives mean by partnership in industry, what some Liberals mean by co-ownership, and what some socialists mean by common ownership or social ownership. There are more industrial or workers' cooperatives in Italy than in the rest of Western Europe and more members of such cooperatives in Poland than in the whole of Western Europe. It is a form of ownership which seems to accord with the teachings of Papal encyclicals as well as with those of members of the Communist Parties of Italy and Poland. It is interesting that the Soviet government has at last decided to legitimize workers' cooperatives in the Soviet Union. If the growth of ESOPs in the U.S. is followed by the kind of structural changes in major U.S. corporations of the kind that Stuart Speiser would like to see, there could be a reduction in international tensions that derive from ideological antagonisms and a real chance of enduring peace in the 21st century.

If basic changes in major U.S. corporations were to bring a more equitable distribution of property *and* make more and more people *owners* of the productive resources with which they work, it would not only help to reinforce the cornerstone of American liberty but also help to promote liberty elsewhere. It would reinforce the idea that even basic changes can be achieved by democratic process if people are clear enough about what they want.

9

USOP AND IMPLEMENTATION CRITERIA

by

Alan Byron Potter

Editor's Note: *Alan Byron Potter of Knowlton, Quebec, a graduate of the London School of Economics, is an economist and a practical businessman with decades of experience in the chemical and construction industries. He is now economic consultant to the largest engineering company in Canada, specializing in socioeconomic assessment of construction projects in underdeveloped nations. He is the author of several books and papers. His essay treats several practical accounting and tax problems inherent in the USOP concept, as well as the economic theory of shareholding and the distribution of corporate profits. He proposes that corporate management be allowed to control the disposition of some retained earnings, thus answering some critics of the SuperStock model who believe that management's expertise in deploying retained earnings is an important element of stock market value.*

ABSTRACT

The USOP Handbook frequently uses the terms "share ownership" and "ownership of the means of production" as if they were synonymous. This essay demonstrates that there is no necessary connection between the two concepts, even in the case of existing shareholders who purchased shares with their own savings.

In the case of USOP shareholders, it would be unrealistic and unnecessary to pretend that they own the means of production. They will own shares that entitle them to dividend payments. Once this distinction has been accepted, many of the problems associated with the implementation of USOP disappear.

In this essay, the criteria to be considered by USOP designers are discussed and analyzed in relation to economic and social feasibility. A mechanism is proposed which should be acceptable to businessmen and tax authorities.

On the basis of this analysis, it appears that USOP, properly defined, can be designed and implemented without confiscation or increased taxation, and that it is feasible to replace the existing welfare transfer payments with the USOP system.

Introduction

A plan to make capitalism work for everyone has been developed by Stuart M. Speiser. He calls it the Universal Stock Ownership Plan (USOP) because it would make corporate stock available to everyone. The purpose of the plan is to spread the ownership of capital throughout society, thus providing a substantial annual payment of dividends to Americans who presently own little or no capital.

This essay examines the meaning of ownership in respect to existing shareholders and demonstrates that the people who provide investment capital to public companies do not own the means of production, except possibly in a very restricted and artificial sense.

It is proposed that it would be unrealistic and unnecessary to refer to USOP recipients as owners of the means of production. They will be the owners of shares and, in that capacity, they will receive dividends adjusted annually in accordance with the profitability and tax liability of the participating companies.

If it can be accepted that the ownership of shares is not synonymous with ownership of the means of production, many problems associated with USOP implementation disappear. In particular, there is no objection to making the USOP shares non-voting and non-transferable.

This essay, then, identifies certain accounting problems and resolves them by leaving matters to stand as they are at present. USOP shareholders should not be considered as being even partially responsible for corporate decision making in respect to generating profit, accounting for it, distributing it, or deciding how much profit should be retained by the corporations that produced it. These questions may be left to the tax authorities.

Assuming this proposal will be acceptable to USOP designers, a mechanism is described which resolves most of the potential problems identified in *The USOP Handbook*. The resources available for funding that mechanism are then identified and found to be adequate.

The conclusion of this essay is that, properly defined, USOP can be designed and implemented without confiscation or increased taxation. It is economically, legally, and financially feasible to replace the existing welfare system with USOP.

All of the factors described in this essay should be considered as USOP design criteria, and should eventually be communicated to USOP shareholders to ensure a smooth implementation and full understanding of USOP by the beneficiaries, business corporations, and the general public.

Ownership

Entrepreneurs who manage their private, wholly-owned companies can exercise their legal right to sell their assets and discontinue corporate activity at any time. In such cases, the ownership of shares can reasonably be interpreted as "ownership of the means of production." USOP should be introduced in such a manner that it does not inhibit entrepreneurial initiative or willingness to continue in wholly-owned businesses.

In the case of companies with minority holdings, however, whether they are public or private companies, shareholders are not necessarily in a position to demand the dissolution of the company, nor even to sell some assets and buy others. Every registered company is a legal entity which can dispose of its assets (through its accredited agents), quite independently of its shareholders. Companies own their assets, not the shareholders.

Voting shares entitle shareholders to express their confidence or lack of confidence in the board of directors and management, but not to make entrepreneurial decisions. Most shareholders do not contribute to corporate decision making in any way. If they are dissatisfied with managerial performance, they sell their shares.

It is therefore incorrect, except in the simplest of cases, to state that shareholders "own the means of production." They own shares that entitle them to a return as the providers of investment capital as long as the company operates profitably. That return may be in the form of dividends or an increase in the market value of their holdings, or both. In any case, the return is a reward to capital, and must be paid if the company wishes to remain investment worthy in the minds of potential investors. Dividends and interest paid to the holders of common shares and bonds are not, and never have been, a reward to entrepreneurial decision making or ownership of the means of production. They are the reward to savings which become investment capital.

It is, therefore, a major potential source of misunderstanding to expect USOP shareholders to acquire "economic power through ownership of the means of production." Shareholders who saved and invested their own money do not have that.

USOP shareholders will be entitled to dividends (within the capacity of the economy to operate profitably) because they own shares, and not because they own the means of production. It would be even more difficult to bring them into corporate decision making than it is for management to consult all existing shareholders concerning the day-to-day conduct of the business. But that is not necessary, nor desirable and expected by the shareholders.

Regarding returns to capital provided by private investors or by entrepreneurs, a distinction must be made between the provision of new investment capital when a company makes a new issue of shares or negotiates a new loan, and the repayment of that capital by other investors who purchase shares or bonds from the present owners. In the latter case, none of the money accrues to the company concerned, and normal fluctuations in the market price of its financial instruments do not affect the company's ability to conduct its affairs profitably. The most that can be said is that a good performance of its shares on the stock exchange may improve its ability to raise additional capital at some future date.

In the case of new share or bond issues, individuals are abstaining from immediate consumption and are directly contributing funds for the procurement of new capital assets. Nothing should be done by USOP systems to reduce the propensity to save, which will remain the essential source of new investment capital in a free market economy, whether or not a USOP system is introduced.

In the case of USOP shares, the new investment has already been made on behalf of the USOP shareholder, via the government guarantee and the banks. USOP shareholders are not themselves abstaining from consumption. Therefore, they cannot be considered as contributors to the national propensity to save, nor should they be able to sell their shares to make a capital sum instead of a right to receive dividends.

The best way of ensuring this is to pay the dividends only to the person who was originally issued the USOP shares, in order that the shares themselves will have no market value. The question of ownership or part ownership of the company as a marketable asset will then not arise.

At present, no problem is foreseen in respect to corporate management under the direction of a board of directors. Contrary to widely held opinion, however, it is not the responsibility of directors to act in the best interests of the shareholders or of any one of them. The director's responsibility to shareholders is only to act in good faith. His or her duty is to act in the best interests of the company as a whole. The board should be described as representing the shareholders (the providers of investment capital) and, simultaneously, as representing the owners (the organization). In regard to good corporate citizenship (long-term profitability), the board can also be expected to represent the ultimate interests of the employees, the suppliers, and of the general public, including USOP shareholders.

The board will provide advice and guidance to corporate management on all matters of policy and business strategies, as it is supposed to do at present. If the advice is not accepted, the board has the alternative of replacing the chief executive officer. The board will continue to make recommendations each year in respect of dividend distribution and retained profits, as at present, but those recommendations will be made in the context of the USOP system and the corporate tax system as it operates in respect of USOP policies.

To ensure the continued viability of the private enterprise economic system, USOP should be designed in such a way that it will not inhibit new share issues in the private sector, reduce the value of existing shares in the marketplace, nor inhibit the exercise of legitimate functions by the board of directors.

Accounting Problems

Profit, as measured by corporate and tax authority accountants, is supposed to be a simple calculation of gross revenue minus the costs incurred to produce that revenue. In practice, many difficulties arise.

Revenue is easier to calculate than cost because there is a certain amount of money in the bank and cash in hand at the beginning and end of each year. However, some of the money earned will prove to be not collectible, and some of the money collected will subsequently have to be returned (to retain good will or to settle legal disputes). The value of inventory at the beginning and end of each period also presents certain problems, especially when inflation affects selling prices and replacement costs.

Costs are even more difficult to identify and allocate to particular periods, particularly in respect of the value of capital assets used up during each period. Many other costs are equally difficult to calculate and to allocate to a particular period on a basis that will be comparable for all companies. Accounting for the damage done to the environment by industrial processes especially requires judgments concerning cause, effect, long-run social costs, and provision for meeting those costs through regulations (making the polluter pay or through general taxation and environmental control agencies).

Deferred taxes or tax rebates receivable add to the complexity of tax accounting. Furthermore, in order to arrive at a profit figure, the cost deducted from revenue should be only those costs that are directly related to the conduct of the business.

Who is to judge these matters? There appears to be no alternative to complete reliance on the wisdom and experience of the tax authorities. The following quotation is taken from John Maynard Keynes, *The General Theory of Employment, Interest and Money.*

> It will be seen that our definition of *net income* comes very close to Marshall's definition of *income,* when he decided to take refuge in the practices of the Income Tax Commissioners and—broadly speaking—to regard income as whatever they, with their experience, choose to treat as such. For the fabric of their decisions can be regarded as the result of the most careful and extensive investigation which is available, to interpret what in practice, it is usual to treat as new income.[1]

It may be assumed that the tax authorities will continue to provide those accounting rules that identify revenue, acceptable costs (including USOP dividend distribution), corporate tax, and the profit which each company will be permitted to retain each year

In the future profit-and-loss statement, it is suggested that there should be no mention of "gross profit," "profit before tax," "profit before dividend distribution," or "profit before USOP." There is only one profit, and that is the sum of money retained by the company after all permitted deductions have been made from gross revenue. The word profit should be used only once—on the bottom line.

Accounting problems will remain, and new problems will no doubt arise, but USOP as described in this essay should not make them better or worse.

USOP Mechanism

USOP Handbook Proposal

Under the proposal presented by Stuart Speiser, federal legislation will establish a government-guaranteed, long-term loan program for 2,000 leading American companies. Thereafter, the companies needing new investment capital will be required to obtain the funds from the banks participating in the program, instead of issuing new common shares, bonds, or using their own internal funds.

Against the bank loans, each company will issue special USOP shares (at the current market prices for common stock) to be held initially by the banks which provide the loans. When the loans have been repaid by the corporations, the USOP shares will be distributed by the government, free of charge, to those households eligible for the USOP program. Participating companies will be required thereafter to pay out all of their earnings as dividends, after allowing for "necessary expenses," (a) to existing holders of common shares, (b) to the banks until the USOP loans have been repaid, and finally (c) to USOP shareholders.

USOP shareholders would probably hold a sort of composite share, rather like a mutual fund, which would entitle them to a dividend calculated on the basis of annual profitability of the 2,000 companies combined, and companies would pay into the mutual fund on the basis of their individual net revenues. It is expected that the USOP system will eventually eliminate other forms of transfer payments and reduce taxation, as dividend payments will make it unnecessary for the governments to pay for many, if not all, of the present social security and welfare systems.

Speiser admits that some difficulties will arise in the selection of the USOP participants:

> We might start by excluding all households, [the] current net worth
> [of which] equals $100,000 or more. Or we could establish a point
> system for eligibility. Points could be awarded for low wages, lack
> of savings or capital ownership, physical disability, and many other
> criteria.[2]

This proposed solution to the problem of identifying USOP participants
at the commencement of the system, and on a continuing basis as participants become better off, would probably conflict with other stated
objectives, for example, "to check the growth of government
bureaucracy, while preserving private ownership and existing financial
institutions, and supporting business."[3]

Other potential problems include the following:

- For USOP to work, someone has to refrain from immediate
  consumption. *The USOP Handbook* assumes that the surplus
  funds generated by the corporations will be sufficient for all
  purposes, but a major source of investment capital at present is
  the saving of part of their income by salary and wage earners.
  That source must be preserved if tax rates are not to be increased.

- *The USOP Handbook* requires participating companies to pay
  out all of their earnings as dividends, except those reserves actually needed to run the company. However, it will be difficult
  for the tax authorities to identify minimum company "needs."
  That problem would not arise if the government took the minimum tax required to finance the welfare system (including
  USOP), leaving the remaining earnings (as at present) to be
  used by the company as it wishes.

- If the government made all reinvestment decisions, it would be
  tempted to give investment capital to companies that are in
  financial difficulty and thus discriminate against the more successful and prosperous companies.

These and other difficulties can be resolved, or adverse impacts can
be minimized, by reserving the USOP system for people who would
otherwise receive welfare. All other members of society could enjoy
the benefits offered by USOP through a parallel extension of normal
share issues with the support of the taxation authorities.

The following proposed mechanism is designed to retain the essential concept of USOP, to maximize the likelihood of obtaining corporate
acceptance and effective legislation, and to minimize the potentially ad-

verse impact on the free enterprise economy as it operates at present.

Wage and Salary Earners

People in employment are not considered to be needy, although they may become needy when they are sick, unemployed, or too old to work. At that time, they may become eligible for USOP. Until then, however, employee stock ownership plans (ESOP) should be developed in parallel with USOP, duplicating as many of the USOP characteristics as possible. A new concept emerged from the 1984-85 Speiser essay contest—"employee convertible debentures"—which should also be considered.

ESOP is a matter for negotiation at the bargaining table. If the tax authorities would encourage the postponement of wage and salary payments by treating the issue of shares to employees as a corporate pre-profit cost, trade unions might prove more receptive to ESOP than they appear to have been in the past.

Generally, employees should receive the shares issued by their own company. People working for themselves, for government agencies, or for entities that do not issue shares that are traded could be considered as a special USOP category, once the needs of the disadvantaged have been met.

No distinction should be made between wage and salary earners. Both contribute to corporate revenue, neither are owners of the means of production, and both should be rewarded in economic terms as the labor factor of production.

Existing Holders of Bonds and Common Shares

To avoid any disruption of the ability and willingness to save (to abstain from immediate consumption), ESOP and USOP should be financed by a reallocation of wages, salaries, taxation, and retained earnings to the required extent, and not by a reduction in the expected levels of return to capital. Above all, corporate taxation, and retained earnings (the bottom line) must be fair and be seen to be fair, both as absolute figures and on a comparative basis between different companies in each industry.

All wage and salary earners—and all USOP recipients to the extent that they are able to save—are free to purchase bonds or shares on the open market, and to receive interest, dividends, and increases in capital value, in addition to anything they may receive in respect to USOP or ESOP shares. USOP is a redistribution-of-income system, including income from wages, salaries, interest, dividends, and rents. But to be self-sustaining, USOP must not prejudice the ability of the private enterprise system to generate the profits and savings on which the USOP system itself will permanently depend.

USOP Recipients

The sooner USOP shares are distributed, the better. This means that the sooner the original bank loans are repaid, the better. Not much would be gained by a partial distribution of shares, which would provide less than the value required to replace existing welfare payments. Retaining the present social security system and all of its administrative costs, while administering a partial USOP, would not be economically sensible.

For that reason, it is proposed that the USOP system should be designed, legislated, and initially implemented as a government/bank/taxation authority measure without particular reference to the ultimate recipients. If it can be fully implemented by early in the 21st century, it will be an administrative triumph and public expectations should not be encouraged prematurely.

The objective of management will remain, as at present, to maximize the profit retained by the organization *after* deduction of all of these costs and after taxation. However, two differences of emphasis may be expected: (a) retained profit required for reinvestment will be lower to the extent that USOP loans will be available from banks at an acceptable rate of interest, and (b) retained profit required for long-term personnel purposes may be less to the extent that some part of the wages and fringe benefit obligations have been replaced by ESOP and USOP.

Taxation authorities, convinced of the desirability of USOP as an alternative to welfare payments, should be encouraged to maximize that proportion of corporate income devoted to ESOP and USOP. The greater the percentage of gross revenue devoted to these plans, the less the corporation will pay in tax as a percentage of income, and the less it will need to retain income.

USOP shareholders will eventually receive dividends (proportionate to national profitability) instead of social security benefits. When the guaranteed annual income reaches a predetermined level (equal to $20,000 per year in the Speiser suggestion), the tax authorities will no longer need to apply corporate taxation to pay for social security. That prospect can be a major factor in obtaining corporate approval to the USOP program.

Available Resources

Profit Tax

All of the taxation presently extracted from corporations may be considered as potential input to the USOP system. Most, if not all, of the money required for government purposes other than welfare transfer payments could be financed from personal income taxes and sales tax revenues.

To the extent that corporations would use USOP bank loans for expansion instead of internal funds or new debt from private sources, existing revenues from corporate taxation could be increased without adversely affecting the economy.

Tax revenue would also be greater if employees agreed to accept part or all of their annual salary increase in the form of shares, thus reducing current salary costs in exchange for the right to dividends which would continue after employment ceases—for as long as the company remains profitable.

Employees would be more likely to negotiate for long-term benefits if they were convinced that the government would channel the additional profit tax into USOP, and eventually reduce or remove their Social Security deductions and taxes.

Social Security and Pension Fund Deductions

All deductions from salary and all corporate payments in respect to Social Security, health and welfare administration, unemployment, pension funds, and so forth can be considered as resources available to the USOP system which will eventually replace them.

Commercial Banks

Banks could provide all or most of the investment capital required by corporations without any USOP system. The reason they do not do so is that corporations can obtain the funds they need on cheaper terms, or on longer term repayment schedules, than the banks are normally willing to provide.

However, a government guarantee would no doubt persuade all banks to provide loans to the limit of the USOP requirements, even though a special rate of interest and repayment terms would apply.

Private Investment Funds

Some of the money that would otherwise be invested in corporate bonds or shares may be attracted to USOP by a higher rate of interest, greater security, or by lack of suitable investment opportunities elsewhere. However, it would be a great danger to the free enterprise system if all or most investment should become government-guaranteed and government-controlled. The problem of deciding which corporations would be considered credit-worthy and how much USOP money each company would be entitled to borrow, and at what rate of interest, would be practically insoluble.

On the other hand, if corporations had the choice of (a) USOP loans up to a limit appropriate to their corporate size and at an interest rate slightly lower than the free market; and (b) private loans, share issues, and self-generated funds at present free market prices, it may be expected that all of the USOP money would be taken up and the present system of private funding would continue to make the decisions concerning the allocation of funds.

Improved Productivity

If social stresses and misunderstandings concerning the distribution of "profit" were reduced through the introduction of ESOP and USOP, it may be expected that productivity would increase at a faster rate than would otherwise be the case.

As output per capita increases, the postponement of consumption through universal stock ownership would release additional resources for the supply of capital goods.

At the next stage of economic development, each factor of production could receive an increased return and the entire economy would become more prosperous. The funds generated for USOP shares and for the payment of dividends would increase proportionately.

It should be noted that, contrary to *The USOP Handbook* proposal, the above sources of funds for USOP do not include "all corporate earnings" after allowing for "necessary expenses." Managers should still try to maximize profit, interpreted as net revenue after payment of all expenses and taxes, including dividends paid to existing shareholders and USOP shareholders. The tax and USOP dividends should be the minimum required for the specified social purposes. All corporate income in excess of that minimum should remain "retained earnings"—the famous and essential bottom line.

Conclusion

This essay confirms that there is nothing in capitalism that would prevent us from spreading the ownership of shares to all of our people, although the ownership of shares should not be confused with ownership of the means of production.

The implementation criteria include the definition of accounting procedures designed to ensure the continued profitability of public corporations; the restriction of the USOP mechanism (at least initially) to the present recipients of welfare payments; and the need for a parallel development of Employee Stock Ownership Plans.

On the basis of the design criteria proposed in this essay, no problem is expected in attracting adequate resources to make USOP economically and financially feasible.

The message to give to the country is very simple. If the productive efficiency of the entire economy goes down, everyone suffers. In the future, if profitability improves, everyone will benefit.

Notes

1. John Maynard Keynes, *The General Theory of Employment, Interest and Money.* London: Macmillan, 1957, p. 59.
2. Stuart M. Speiser, *The USOP Handbook: A Guide to Designing Universal Share Ownership Plans for the United States and Great Britain.* New York: Council on International and Public Affairs, 1986, p. 36.

10

THE UNIVERSAL SHARE OWNERSHIP PLAN: A PATHWAY TO PEACE

by

Donald A. Newey

Editor's Note: *Donald A. Newey of Santa Cruz, California, has devoted his career to community development work and the cooperative move-ment. He was one of the organizers of the Northern California Regional Land Trust and the Santa Cruz Community Development Credit Union. He has served the National Cooperative League in various positions, including Associate Director of Community Development. The func-tions of the Santa Cruz Community Development Credit Union are reflected in his essay.*

ABSTRACT

This essay depicts the course of societies motivated by greed and selfishness, as is implied in the concept of private profit. It recog-nizes the fact that this concept has run its course and is about to end in worldwide collapse. Fortunately, there has been a different con-cept existing concurrently which now has an opportunity to capture the imagination and take the lead in organizing society.

The essay portrays a brief outline of how USOP can be the mechanism for bringing about that change through creative use of some of the techniques employed by the private profit motive.

It also points out how, by basing its operation on moral principle, the USOP program can bring to humanity the peace which has been so elusive in the past.

There are no references in this essay because the author has based it solely on his own education and hands-on experience in cooperative economics.

Since the beginning of civilization, every society has become polarized into a structure, where the power, control, and wealth is centralized into a small percentage of the population with the majority becoming slaves to the system. First, it was the religious hierarchy, then the monarchy hierarchy, then the industrial hierarchy, and now it is the political/industrial hierarchy. The result is the same: the rich get richer and the poor get poorer. Each society evolved into a system in which the majority lived on subsistence income and the minority enjoyed affluence and great wealth. There were a few who sank below the subsistence level, but not many were allowed to do so because workers were needed to produce for exchange. During the industrial revolution, a large middle class developed which enjoyed relative wealth and prestige above the subsistence level; however, with the rapid increase in technology it became possible to produce without much human labor. As a result, it no longer became necessary to maintain all workers at a subsistence level, so the jobless, homeless, and destitute increased and the middle class gradually lost their relative wealth and prestige and became the new subsistence class. This process is still going on and is the reason for the need to establish a basis for income not directly connected to the work ethic.

Now that humans are expendable in the workplace, why is it necessary to keep them at subsistence level? Welfare has failed to do so and supply-side economics has failed to do so. The reason is that capital formation is the mechanism by which production is maintained, but consumerism is the reason for maintaining production. Without buyers, all production would stop, no matter how much capital was accumulated. By eliminating workers, industry is also eliminating consumers. The problem now is to maintain people as consumers without providing them with work.

Having a strong allegiance to the work ethic and the justice ethic of producing something of value to exchange for something of equal value, it is difficult for me to consider the separation of work from income. The reason for this is that I believe all the inequities in our economic system, where the rich get richer and the poor get poorer, are due to the fact that it is easier to acquire wealth without producing anything in exchange than it is to work hard for what you acquire and make mutually satisfying exchanges.

Also, it is difficult for me to consider a plan that does not include confiscation because it is like saying to the bank robber, "You can keep what you took and continue to take it provided you cut me in on a share of the profit." The means by which people acquire wealth without paying for it by producing its value in exchange are legal under our present system, even though they may not be morally just in result. So although inadequate, the bank robber analogy will serve to state my convictions. To devise a plan that does not increase taxation is quite acceptable because I believe that the power to tax is the power to control and to destroy, as is fully demonstrated in our present economy, and also that it is possible to eliminate taxation by government and return power and control to the people. So after this preamble, it is possible for me to consider a plan that will not confiscate or increase taxes. There is a glimmer of hope that the USOP program can be devised in such a way that not only will the profits of production be universally shared (whether people work or not) but a mechanism can be developed to eliminate the ability to accumulate wealth without justice, and further render the government subservient to the will of the people rather than have power over the people.

The key to my belief that USOP can be designed to bring justice to our economy lies in the fact that the mechanism to do so is in existence in our present system and only needs to be recognized and used with the right motivation to succeed.

The power to control the economy and the political structure rests with the consumer. The consumer is everybody.

The consumer presently finances all production and exchange and pays all costs involved in production and exchange. Under our present system, consumers deposit their income into banks which not only lend this money to business but also through the fractional reserve system use this money as leverage to create a much larger money supply to lend to business, governments, or speculators. The reason that the banks lend the money is to create profits for themselves and not to maximize the return of the depositor. They lend the money where the most profit is.

Whether it is harmful to consumers through financing of drugs, munitions, gambling, speculation, unhealthy foods, etc. is not the primary consideration. To the banker, profit is the primary goal and this stands in the way of consumers realizing the full return on their investment or to having control over the type of investment their deposits finance. The latest ploy of the banks, which hastens the debt-credit rush toward bankruptcy, is to issue a credit line to consumers through credit cards in the knowledge that most users will choose to pay the minimum required and give usury profits to the bankers. The credit is issued against non-existent assets generated by the fractional reserve system. The solution to this is to organize community development cooperative banks that operate on a non-profit basis for the benefit of the consumer depositor and only charge for the expenses involved in proper operation. A cooperative bank would be an agent for the consumer and the producer, bringing them together in a harmonious cycle which would benefit both rather than channeling profits to speculative middlemen. Workers in the bank would receive fair compensation for their work while the profits from investment would go to the consumer depositor. The fact that consumer deposits presently finance directly or indirectly most production is justification enough to share profits and new equity with all consumers.

Another justification is that all expenses in any economy are averaged out in consumer prices. An acre of land in New York City, which may be sold for $1 million, is paid for through the prices charged by whatever business is operated on that land, and these prices affect all prices in the economy.

Expenses of government are not paid for by the taxpayer, but are passed on to the consumer. Individual income taxes are paid out of income received from production and are a cost of production included in consumer prices. Business taxpayers merely collect taxes by adding them directly to consumer prices and acting as a tax collector for the government. All government expenditures, whether collected through taxes or borrowed through printing fiat money, are eventually averaged out in consumer prices. Since all costs of production and exchange, whether economic or political, are reflected in consumer prices, it follows that consumers are not only financing production but are also paying all the costs of production, exchange, and government. This is a second justification for sharing the profits and equity with all consumers.

The third justification for sharing the profits with all consumers is the fact that business could not function without the community. Business needs consumers to buy the products. Business needs consumers in their productive worker role to help run the business. Business needs community education to train employees. Business needs community traffic and highway systems for transportation, community fire and police protection, community monetary systems, and so forth. So there is already a partnership between business and the community that justifies sharing profits and equity with all consumers in the community. The power lies in consumer purchasing power. Special interests have usurped that power for private profit because the consumer is unorganized and therefore impotent. A few changes in our basic institutions will correct this situation and create an equitable production, exchange, and governmental structure that will benefit all in relation to their participation. USOP can be the mechanism for bringing about that change.

The basic institutions are:

1. Land tenure.
2. The monetary system.
3. The method of government.
4. The unions.
5. The education system.
6. The method of wealth distribution.

Land Tenure

There is a commonly used expression that all people are created equal and are entitled to life, liberty, and the pursuit of happiness. This expression is all right as far as it goes, but there is one element left out which causes our basic inequities. We may be born equal but our current land-use policies create inequality very quickly. Since no person is responsible for the creation of land, no person has an inherent right to claim ownership of the land over any other person. It is a common heritage which should be managed by the community through trusteeship. The community trustees should grant ownership rights to private individuals, provided that those individuals pay for the privilege of using the common land and its resources, such as timber, minerals, or oil, for private monetary gain. Private landowners should also pay to the community a prorated share of the expenses of maintaining the community, determined by the relative value in production of the land involved. The land is the basis and source of all productive income and therefore should be the basis and source of community revenue. No private individual should have the right to charge or exact tribute for the use of land which all individuals have an equal right to. This process creates inequality and makes one individual dependent upon another. The individual paying tribute to another for the use of land becomes involuntarily subservient to the person demanding tribute until the imposed debt is paid. Land is essential for survival. No individual should have the power of life or death over another. This is the basis for most of the inequality in the world and must be resolved before there can be peace and justice and equality. There should be private property in land, but it should be granted by the community and not by one individual to another for monetary gain. Involuntary servitude of one individual by another is outlawed under the 13th Amendment of the Constitution.

Under the USOP program, it would be established that the community has trusteeship priority over land use. This concept is already established in our eminent domain laws. The existing private ownership deeds and other evidences of ownership would be honored so as to conform to the principle of no confiscation.

Instead of taxation (which will be covered under the heading of government reorganization), each community will establish a formula for appraising the land in order to determine how much of the community expenses each landowner should pay for the right to use the common heritage for private use and profit. Since land is a common heritage, each individual in a particular community should be assigned equity in an amount of land determined by dividing the total amount of land by the total population. If any individual or group presently owns more than the equity share arrived at by this procedure, this can be compensated for by having the present landowner pay into the community fund the amount required for each prorated equity share. In this way, the present owner can keep the land and the person without an equity share will benefit by not having to pay community expenses. As long as the owner can use the land productively and pay its share of community expense, ownership will not change. However, if the landowner cannot pay the share of community expense assigned to the land owned, then the land would have to be sold just as it is under the present mortgage agreement.

The Monetary System

The backing for money is an abstract. The abstract is the capability of human energy to produce and exchange goods and services. The actual money unit used to facilitate exchange does not have to have any value in and of itself because it merely represents something. It is a negotiable record of the relative value of goods and services in production and exchange. The actual value is determined by the buyer at the point of sale, provided no coercion or monopoly is involved. As long as money represents real values in goods and services and is in dynamic equilibrium with them, we have a stable economy. Under the present system, the government and the banking industry cause inflation by creating money in excess of the real values in existing goods and services. For the USOP program, I would recommend that a two-tier monetary system be established. The government would adhere to the constitution and be responsible for coining the monetary unit and be returned to the Gold Standard so that this unit would always be covered by something of real value. The federal government could only issue money to cover its authorized expenses by Congress and would put it in circulation by spending it for those authorized purposes. By this method, all consumers would share the cost of government through direct inflation of consumer prices and there would be no unearned interest for private bankers or any national debt.

There would also be no taxes necessary and therefore no I.R.S. with its satellite organizations. The effect on consumer prices through inflation would be a small percentage of what it is now, particularly if Congress kept government spending down to the services that could not be performed by individual states or private enterprise. Since USOP would replace the need for welfare, the whole bureaucratic structure used to redistribute the wealth to the poor would be dismantled with great savings to all consumers.

The second tier would provide the medium of exchange for private enterprise and local governments. This monetary unit would be created by the cooperative community development bank against existing individual, business, and community assets. It would be limited to real assets and could not be used to finance speculation. It would be placed in circulation through lending against existing assets or through certificates of credit to finance new production. Certificates of credit would be backed by the USOP fund, which will be described under the below section, The USOP Method of Wealth Distribution.

Consumer and business depositors would be issued lines of credit according to their ability to repay. Since funds allocated to depositors through lines of credit would always be on deposit in the bank, or be represented by goods or equipment purchased or income from business activity, there would be no need for the expense of formal loan arrangements and regular payments. Payment would be accomplished when a profit is made and the account shows a surplus.

To facilitate efficient operation of business, the bank would help arrange for efficient bookkeeping and business management services. The main function of the bank would be to increase consumer equity and decrease business expense.

Government Reformation

When the Congress of the United States does not know what is being done with the money it authorizes, it is obvious that the government is out of control. Not only is it not of, by, and for the people; it is not even of, by, and for the representatives of the people.

We now have a world economy that is run by the international banking systems for private profit and most of the governments in the world are pawns of that system. The private profit motive, operating without regard to justice and equity, has run its course and the world is about to experience the greatest economic collapse in history. Trying to return a government to the control of the people in the face of such overwhelming odds is a discouraging task even to contemplate. It would take much more than 5,000 words to discuss this problem alone. So I will confine myself to the merits of USOP in the hope that such a plan could be implemented after the collapse.

One encouraging fact is that technology has now made it possible for every voter to sit in on the deliberations of Congress and to know from day to day what is taking place. With this in mind, it would be possible for the elected representatives to be information gatherers, who would debate and discuss the issues and leave the voting to the people after all alternatives are explored. With touch-telephone technology, the voters could vote on each issue and the representatives would be able to implement action with direct authorization of the majority.

The Unions

Unions have historically always created confrontation between labor and capital instead of cooperation. This has been in keeping with the prevailing profit motive. If USOP is going to promote cooperation and sharing between the forces of production and exchange, it will be necessary to change the objectives and methods of labor unions.

I have always believed that labor unions should function for the purpose of improving the efficiency of workers and teaching them how to reduce the cost of production. Along with this should be a profit-sharing plan which would equitably distribute these profits and/or equity buildup. In order for USOP to function, the unions will have to change their policies and cooperate with a program that will produce more for everyone to share.

Education

Our educational system reflects the attitude of the economy and serves to prepare individuals to compete in a profit motive economy. Since the profit motive is not based on justice, equity, sharing, or cooperation, there is little taught in our educational system regarding these values. USOP proposes to extend the benefits of the profit motive capitalistic system to all the people. This implies cooperation and sharing, and therefore runs counter to the existing procedures. In trying to justify USOP in our profit motive society, I have come to realize that we are not really talking about extending the profit motive but about inserting justice into the system. Can this be done?

The profit *motive* implies that each will do what serves that individual best, even to the extent of taking advantage of every other individual. There is no room for justice in this concept. What USOP is really trying to do is to change the profit *motive* to the profit *method*. There is a big difference. Under the profit *method,* the techniques of capitalism can be used to produce more through cooperation and efficiency, with the prospect that everyone will be better off by sharing the profit. This is a concept I can agree with and can enthusiastically work to bring about. If this concept can be implemented, the education system can make justice, morality, and ethics a priority by teaching how to cooperate and share in the benefits of the economy.

The USOP Method of Wealth Distribution

Before elaborating on my proposed method for distribution of the wealth, I would like to emphasize again the justification for sharing the wealth.

Presently taxpayers, particularly the landlords and large equity holders, think that they are paying the costs of government and therefore should be entitled to the benefits, rather than the poor, low-income people. As explained earlier, the fact of the matter is that all taxes as well as all expenses in the economy are paid by consumers. This means that all equity buildup, including government holdings, private and corporate equity, and improvements to the land, have been paid for by consumers. This includes the destitute, the low-income, the middle-income, and the high-income consumers. At some point, even the destitute have contributed to the buildup of community equity, and they should be able to draw against that in time of need.

Every community has accumulated equity in the form of buildings, equipment, parks, improvements to community land, capital funds, and government operational funds. These have all been paid for by consumers and could be used as the basis for community equity in the Community Cooperative Development Bank. Also included could be the present value of land and natural resources which rightfully belong to all citizens.

By totaling the value of all community equity and dividing it by the total of individual consumers in the community, we would come up with an individual share in the community equity. The Community Cooperative Development Bank would use this equity as backing for the money it creates to finance a credit line for consumers. In this way, even the destitute and unemployed would have something to borrow against to finance education, housing, development of a craft, or even to live on until conditions improve. This would be far superior to the present welfare system.

This equity fund would also be the basis for borrowing to finance the purchase of stock in the nation's largest corporations. The profit from the stock would replace the money in the equity fund and then be available for improvement in living conditions. Particularly, the people in the greatest need could purchase stock this way and eventually become productive consumers. This plan would be much more appropriate than having the government borrow the money from private profit banks at interest, thereby perpetuating the present system where the rich benefit from the problems of the poor.

By using the community equity fund for backing the community monetary unit and lending it into circulation only for productive purposes, we would establish a program of constant expansion of the fund, as the capabilities of the people are expressed in creative production and exchange. Cooperation and sharing by the profit *method* would replace the greed and selfishness of the profit *motive*.

There are at least two ways in which the community equity fund could be used to invest in large corporations and eventually all businesses. Individual members of the Cooperative Development Bank could borrow against their equity in the fund and then invest in the shares of corporations of their choosing, or the bank itself could invest the fund in the most profitable corporations and then distribute the profit by adding it to the fund, thereby increasing everybody's prorated share.

On this basis, since it has already been established that businesses depend on community support in many ways, it would make sense to establish a ratio by which businesses would share profits with the community equity fund. Working out the process would involve much thought and analysis. This essay can only establish a justification for a new concept and brief guidelines for its operation.

With community equity could come the concept of "community birthright," which would provide a basis of support for all new additions to the community, just as individual families provide that support to additions to the family. Every new citizen must be supported by the community for at least one-third of expected life span before becoming self-sustaining, and repaying to the community fund the amount needed to reach that point. We all need to receive before we can give, and we all need to learn that a balance between the two is the ideal. An economic system that practices balanced giving and receiving would provide the basis for establishing peace on earth.

Some people seem to think that peace will come through wishful thinking or praying to some outside force to bestow it upon us. But the condition of peace is the result of dealing with each other with respect, love, cooperation, and justice. If the USOP program could be developed on these principles, rather than just giving the underprivileged some share in the profits of a system that negates these principles, I would feel more comfortable in helping to develop the program.

One of the most important benefits of the USOP profit distribution plan would be the elimination of unemployment and a solution to the problem of the substitution of automation for human labor. There will always be a need for a certain percentage of human participation. Under USOP, consumers could retire earlier from their worker role and live on the income from their investments, particularly if they are content to live simply on modest means. This would leave more jobs for the young and ambitious. By reducing the number of applicants for jobs, employers would have to offer incentives to acquire the personnel needed. This would increase the value of productive work.

Consumers could go in and out of the work force at will for vacations or sabbatical leaves, to be creative in raising a family, or for further education—secure in the knowledge that their consumer purchasing power is what supports industry. When not working, the purchasing power available from their investments would still be supporting industry.

The average life cycle would tend to be (a) one-third receiving support from a birthright share in community equity while growing, learning, and developing the ability to be self-supporting; (b) one-third being self-supporting and replacing the equity borrowed from the community equity fund; and (c) one-third retirement to enjoy the benefits of a productive life, knowing that even at this stage the purchasing power of the profit from investments is still financing production and government.

To implement the restructuring of our entire political/economic system, as I have outlined, would require much planning and time, but the USOP could be implemented in any community fairly quickly. After careful development of ideas and procedures, the USOP program could be presented to consumers in a community. Since consumers technically hold the power and would benefit most, a carefully prepared referendum by any political party or socially active group could be the organizing force that would secure a majority vote. If this happened, no private power elite could maintain its control of the community.

In America, we already have a National Cooperative Bank which returns its profit to its member-borrowers. This organization could be approached as the medium through which USOP and monetary change could be implemented. They have the facilities and structure to set up a branch in any community.

And in Santa Cruz, California, there already exists a progressive, community-owned Community Development Credit Union. By using the resources of this and a National Cooperative Bank in a progressive area such as Santa Cruz, it should be possible to establish a USOP program that would be a model for other communities to follow.

11

LAND-BASED SHARES

by

Oscar B. Johannsen

Editor's Note: *Oscar B. Johannsen of Roselle Park, New Jersey, is ex-ecutive director of the Robert Schelkenbach Foundation in New York City. He is also vice president and a director of the American Journal of Economics and Sociology, and winner of first prize in the 1976 essay contest on the benefits of the free enterprise system, sponsored by the National Association of Manufacturers.*
The following essay draws on the economic theories of Henry George, which are further discussed in Chapter 12.

ABSTRACT

This version of the Universal Share Ownership Plan is based on the lands owned by the federal government in the western part of the continental United States. Thirteen public corporations would be established, one in each of 13 states, and be given title to the federal lands in those states. Shares of stock in each of these 13 corporations would be given to all living Americans.

The 13 corporations would not produce goods. Instead, their function would be to lease the federal lands to the highest bidders. These corporations could delegate the auctioning process to the local communities which are contiguous to the federal lands. The income from the actions, after deducting administrative costs, would be distributed by the 13 corporations to the shareholders at periodic intervals.

This plan is fair because all would participate, regardless of wealth or position. It is non-inflationary since no funds are needed to purchase the shares, as they will be given to all Americans. Because anyone, whether an individual, partnership, or corporation, may participate in the auctioning process, the concept of freedom is maintained.

Land-Based Shares

Any plan to spread the ownership of America's productive assets among the people should be based on four criteria. First, and probably the most important, is justice. The plan should be one which benefits everyone without exception. No one should be excluded, regardless of wealth or position. Second, the plan must be one which does not cause monetary inflation, for inflation is one of the most insidious forms of disguised taxation there is. A third fundamental principle of the plan is that it should be predicated on the free and open marketplace. And the fourth criterion is freedom. The plan adopted must not restrict the activities of any individual, corporation, or other organization from establishing any fiscal or financial policies that are adapted to the plan, as long as they do not conflict with the principles of justice.

The assets on which this version of the Universal Share Ownership Plan is based would consist of the land of the United States which does not belong to any individual—the land which is usually called the "public domain" or "federal lands." At present, this constitutes about 740 million acres. It is about one-third of the land of the United States, 90 per cent of which is in the West. While most of this land is far from population centers, it nonetheless contains valuable resources in the form of forests, grazing land, minerals, oil, coal, fisheries, and parks.

This Universal Share Ownership Plan could start with federal lands in the 13 states west of the Hundredth Meridian—Montana, Wyoming, Colorado, New Mexico, Idaho, Utah, Oregon, Arizona, Washington,

Nevada, California, Alaska, and Hawaii. If shares of stock based on the federal lands in these states are issued to all American citizens, it will not only arouse people's interest in stock ownership, as all would be shareholders; it will also result in more active interest in how these lands are administered. At present, the people appear to be relatively indifferent as to how these acres are managed because they are not conscious of owning them.

One of the aims of this Universal Share Ownership Plan is to vest in the people individual ownership of an important productive asset— namely, land now in the public domain. It also seeks to assure that these productive assets under private control shall be utilized to benefit future generations as well as the present one, and to improve their administration which at the present time is far from satisfactory.

To accomplish these aims, independent public corporations would be established in each of the 13 states. Each corporation would have title to all the federal lands in its state.

Every American would receive a share of stock in each of the 13 corporations. Upon the individual's death, his or her shares would revert to the corporations. Each newborn child automatically receives 13 shares of stock upon birth. While not necessary, it may be wise for psychological reasons to give each American tangible evidence of share ownership in the form of the traditional stock certificate.

The objective of the corporations would be to obtain the optimum income but with due concern for environmental sustainability. Today private forest products companies harvest timber so as to maximize their returns, but are beginning to show greater concern for the environment and resource renewal by planting new trees.

These 13 corporations would not engage in production. Their function, instead, would be to lease the land by public auction to private entrepreneurs with lease renewal at reasonable intervals. The corporations would be encouraged to delegate the leasing function to local communities contiguous to the federal lands in each of the 13 states. These communities would be more likely to insist that the lessees' production practices followed sound environmental and esthetic principles because the people in these communities obviously wish to live in a healthy environment.

At the same time, since the federal lands in these 13 states would come under private control through leasing, it is more likely that the lands would be managed in order to maximize income.

After deducting administrative costs, the income from the public auctions would be distributed by the 13 corporations at periodic intervals to the shareholders—i.e., to all living Americans. (This would be similar to the annual distribution of income from the Alaskan land leases to Alaskan residents.)

The very fact that there are 13 corporations involved should lead to competition among them to determine which is doing the best job. Comparisons of administration costs will be one means of controlling unwise expenditures.

The determination of criteria for selection of the directors of the corporations would ultimately be decided by experience. Initially, each of the 13 state legislatures might determine how many directors its corporation would have and who they would be. Later, selection of the directors might be through ballot by all the shareholders, which means by all the people.

This Universal Share Ownership Plan would meet all four criteria enumerated earlier. It is a just plan since every American, regardless of race, color, wealth, or position, would have an equal share in these corporations.

Since no funds are necessary for the participants to acquire shares as the shares would be given to them, it is non-inflationary. Because the parcels of land would be auctioned off publicly, the plan operates in the open marketplace. And the principle of freedom is maintained, inasmuch as anyone wishing to participate in the auction process can do so.

Thus, this Universal Share Ownership Plan is one which is straightforward, easily understood, fair, and workable. The necessary federal and state legislation to put the plan into operation would be relatively simple.

Finally, this plan would help spread the concept of capital ownership to all Americans. It would no doubt induce many Americans, once they became accustomed to owning shares of stock in these 13 corporations, to consider the purchase of shares in other companies. It would be a big step forward in enhancing an understanding of belief in the importance and value of capital share ownership.

Reference

Junkin, Elizabeth Darby. *Lands of Brighter Destiny: The Public Lands of the American West*. Golden, Colorado: Fulcrum, 1986.

12

NORTH AMERICAN ESSAY ROUND-UP

In addition to the foregoing essays, many others contained innovative ideas. Quite a few entries in both the 1984-85 and 1986 essay contests were from proponents of Henry George's land-based economic theories. George's 1879 book, *Progress and Poverty,* was an all-time best seller. In it he proposed a *single tax* on land that would tax away all "economic rent" and would abolish the need for any other taxes. George argued that economic progress created a growing scarcity of land, with the owners of idle land reaping great returns at the expense of the real productive factors—labor and capital. He considered this to be "unearned economic rent" that should be taxed away by the state. (The tax was to be on the land itself but not on its improvements, thus encouraging the productive development and use of land.) According to George's calculations, government revenue from the single tax on land would be so great that there would be a surplus for public works. He had a strong following among humanitarian and religious groups interested in social welfare. Most of the Henry George adherents who submitted essays believe that USOP is complementary to the Henry George single-tax and land-use philosophy. This is especially true of those who think of land as a common heritage.

Another group of essayists find common ground between USOP and ESOP—Employee Share Ownership Plans. Robert J. Massey of Arlington, Virginia, submitted an essay entitled, "On Broadening Ownership of Productive Assets Through Work Team Co-Creation of

Capital." His main innovation is DTSM (Democratic Team Self-Management). DTSM would enable workers to buy their enterprise with a fair share of the capital that they create through their own self-management efforts. He proposes that management of large companies help workers to organize as self-managed work teams for both operating and improvement functions, with all new profits to be reinvested in improvement. The work teams would control the reinvestment of half the profits, while the corporate management would control reinvestment of the remaining 50 per cent. Thus, increases in the value of the company flowing from their improvement efforts would be split 50-50 between workers and owners in the form of stock or stock options. Eventually, an ESOP would be established under which the workers would get 100 per cent ownership of their shops and become franchisees of the original corporation. In Massey's view, the DTSM model would greatly expedite training, which most American enterprises today grossly neglect because it is viewed as a drain on profits. As Massey sees it: "In the DTSM organization, the employee is powerfully motivated to make sure he is still with the company when the ESOP is established." Thus, the major incentive for team members is not the weekly pay check but growth of his or her share in the enterprise.

While Massey's essay addresses the problem from the standpoint of workers, and thus benefits mainly people fortunate enough to be employed by growing organizations, another ESOP-based paper by Vincent J. McGrath of Woodbridge, Virginia, takes a broader view by working Shareholders In America (SIA) into the picture. In his essay, "Personal Income in a High Tech World," McGrath observes:

> Over the period of a few years we will phase out Social Security and other tax-supported welfare programs. The phase-out period will correspond to the buildup of citizen equity in SIA.
>
> We will link privatization of government economic enterprises (federal, state, and local) to SIA. Such linkage will provide SIA with its initial capitalization and liquidity. Transfer of government-owned assets to SIA will involve no liability on the part of SIA. The transaction merely represents a change in custodian from the federal, state, or local government to SIA, the private sector trustee. The obvious rationale is that the citizens already have equal individual ownership interests, but control resides in the government bureaucracies.
>
> SIA will be organized into 435 private-sector, free enterprise zones corresponding geographically to the 435 congressional districts. Each zone will receive proportionate amounts of direct investment capital and low-cost productive credit. . . . Churches and other tax-

exempt charitable institutions should be encouraged to make direct investment in SIA. Economic and social justice really demands that they lead the way. . . .

[We should also] establish an integrated moral, social, and scientific futuristic research arm of SIA to seek ways to make high technology serve individuals according to their aspirations and participation with their labor and capital, and balance economic representation with political representation through increased opportunities to participate economically within each SIA free enterprise zone.

Dr. Mary Timney Bailey of Cincinnati, Ohio, submitted an essay entitled, "SIA: An Opportunity to Integrate Economics and Democracy." She argued that SIA can be made a vehicle for achieving pure democracy as well as a just economic system. In connection with the implementation of SIA, she suggested a method of calculating user fees:

Identify all costs related to individual economic decisions and the impacts, negative and positive, and allocation of the impacts and potential rippling effects. Once identified, those who benefit would also be expected to pay for the costs imposed on society. This might mean an assessment of "user fees" for public goods and the costs of corporate decisions exacted on entire communities. This would provide an incentive for companies to make a commitment to the workers and communities which have provided the benefits.

Dr. Bailey also had some interesting ideas on organizing SIA to foster participative democracy:

The implementation of this plan would be astounding in its simplicity, yet as intricate as the complex world in which it would operate. It involves, as a primary element, the development of groups of interested and affected people at all levels, trained to work together to define problems, identify alternatives, and develop workable solutions. The groups would be organized and trained as part of the work of SIA, which would also provide educational materials and staff services.

The basic organizing work would be done at the local level where neighborhood groups would be organized to evaluate local needs and determine preferred plans and programs for meeting them. Each group would be unique since each area of the country has a set of problems which is unique [to] it. The groups would involve all members of the community who are affected by the problem and would have a stake in the solution.

As groups identify intricate problems or expand to encompass a larger area, such as a city, they could be organized into teams or subcommittees. Division like this, however, can lead to fragmentation and loss of connections. To overcome this problem, there should be a mechanism to tie the groups together. Perhaps the "linking pin" model proposed by Rensis Likert would be appropriate. This model, also called "System 4," is characterized by small groups of decision-makers which are each linked through a joint member. In this way, all decisions are linked to all others in the system. (Rensis Likert, *The Human Organization,* New York: McGraw-Hill, 1967.) . . . Linking the groups at the national level will be more difficult, but could be attempted through the use of communications technology which enables people at various locations to be joined through satellite television transmission and downlinks. These national "town meetings" would permit the interaction of people all over the country, working face to face to identify ways to produce economic wealth for all areas and improve the physical and social structures of our communities for the benefit of all citizens. They would also break down the barriers which currently exist between regions of this country since they would eliminate the need for competition which enriches one regional economy while beggaring another.

Another movement, the adherents of which show an affinity for USOP, is the Social Credit theory of British economist Clifford Hugh Douglas (1879-1952). Douglas's theory, first published in 1919, sought to bolster purchasing power by issuing additional money to consumers and providing subsidies to producers in order to free production from the price system, while maintaining the private enterprise and profit systems. The Social Credit Party of Canada, founded in 1935 by William Aberhart in Alberta, won a majority in the Alberta assembly in 1935 and remained in power for 36 years until 1971. The Social Credit Party also governed British Columbia for most of the time between 1952 and 1975. In addition, it had some following in Great Britain in the 1920s and still holds a few seats in the New Zealand Parliament. By the late 1930s, the Social Credit Party had modified or abandoned many of Douglas's theories, and it now concentrates on such policies as employee profit-sharing and the broadening of share ownership.

Our 1986 essay contest received entries from two prominent Social Credit writers: J. Martin Hattersley, Q.C., leader of the Social Credit Party of Canada, and Victor R. Hadkins, secretary of the Social Credit Centre of Great Britain and editor of its quarterly publication, *Abundance.* Both the British and the Canadian groups have informally endorsed James Albus's National Mutual Fund concept, and therefore both groups are open to the idea of Universal Share Ownership.

Hattersley, who is the senior member of a prominent firm of barristers and solicitors in Edmonton, Alberta, devoted much of his essay to explaining why the Douglas Social Credit theories must be revised and brought up to date. He concludes:

> The need within the Social Credit movement at this time is for a rigorous intellectual housecleaning to recapture the importance of Douglas's insight, without at the same time becoming so hidebound that the solutions of the 1920s to problems perceived at that time are treated as the only possible ways to deal with a vastly changed and better understood world. In truth, Douglas, and other reformers advocating 100 per cent state-issued fiat money, such as Soddy and Irving Fisher, all point in a direction it would be wise for the world to follow. The components of the new order will have to be:

> (1) Close control of the quantity of the monetary mass to relate it to physically attainable and desirable levels of production.

> (2) State receipt and distribution in the name of the general public of all profit from the creation of financial credit instruments.

> (3) Creation of the national money supply against the backing of the nation's credit as a whole, rather than the pledge of individually owned assets.

> (4) A system of income distribution, where more is received by the average person from holdings of investments and fully paid for capital assets, and less from wages, which could well fall to lower levels.

> Implementation of these four proposals will yield employment for all who wish it, a competitive position in international markets, adequate welfare levels without excessive taxation, lower prices, a stable economy, more personal leisure, and an adequate standard of living for all.

> It is physically possible. It could be made financially possible.

Hadkins' essay reflects his strong feeling that the issue of all our money—not only currency—should be done by government, instead of by banks which now create much of our money. He is also concerned that such USOP programs as the SuperStock/Kitty Hawk Model might cause inflation due to the lag between the creation of credit and the increase in production that eventually will offset it. Therefore, he combines the SuperStock principle with the anti-inflation mechanism created by James Albus ("Demand Regulation Policy"). Hadkins summarizes the financing and monetary steps required by a USOP program such as SuperStock:

> (1) Because of the nationwide distribution of the branches of the commercial banks, these would be allowed to distribute all the loans re-

quired by the SuperStock program. No interest charge would be made on loans. Government would pay the banks a service charge for all the checks issued.

(2) From the issue of the first loan, government monitors the inflation rate continuously, and the Albus method of savings withdrawals to minimize inflation would be applied.

(3) Banks would no longer demand either interest or repayments of SuperStock loans. This has been made unnecessary by government maintaining non-inflation throughout. By this means, the money supply is made to conform with available goods and services at all times.

(4) However, for the period of the exercise, all other bank loans would be vetted by government to prevent a bank-inspired inflation, and instead of interest charges on such loans, the same service charge would be made by banks.

It will have been noted that no "interest" has been paid to the banks, nor has the value of any "loan" been returned at the end of the loan period, in cash. Instead, the total cost of the issues to the banks has been met by government representatives in the service charges made in respect of every "loan" arranged.

No bank money has been involved. There has been widespread cashing of checks into national currency, notes, and coin—supplied to every bank by government—which is a necessary element in the SuperStock exercise to increase productive capacity. The prevention of inflation has been assured by the Demand Regulation Policy.

Marlan M. Smith of Roseville, Minnesota, suggested in his essay that government-operated lotteries or gambling programs be used as a source of additional funds for USOP. The lottery prizes could be paid in cash or in USOP shares. This would be a method of popularizing the USOP idea and educating the public on the advantages of Universal Share Ownership.

Robert A. Carlton of Rochester, New York, did not submit a formal essay, but he made a valuable contribution after reading the contest material. He suggested that the federal government should elicit a *quid pro quo* for various forms of assistance to business by requiring the beneficiary businesses to issue an appropriate number of their shares to a USOP which would be owned by all Americans. For example, government funding of research and development projects should stipulate that profits derived from such research should be "shared by the people of the United States as part of the USOP pool." And when the government bails out a failing company (e.g., Chrysler, Lockheed, Continental Illinois) or an entire industry (e.g., semi-conductors) the USOP pool should receive shares of the companies involved to compensate for that government assistance.

Diana Sue Christ Mathews of Gainesville, Florida, devoted a considerable part of her essay, "The People's Economy," to the important subject of ways in which people could *earn* USOP shares. She suggests the establishment of "Community Service Units" through which people needing public assistance could provide community service and receive USOP shares in return. Such USOP shareholders should lose their shares if they do not continue to participate in the community service needed in their areas in the future. Mathews cites the foster grandparent programs as an example of the use of lifetime skills to solve social problems in this way. She also suggests that welfare mothers could earn community service credits simply by raising their children, rather than being required to work at menial low-paying jobs that may actually hinder their ability to raise their children properly. This program should be accompanied by some training of the welfare mothers in human development. Mathews further proposes "Community Education Units" which would earn USOP shares. Those who earn USOP shares through Community Services Credits should first be required to obtain Community Education Units in order to assure their proper preparation for community service.

Terry Mollner, founder and president of Trusteeship Institute of Shutesbury, Massachusetts, and one of the founders of the highly successful Calvert Social Investment Fund of Washington, D.C., submitted an essay on trusteeship trusts. He sums up the concept of trusteeship trusts as follows:

> The "original American dream," the dream of the first European settlers to this new land, was of a society based on freedom and cooperation, not freedom and competition. This essay proposes the establishment of "trusteeship trusts," initially for every new baby born into a family, group, church, company, township, or nation, and eventually for everyone. A "trusteeship trust" is a trust where the beneficiary is primarily the entire human family and secondarily an individual.

> Members of a group would loan $10,000 to the trusteeship trust for a particular beneficiary at money market fund rates. The capital would be invested in mutual funds. The loans would be repaid, plus interest, in one payment to each creditor when the return on investment would leave a balance of $10,000. Every year thereafter, 25 per cent of the net profit would be loaned by the beneficiary to start or increase a trusteeship trust for another, to the equivalent of $10,000

in 1986 constant dollars. At the age of 20, the beneficiary begins receiving 25 per cent of the net profit each year. At the age of 30, this amount increases to 50 per cent each year until death. Upon death the assets of the trust become the property of the "Trusteeship Trust Club of Earth" which loans the capital to start new trusteeship trusts.

Because any existing group of any size—a group of friends or a nation—can begin such a program, and because of the built-in geometric growth of the number of trusts as a result of the required loan of 25 per cent of the net profits, everyone on the planet could end up with a trust within one generation. Finally, to start the trusts, individuals, churches, corporations, townships, and the like would only need to sign a paper guaranteeing the loan, which could be made by a bank or money market fund. Thus, it can be easily begun as well.

Dr. Mollner stresses that government involvement, if any, need not be at the national level since even a local township could implement a trusteeship trust program:

This proposal can be presented to a local township. It could establish such a program for all children born in its borders, which would make it a more attractive community within which to live. The town would simply have to guarantee money market loans to the trusts. Money market funds, such as the Calvert Social Investment money market portfolio of which I am one of the founding board members, would be very interested in speaking to any municipality about such a program.

If all goes well, the municipality has done nothing but sign its guarantee. Only if a trust account goes completely broke would the municipality be responsible for repayment. There will be volatility in the trusteeship account, but the odds that it will go completely bust are small. The municipality would normally have very few defaults and it could place restrictions on its guarantees, such as only allowing the investments in approved mutual funds managed by professionals with five years experience and successful track records.

Once such a movement has proven itself at the individual, church, corporation, and local township levels, it would be an obviously credible program to recommend to the Congress as a national program. We could begin to locally propose it immediately, but we can initiate it locally at the same time.

This proposal also avoids some of the problems sure to arise in similar proposals I have read. It does not demand that stockholders of existing large corporations give up anything or even be concerned. It does not seek to have people representing the trusteeship trusts on the boards of trustees of major corporations, it does not ask that their future capital gains be directed toward the program, and so forth.

Its shortcoming is that it is a slow growth program which will take at least 20 years for everyone to have a trust of more than $50,000. On the other hand, it might take more than 20 years to get a hearing on proposals which significantly effect the operations of major corporations. This proposal will have the aggressive support of big business and big finance because it will bring them investment dollars and increase the buying power of consumers.

Let's do it! If you are interested, please write us. It is time to return to the path of the original American dream. Only this time we will do it not by running away from the people on other continents but by extending equal partnership to them. This way we will not lose our way as easily.

Readers interested in starting trusteeship trusts or getting further information should contact Terry Mollner at the Trusteeship Institute, Baker Road, Shutesbury, Massachusetts 01072.

PART II

THE BRITISH ESSAYS

13

A FISCAL BOOST TO THE SHARE-OWNING DEMOCRACY

by

Andrew Greenwood

Editor's Note: *The first-prize winning essay in the British competition was submitted by Andrew Greenwood of Heston, Middlesex, a financial officer in a London firm. The British judging panel were strongly impressed by the simplicity and pragmatism of his approach, which builds on established structures to achieve a more egalitarian spread of share ownership while maintaining revenue neutrality.*

ABSTRACT

Following an examination of the need to revive the economy and to distribute share ownership more equitably, analysis is made of recent moves to increase the number of individuals owning shares in U.K. companies, including the Personal Equity Plan, Profit-Related Pay, and Employee Share Ownership. Through this examination, shortcomings of the existing schemes are revealed, and various necessary characteristics of any more ambitious and egalitarian scheme are identified.

Having examined the experience of France with its savings-based Loi Monory scheme in the late 1970s, and having justified the need to simultaneously further encourage Employee Share Ownership, the scheme proposed is outlined. The main incentive to increase savings-based shareholding is immediate tax relief on up to £600 per year of investment in U.K. companies with full tax relief if the shares are held for five years or more, scaling down to 25 per cent tax relief on shares held for two years. In addition, to encourage employers to broaden employee ownership, they would be permitted to issue up to £600 worth of shares per annum to each employee, 50 per cent of which (maximum of £300 per employee) would be subject to tax relief.

Finally, costings of the proposals are presented, together with suggestions as to how financing could be undertaken so as to ensure that the overall effect (from a revenue point of view) was either positive or neutral. The cost of the broadened employee ownership scheme would be offset by higher corporation taxes on those companies that do *not* issue these shares to their employees.

The Issues in Question

Economics is an obliging science. Among the abundance of economic indicators prevalent in the economy at any time, there will generally be those sufficient to compile political propaganda for each of the parties. Moreover, for the party in power, commitment to a small number of economic objectives will usually result in their achievement. As evidence that the nation has finally seen the light at the end of the proverbial tunnel, these can then be waved under the noses of the electorate at every opportunity, together with a promise that if everyone can just wait until the election result is determined, everything will start to fall into place.

It is perhaps fortunate for politicians of all persuasions that the life of a Parliament is only about five years. Looking at the British economy over a longer time span presents a consistently more dismal performance in most areas if compared with our major competitors. A particular cause for concern in recent years has been the state of the British manufacturing industry. Rising unemployment, combined with declining manufacturing output, have been a particular feature of the 1970s and 1980s. These conditions manifest themselves in a variety of ways.

Official Department of Employment statistics show that the proportion of total employment engaged in manufacturing declined from nearly 36 per cent in 1960 to just 22 per cent in 1985. Although manufacturing in most Western economies suffered at the same time, there is evidence that the British economy fared worse than most. World industrial output between 1973 and 1980 rose by 13 per cent. In Britain, output fell by 10 per cent. A more visual presentation of the changes taking place is provided by the weekly ITN (television) jobs survey. Week after week the underlying rise in unemployment, combined with the trend toward Britain becoming a nation of supermarkets and DIY (Do It Yourself) stores, is vividly illustrated. That the economy needs revival should not be a matter of contention. Discussion should rather center around whether the responsibility for instigating this revival lies solely with the government, whatever its persuasion, or whether the community generally has a role to play.

Of all the various categories of wealth, there are few where ownership is more concentrated than is the case with the ownership of U.K. companies. This fact is well illustrated by Inland Revenue comparisons of wealth. In the following table, the first column gives the value of the average holding for persons owning the item concerned. The second column gives the value per adult (21 years and over) in the whole population. All figures relate to 1983.

	Average Holding	Average Per Adult	Per Cent
Total Net Wealth	£26,400	£13,917	52.7
Extracted from Above:			
U.K. Securities			
Listed	15,860	837	5.3
Unlisted	20,440	316	1.5
Bank/Building Society Accounts and Cash	4,823	2,142	44.4

Looking therefore at the two issues of Britain's declining industrial base and the concentration of its ownership, consideration needs to be given to whether a revival could be assisted by combining government fiscal policy with the appetite that the electorate has clearly demonstrated for investing in the economy during the past few years.

Recent Experience

Since 1979, a greater appreciation of the benefits of a broad base of share ownership has been developed. It is now estimated that about 17 per cent of the adult population are shareholders, although many hold only a nominal shareholding in one or more of the recently de-nationalized public utilities. Share ownership has already become a major issue of the next election (1987). Given that it is easier to identify with a monetary stake in industry than it is with some rather more general and vague idea of social ownership, it is likely that parties encouraging the spread of share ownership will benefit in electoral terms from that policy. However, criticism can be leveled at the perception and extent of share ownership that has been created in recent years. The words of David Blunkett, member of Labour's National Executive Council, strike uncomfortably near the truth: "These share offers create money out of money without creating new wealth or jobs, and help to create a betting shop economy with [Chancellor of the Exchequer] Nigel Lawson as the bookie's runner."

Prior to the recent British Gas share issue, a number of newspapers carried detailed articles explaining how individuals privileged with a "gold" credit card should use the extensive overdraft facilities available with such cards to "stage" the forthcoming share issue. Is this really the concept of share ownership that ought to be created? Moreover, it should not be overlooked that if 17 per cent of the adult population owns shares, 83 per cent do not. Included within this larger group will necessarily be many of the less-privileged sections of society. Despite what appear to be genuine attempts to allow as many people as possible to share in the fortunes of those public utility industries that have been privatized, the fact remains that many will not be able to avail themselves of the opportunity to invest.

Features of a plan to revive the economy through wider share ownership of productive assets should draw on recent experience. A level of commitment should be required well beyond that of buying shares in the hope of an immediate capital gain. The notion that share ownership is alternative terminology for a national lottery must be dispelled. As most newly elected governments are quick to point out, British industry is not going to be revived overnight. Additionally, as the fortunes of each and every one depend to some extent on the state of manufacturing industry, the financial involvement of all shades of the political and income spectrums should be a central objective.

The Personal Equity Plan

It is difficult to be anything other than critical of the Personal Equity scheme introduced in the 1986 budget. As there seem to be few people who understand it, and even fewer who believe that it will have any quantifiable impact, it is worth summarizing. From the 1st of January 1987, U.K. residents will be able to invest up to £2,400 per annum in a Personal Equity Plan. The funds must be used for investment in a company registered either on the stock exchange or on the unlisted securities market. They must be held in the custody of an authorized manager. Providing that the shares are held for a qualifying period, all capital gains and reinvested dividends arising will be tax free.

There are several reasons why the scheme can be considered a non-starter. The most important is that for the majority of people it offers no significant tax concessions. For the tax year 1986-1987, the first £6,300 of capital gains for individuals are exempt from taxation. This is in itself a significant tax concession and one which will amply meet the requirements of all but the largest of personal investors. The aim should be to attract money from those who would not normally invest their money in industry, rather than to give further tax concessions to those who would probably do so anyway. For the small investor, it is unlikely that the tax concessions on dividends will compensate for the administration charges levied by trustees. The degree of commitment in terms of time and the requirement to invest in the U.K. are desirable features. Overall, however, the scheme fails in two important areas. Firstly, it is too complicated to appeal to a broad section of the community. Secondly, it does not offer "up front" tax concessions on the money invested. Consequently, any scheme which aimed to make a serious impact would need to possess the following characteristics in addition to those previously identified.

(1) It should be simple to understand and simple to administer.

(2) It should offer generous tax concessions of the money invested.

(3) Although generous, tax concessions should only apply to a comparatively small annual sum.

Critics may well argue that the British people have fixed ideas about saving and investing money and are more risk-averse than others. The evidence does not support this hypothesis. It is estimated, for example, that in 1985 the average adult spent a total of £96 on horse and dog racing. Regarding investment, it should be considered that for several months in 1986 more money has been invested in unit trusts than in building societies. Moreover, some of the best growth areas for unit trust investment have been in the U.K., particularly in small companies and recovery situations. Building society investment is favored through the composite tax system. Nevertheless, £1,000 invested ten years ago in a building society would now be worth about £3,000, whereas a similar sum invested in a U.K. growth unit trust would be worth in excess of £6,000. Building society deposits currently stand at around £91 billion. Direct investors in British-listed companies are estimated to hold ordinary shares to the value of £65 billion. It is quite probable, therefore, that redirection of funds away from housing and toward industry would have the threefold beneficial effect of assisting industrial growth, improving investors' returns, and slowing down the growth in property prices.

Employee Share Ownership

Whether such major public utilities as British Telecom or British Gas are in private or public ownership will probably make little overall difference to the average individual. Certainly after two years in private ownership, there is little tangible evidence that British Telecom has improved its level of service to domestic customers. For employees given shares at concessionary rates, there is also probably little opportunity for them to identify with their employer. Large monopolistic corporations have problems of their own which will occur whatever their ownership. Despite this, it is surely reasonable that employees of a firm should have a "piece of the action." Quite clearly, such involvement can only have a beneficial effect on industrial relations. There is also empirical evidence that such financial involvement encourages motivation and loyalty.

Jaguar Plc is so frequently exalted as the jewel in the British crown that after a while one begins to wonder what else the crown is actually made of. Nevertheless, it possesses a number of characteristics that make it particularly appropriate when examining the concept of employee share ownership. John Eagan has identified four key factors to which he attributes the recovery of the company in recent years, none of which is share ownership! These factors are: improved quality, timing, customer sovereignty, and increased productivity. However, since the recovery has occurred at a time when the company has had a marked absence of new products, it is likely that fundamental changes have occurred throughout the company. To an extent this will have resulted from the notion that nothing succeeds like success. Most people would rather work for a successful company than a mediocre one. Particularly in the West Midlands, which does not appear to have had much in the way of prosperity during the 1980s, it must be uplifting to work for a company, the products of which are unquestionably among the finest in the world. In addition to sharing in this success by being among the highest paid of the U.K. motor industry, over 90 per cent of employees hold Jaguar Plc shares with an average holding that exceeds £2,000. The value of shares on the date of issuance (8th August 1984) was £1.65. Since that date, they have risen as follows:

1st April 1985	£3.39
30th April 1986	£4.50
End of 1986 (approx.)	£5.15

The basis of the Jaguar scheme is that each year, depending on the profits of the company, the directors will set aside a profit-sharing fund. Trustees will then acquire shares either by subscribing for new shares or by purchasing the shares on the Stock Exchange at arm's length. There are no costs to the employee. Entitlements must be held for a minimum period of two years, after which they can be sold. However, such an early sale would involve a 100 per cent liability to tax on the lower of the price of the shares when they were first allocated and on the sale proceeds. Only when the shares have been held for a full five-year period does the employee escape any income tax liability.

These are statutory rather than company provisions and would seem to be a fair representation of the desirable level of commitment to be sought in return for tax concessions. There are stories of the Jaguar share price being announced daily at the workplace and there is currently pressure from employees for an extension to the scheme. It would be an interesting exercise for an analysis to be undertaken of the revenue effects of the Jaguar recovery over the last five years, considering such factors as increased corporation tax paid, incremental VAT received on improved sales, increased national insurance, and income tax paid from a higher number of better-paid employees.

When considering the costs of the introduction of a tax-based scheme of share ownership, the financial spin-offs resulting from bet-

ter industrial relations and improved motivation should not be overlooked.

Profit-Related Pay

Employee share ownership is only one method by which a link can
be introduced between the employee and the financial situation of their
employer. The idea of profit-related pay (PRP) is one particular suggestion that has been considerably discussed since hints were given in the
1986 budget that such a scheme was receiving consideration. The basic
mechanism of this type of scheme is that employees share in the success and failure of their company through cash bonuses that vary according to profits, sales, or other criteria.

There are many reasons why this type of scheme, although desirable
in theory, should not form the basis of a scheme to revitalize the
economy. First, it would not be relevant to the majority of people.
Groups such as the retired, temporarily unemployed, and employees of
the public sector would not be able to participate. Second, it is based on
the premise that employees can directly affect the profit of their company. This is not necessarily so. Employees frequently have little control over non-production overheads. Third, in many large organizations
which produce a wide range of product, each with a different degree of
profitability, it would be difficult to fairly apportion the profit between
different groups of employees. The final drawback of the scheme under
consideration is that the tax effects are too small to be of significance.
The Green Paper proposals state, "one-quarter of PRP received would
be exempt from income tax up to a limit of 5 per cent of pay . . . this
relief could be worth up to £12 per month." On top of a requirement for
80 per cent of qualifying employees to participate before tax relief
would be granted, these minimal concessions are unlikely to have any
significant impact.

Wages and the ownership of assets are essentially different issues.
It is, of course, right that employees should not price themselves out of
jobs, but the free market is the basis on which wage rates ought to be
determined. There are many examples of private sector employees
taking wage cuts to ensure continuity of employment. Efforts of central
government would be better directed toward the introduction of some
kind of "efficiency-related pay" for the public sector, where all too often
there is little relationship between wage rates and the ability to pay.

To Lead or to Follow?

There have been several schemes introduced by European countries since 1978 designed to encourage private individuals to take a direct stake in the industrial base. The majority of these are based on the French "Loi Monory" scheme introduced in 1978 and it therefore is that particular scheme which should be examined to see the extent to which Britain could copy or adapt its characteristics to suit the slightly different circumstances and tax regime that exists in this country.

In essence, the Loi Monory was a plan which allowed each French household to set up to Ffr. 5,000 per annum of net new investment in the shares of French companies against its taxable income. A "household" was defined as husband and wife, although there were additional small allowances available for children. Shares could be purchased either through the Bourse (the largest stock exchange in France) or via units in any of the designated funds, the so-called Monory Sicavs. These funds had to keep at least 60 per cent of their portfolio in French equities. The tax benefits were available for four years (1978 to 1981), although the newly elected socialist government extended the scheme for a further year. To escape tax liability the investments had to be held for a minimum period of five years. In conjunction with the introduction of the scheme, various concessions were offered to industry in the form of abolition of price controls and making interest and dividend payments on new capital-raising exercises fully tax-allowable against profits for a period of seven years. It was, therefore, an ambitious and innovative scheme, and has already been used by Belgium and Norway as the basis for similar schemes.

One of the main reasons for the introduction of the scheme centered around the fact that the French government believed that industry was undercapitalized. In other words, too great a proportion of the financing of companies relied on expensive loans and overdrafts. It was hoped that the introduction of the scheme would result in firms relying less on bank financing and, at the same time, improve their performance so as to be able to distribute reasonable dividends to their newfound investors. Further, the government also aimed to influence the way in which individuals invested their money. As with Britain, most personal savings found their way into short-term deposits with banks. This in turn meant that industry was dependent on the banks.

Comparisons can be drawn between the problems of France and current British difficulties. Although undercapitalization is probably not a difficulty, a commonly heard criticism is that high British interest rates stifle manufacturing industry. Furthermore, the pattern of personal saving is slowly changing, yet the level of resources being channeled into traditional savings institutions, such as building societies and banks, is still too high. The tax concessions introduced in France effectively meant that investors had a cushion against their investments falling in value in the short term. This was represented by the amount of the tax concession. The final motive behind the introduction of the scheme was to give the whole of French society a financial stake in the future of their industry.

The French responded quickly to what were clearly substantial concessions. The following table illustrates the growth of savings flow into Monory funds.

Year	New Flow of Savings (in millions of Ffr.)
1978	3,414
1979	4,354
1980	5,548
1981	5,831

It is estimated that half of investors taking advantage of the scheme had not previously owned shares. Financial institutions were also quick off the mark in developing suitable schemes for investors. French companies raised substantial amounts of new capital through new share issues. To a considerable extent these share issues were from firms who were raising equity finance to reduce expensive short-term borrowing rather than undertake new capital investment. However, this was one of the original aims of the scheme.

Overall, despite the fact that the Loi Monory scheme was superseded by the socialist Mitterand government, it must be judged a success. It tended to benefit taxpayers paying high marginal rates of tax and lacked a reasonable trial period, but was nevertheless a brave and innovative venture.

Detailed Proposals

One of the main criticisms that can be leveled against the U.K. taxation system is its complexity. For any tax-induced investment scheme to be successful, a vital characteristic should be simplicity. With this aim in mind, the following are the main aspects of the proposed scheme which relate to the income tax system.

(1) Every income taxpayer should have the right to offset against his tax bill any amount of money up to a predetermined level that he has invested during the course of that year in U.K. companies. The limit of the annual contributions to be made to the scheme should be £600 per annum (£50 per month). Effectively, this means that allowing for basic level tax at the rate of 29p, the cost to an individual of an investment of £600 in terms of post-tax income would be £426.

(2) The right to offset payments against taxable income should be limited to basic-rate taxation.

(3) To cater for circumstances where individuals are temporarily unable to make contributions due to unemployment or other circumstances, the right should exist for contributions to be made in one tax year relating to a previous tax year where such entitlement has not been utilized. This would operate in a similar manner and for a similar length of time to that currently permissible with pension contributions.

(4) Restrictions should be placed on the sale of investments made. These would operate in a similar way to those placed on employee share schemes. Irrespective of when money is invested during a tax year, it should be necessary to hold the investment for a minimum period of two years before escaping 100 per cent tax liability. Thereafter, a scale of liability would apply depending on the time for which the investments are held. The following would be appropriate:

Period Shares Held	Per Cent Liable to Tax
More than 2 years but less than 4 years	75
More than 4 years but less than 5 years	50
More than 5 years	0

(5) The scheme should be specifically aimed at income taxpayers rather than families. This would give a tax advantage to families with two or more wage earners, but this is reasonable because (a) the system of mortgage relief that is directed toward families rather than individuals is already the subject of much criticism, and it would be wrong to introduce a further scheme which could be criticized for the same reason; and (b) it is unlikely that the average married couple would fully utilize both their individual facilities during a tax year.

(6) The decision as to which companies an individual should invest in should be entirely a matter of personal choice. As will be explained

further, there should be tax incentives to encourage firms to offer shares to employees. For a variety of reasons, however, a taxpayer may be unable or unwilling to participate.

(7) The income tax element on contributions should be reclaimable in one of two ways. First, financial institutions wishing to market unit-trust type schemes should be required to register them with the Inland Revenue. Once approval has been obtained, participants should then be able to contribute the necessary net of tax sums with the tax element being reclaimed by the respective institution from the Inland Revenue. The costs of the time lag in this process would be passed on via the management charges of the scheme. Second, individuals should be able to purchase their shares themselves and reclaim the tax element as they would for any other tax overpaid.

(8) Dividends received and all capital gains would be exempt from taxation.

Costs and Financing

Essentially, the above scheme amounts to a sizeable central government subsidy to industry. However, the decisions as to which firms to support are taken by individuals and financial institutions rather than by government. It therefore satisfies the aspirations of both sides of the political spectrum: those who believe that the state ought to do more to assist industry and those who believe that investment decisions are best left to the free market.

The costs of the above scheme will be substantial, but its introduction can be effected without an overall increase in the level of taxation. Based on a total working population of 27.5 million and a maximum income tax concession of £174 per person (£600-£426), the potential maximum cost of the scheme in a financial year would be around £4.8 billion. Given that total income raised from income taxes for the year 1986 to 1987 is estimated at £38.7 billion, the costs of introduction would appear to be high. However, the above unrealistically assumes that all the working population would participate, using their full entitlement. It further assumes that no income tax would be recovered by the Inland Revenue on the early sales of share portfolios. It is, of course, impossible to predict with accuracy the take-up of the scheme. However, it would be unlikely that the first-year cost would exceed half of the potential maximum.

There are many ways in which the above could be financed without the overall levels of taxation being increased. It is, for example, generally accepted that as a result of strict control over spending and buoyant revenue, the present government is likely to be in a position to finance tax cuts to the value of £3 billion to £4 billion next year. This would be sufficient to reduce the basic rate of income tax by 3 or 4 pence in the pound. It would also be sufficient to undertake the proposed scheme in its entirety and still undertake further tax cuts. Serious consideration should be given as to whether the resources available are best used to finance further basic rate tax cuts which will, in all likelihood, lead to a rise in the level of imports, or whether a more imaginative approach is required.

It is envisaged that the scheme outlined would apply indefinitely, instead of only for one year. Having regard to general budget considerations and the state of manufacturing industry, an annual limit for the scheme would be set as part of the budget. This then presents the problem as to how the scheme is to be financed in future years. The previously identified likely spin-offs from the scheme would mean that, in part at least, it would be self-financing. However, the balance of the funding requirement should be met either by being more selective with the application of VAT or by raising the basic rate of income tax. Whichever approach was adopted, there would be a strong fiscal incentive to invest rather than to consume. With a VAT level of 15 per cent, total revenue from this source of taxation is in the region of £20 billion. It would, therefore, be comparatively easy to raise the sum required by either adjusting the VAT rate, extending the range of goods and services on which it is levied, or by introducing a higher rate on selected products.

Expansion of Employee Ownership

In conjunction with the above scheme, it is necessary to encourage employers to have a greater percentage of the equity of companies owned by employees. Legislation has already been introduced along these lines. Specifically, the 1978 Finance Act enabled companies to establish trusts to purchase their own shares for the benefit of their employees and deduct the cost of this from their corporation tax bill. This was a radical development, but was watered down by further requirements of the Investor Protection Committee. In conjunction with the specific proposals relating to income tax concessions, it is therefore proposed that companies offering their own shares to employees be taxed at a concessionary rate on those shares purchased by employees. The scheme would work along the following lines:

(1) During the course of a firm's financial year, it would draw attention to opportunities employees have for investing in their own firm. It may issue shares to employees or purchase them for employees at arm's length.

(2) Subject to a maximum of £600 per employee, the firm would be able to have the equivalent amount of its precorporation-tax profit in the following financial year taxed at 50 per cent of the current corporation tax rate.

With total revenue from corporation tax in the region of £9 billion per annum, and rates for large and small companies currently being 35 per cent and 29 per cent respectively, it is proposed that the cost of these measures be financed by upwardly adjusting the standard rates of corporation tax. These were substantially reduced in the 1984 budget, and adjustment to ensure discrimination in favor of those companies offering employees the opportunity to share in the wealth they have helped to create is fair and reasonable.

It is most unlikely that undue pressure would be put on employees to purchase shares in ailing companies. The large scale of income tax concessions would ensure that there were a large number of institutions prepared to offer sound advice to small investors on where to invest. The need for such investors to seek Inland Revenue approval of the schemes offered would ensure that such schemes were handled only by those sufficiently competent to run them.

Conclusion

The entrenched attitude of British industry is a standard economic textbook reason for Britain's relatively poor economic performance. Even in 1986, the interests of employment and ownership are portrayed as operating in opposite directions. In such organizations as John Lewis, National Freight, and Jaguar where different approaches have been tried, it has been demonstrated that attitudes can be dramatically changed for the better. The proposed scheme, insofar as it is possible, would give a strong fiscal boost to the concept of a share-owning democracy. It is intentionally simple in the belief that it is often the simple ideas that are successful. Although drawing on the political philosophy of all parties, it is probably most closely akin to the current views of the SDP/Liberal Alliance. No apologies are made for that. After all, if there is one lesson that can surely be drawn from the experience of post-war Britain, it is that new approaches to old problems are urgently required.

14

JOHN CITIZEN—SHAREHOLDER

by

Maurice I. Gillibrand

Editor's Note: *Dr. Maurice I. Gillibrand of Tregarth, Bangor, second-prize winner in the British competition, is a Fellow of the Royal Society of Chemistry and a Member of the British Institute of Management. He has published some 32 scientific papers and patents. His plan for National Share Ownership adopts the reservoir of the SuperStock/Kitty Hawk Model, but distributes its flow differently by requiring John Citizen to buy and pay for the USOP shares. In addition to broadening distribution of new capital ownership, Dr. Gillibrand's objectives are to make the economy more accountable to the people and to improve company management by requiring the issuance of new shares each year to pay for capital additions.*

ABSTRACT

Any plan for developing wider share ownership needs to be based on an understanding of the nature of share ownership and the economic environment of our citizens, who are to be encouraged to participate. The essay establishes the characteristics of these two factors. It also proposes that ownership of the wealth-creating processes by our citizens is an alternative to state ownership. It follows, however, that those who have the use of the savings of our citizens' savings must also be accountable to them. At the same time, there is a need to make a substantial number of shares available to the public, and taxation incentives are regarded as being essential to stimulate national share ownership.

The plan itself consists of three components: first, the educational need to create a greater understanding of the responsibilities of share ownership; second, proposals for changes in taxation and company law; and third, adoption of the proposal made in *The USOP Handbook* (the SuperStock/Kitty Hawk Model) for the annual distribution of profits with new capital being provided by additional issue of shares.

Finally, some implications of the adoption of the plan are discussed.

Introduction

Social evolution has resulted in our being members of a democracy which is also a wealth-creating society. The basis of this democracy is that those who are placed in authority are ultimately accountable to the people. Today, John Citizen (and for the purposes of this essay, any reference to him will be equally applicable to his female counterpart, Joan Citizen) can call to account at the ballot box those to whom he has given authority to govern and administer the rules of our society. In contrast, those who control the means of production and other wealth-creating processes have, as yet, not become accountable to the people.

At the center of this issue is the fact that control of the wealth-creating processes is vested in the ownership of the means of production. State ownership of large sections of our industrial heritage has not been successful as a means of bringing the wealth-creating process into the democratic system. This essay is concerned with an alternative form of public ownership in which we, together with John Citizen, will own shares in the enterprises which develop the wealth of our society.

In the first instance, we need to appreciate that we are not dealing with a static system that can be changed to achieve our objective. Share ownership has been developing since the late 17th century, and even today major changes in the stock market are taking place. Likewise, John Citizen's economic environment is the product of a longer term evolution. Therefore, we need in the first instance to establish both the direction and the momentum of these dynamic processes. This will enable us to establish what changes are needed in both if the process is to be directed toward the target of wider share ownership. Our plan will take form when we consider the means of bringing about these changes.

However, these in themselves are unlikely to be sufficient to achieve our objective. We will need to demonstrate that the consequences of the adoption of the plan will be a contribution to the improvement in the social, economic, and democratic life of our community. It will be particularly important to demonstrate that the means of wealth creation will become accountable to John Citizen as part of the democratic system.

The Developing System of Share Ownership

The origins of the shared financing of commercial ventures can be traced to the late 17th and early 18th centuries.[1] At that time, trade from Europe was expanding to the distant parts of the world and the amount of money required to finance these voyages increased commensurately. More and more frequently, merchants found it necessary to combine to provide the necessary capital for these ventures. In this manner, joint stock companies were evolved, based on the principle that those who provided the capital to finance a venture were entitled to a legitimate share of the profits. For the purpose of this essay, we will limit the term "investors" to those who provide capital in this way and have a legitimate entitlement to a share of any profits achieved. In due course, we will also extend the term to those who purchase from the original owners this entitlement to the profits of a venture.

In the main, such joint companies prospered and provided substantial return to investors. Consequently, the possessors of wealth at the time were increasingly attracted to making capital available. This inevitably provided an opportunity for "speculators" to take advantage of the system. Again, we need to attach a somewhat limited but precise description to the term "speculator," and perhaps there is no better way of doing this than by using the modern American idiom as being a person whose aim it was to "make a quick buck." The speculators at the time were able to use the system by creating ever-increasing numbers of joint stock companies of dubious viability. Nevertheless, the visions of financial gain overshadowed the need for prudence, and the possessors of wealth competed to participate. This situation culminated in the catastrophic collapse of the South Sea Company in 1720, which created panic and loss of confidence in joint stock companies. Confidence was only restored by the intervention of Prime Minister Walpole who introduced the South Sea Bubble Act of 1721, prohibiting the formation of joint stock companies without a Royal Charter.

It would be easy to decry the South Sea Bubble Act since its subsequent repeal was to herald a further rapid development in our economic heritage. However, it was very necessary at the time and it enabled us to learn the lesson that investors who do not accept responsibility for the conduct of a venture are prone to lose confidence if there is any evidence of difficulties—a phenomenon that was to be repeated nearer our own time with the Wall Street collapse of 1929.

The repeal of the 1721 Bubble Act in 1825 led to the development of insurance and banking. Insurance in various forms was undertaken by joint stock companies; the London Westminster Bank and the London Joint Stock Bank were established and were offering interest on deposits and cautiously loaning money by the mid-19th century.

Other joint stock companies were concerned with manufacturing, the development of which was being stimulated by the industrial revolution. Such a period of technical innovation had a twofold effect. First, it created a need for ever-increasing capital expenditure. Second, when new technology was not fully developed, progress went hand-in-hand with disaster. Explosions of steam boilers in the Lancashire cotton industry in the 19th century were the equivalents of Windscale and Chernobyl in our own time. Thus, although the majority of joint stock companies in the industrial sector prospered, bankruptcies were also frequent. Such bankruptcies had calamitous consequences for the investors, who were held responsible for the full extent of debts of the company.

Thus, a situation had developed in which substantial funds were accumulating in the financial sector and there was an equally substantial requirement for capital in manufacturing industry. Nevertheless, the former was constrained from investing in the latter by the open-ended responsibility for indebtedness. The dilemma was resolved by the Limited Liabilities Acts of 1855 and 1862 that made provision for joint stock companies which:

(a) had their liability limited to the value of the subscribing shares;

(b) were able to appeal to the public for capital;

(c) were financed by shares which existed in perpetuity; and

(d) were managed by a committee of directors accountable to the shareholders as a whole.

The impact of this provision was profound. In the first place, it released capital for manufacturing industry that had otherwise been accumulating within the financial sector. Also, it initiated a process which was to develop shareholding and management structures as we know them today.

Previously, the industrial companies had been managed by the factory owners and these were gradually assimilated into joint stock companies. The shareholders, in the main, were individuals whose investment was motivated by the knowledge of the commercial opportunities of the business; the institutional shareholders were to remain in a minority for many years. The Limited Liabilities Acts had made specific provision for a board of directors to be accountable to the shareholders, and the annual general meeting of the company was an effective part of the system. In such circumstances, management continued to be direct and close to the enterprise.

Figure 1

DISTRIBUTION OF BENEFICIAL OWNERSHIP OF SHARES

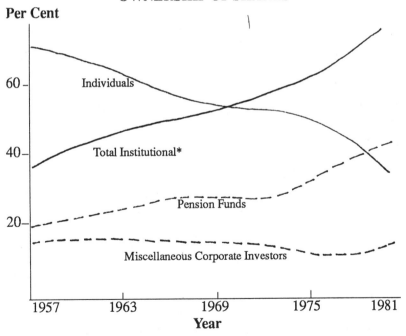

*Insurance, banks, unit trusts, other institutional investors.

Demands for capital eventually could only be satisfied by the institutions (see Figure 1). Individual shareholders represented a majority until as late as 1957.[2,3] By 1981, however, individual beneficial ownership represented only 28 per cent of the total stock market. The increasing participation of the institutional shareholders was to have a profound effect on the system of management. The responsibilities of the institutional shareholders to their policyholders could best be discharged by spreading the risk over a large range of investments. The result is that they do not participate actively in any debate at the annual general meeting and usually support the existing management with their proxies. Such proxies render ineffective any intervention by individual shareholders. Therefore, management policies are not critically examined, inefficient management can survive for some time, and changes only occur after they have been long overdue.

The trend toward decreasing individual ownership of shares may now be reversed by the government's privatization program. A stock exchange survey in 1985[4] suggested that 16 per cent of the adult population were shareholders. This would represent 7 million out of an adult population of 42 million. The privatization of British Gas is expected to attract some 4 million shareholders, but a proportion of these will be within the 7 million who are already shareholders. If we assume that half of these are new shareholders, the shareholder population would be about 9 million. Further privatization projects are likely to be attractive only to the same segment of the population, and the limit of the potential of the privatization policy is likely at the best to be about 20 per cent of the population.

Finally, in this section of the essay, we need to consider that shares are bought and sold and that the price is continually changing. We have already defined an investor as a person who has provided capital for a commercial venture and, in consequence, has a legitimate entitlement to a share in the profits. Now this definition should be extended to include a person who has replaced the capital by the purchase of shares from the original owner and has thereby gained the same entitlement to a share in the profits of the company. Nevertheless, the price of shares does not solely reflect changes in the profitability of the enterprise. It is also influenced by such factors as supply and demand, the political and economic climate, and even by rumors and fashions.

This fluctuation in the price of shares again provides opportunities for the speculator who is motivated by the financial gain, which can be made simply by purchasing shares at a low price and selling again at a higher one. However, unless extra wealth is being created within the system, one person's capital gain is another's capital loss. Undoubtedly, as can be seen in Figure 2, the total market value in money terms has been increasing consistently over a number of years.[2,3] Nevertheless, when the total market value is corrected for inflation,[5,6] it can be seen that the total wealth of the market has decreased.

Figure 2

TOTAL VALUE OF THE STOCK MARKET

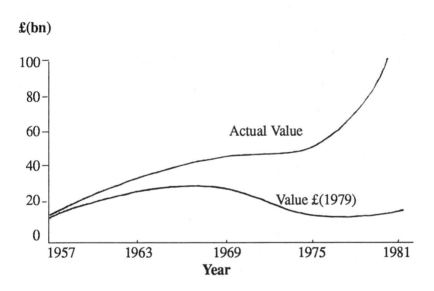

Having established an understanding of the hereditary features of the share market, we can appreciate that when it comes to motivating John Citizen to participate in wider share ownership, we not only need to take into account his proposed role as an individual shareholder in relation to the institutional share owners but also his potential as an investor or a speculator.

John Citizen

Some of our citizens are extremely wealthy, possessing large unearned incomes generated from investment of capital. Other citizens are unemployed and depend on the state welfare services for the well-being of themselves and their families. However, the vast majority do not fall into either of these categories and, at this stage, we will direct our attention to the circumstances of John Citizen as a representative of this majority.

John Citizen's income will be earned mainly from his employment. The main bulk of his income will be used on consumer spending for clothes, food, and other necessities of living, but some will be used in effect to provide for deferred or indirect income not directly related to employment. For example, the state will compulsorily acquire part of John Citizen's income in the form of national insurance contributions in order to provide him with welfare during his lifetime, and eventually a state pension on retirement. Additionally, as a condition of employment, he may be required to participate in the employer's pension fund and, in these circumstances, the employer will be making an additional contribution to a capital fund from which John Citizen will have an entitlement. Furthermore, John Citizen may voluntarily allocate some of his income to capital, for example, in the form of house purchase or superannuation schemes.

John Citizen's income will be taxed, but the rate will be dependent on the purposes to which the income is to be put. Successive governments have used the taxation system to promote the implementation of particular policies. For instance, both John Citizen's contribution to a pension scheme and that of his employer are not subject to tax. Of particular significance is the release from tax on interest payments on mortgages, which has played a major role in stimulating house purchases. We can see from Figure 3 that John Citizen is now more likely to be the beneficial owner of his house than at any time in the past. There is a further consequence of this increase in home ownership in that each successive generation of John Citizens becomes the recipient of an inherited capital, resulting from the fact that their parents were increasingly homeowners.

From the foregoing we can attribute two economic features to John Citizen. First, there is the income factor that is generated mainly from his employment. Second, there is the capital factor, and for this purpose we are not limiting it to that which he owns directly. We also include all monies paid to the state or pension schemes for which he has an entitlement of future income.

To complete our picture of John Citizen, we need to identify the patterns by which both the income factor and the capital factor vary during the course of his lifetime. The simplest manifestation of the pattern will be that the capital factor will be minimal in early years, but will accumulate over the normal lifetime, during which income will be created from employment. Nevertheless, eventually on retirement, John Citizen will be dependent on the income that will result from the investment in the capital factor.

Figure 3

PERCENTAGE OF NATIONAL STOCK OF DWELLINGS THAT ARE OWNER-OCCUPIED[6,7]

Per Cent

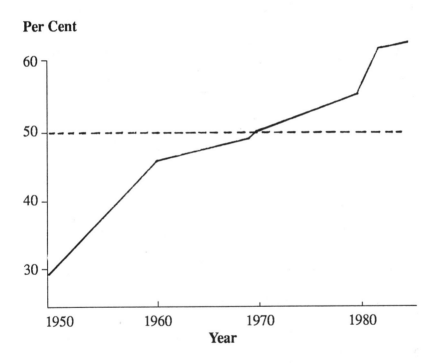

A model, which will reflect the changing pattern of John Citizen's finances during his lifetime, can be constructed from the distribution of average earnings according to age groups.[6] Such a model would not take into account inflation or changes in economic conditions that will affect John Citizen's future. It will establish, however, the general pattern and orders of magnitude sufficient for our purposes. The characteristics of such a model are shown in Figure 4.

Figure 4

JOHN CITIZEN'S INCOME

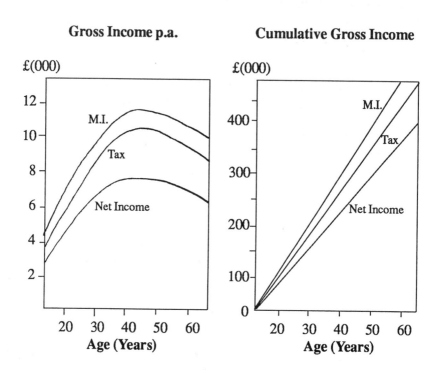

From the diagram on the left, it can be seen that John Citizen's gross income increased up to the age of 40 years but then decreases. This decrease probably reflects the effect of inflation on the earnings among those older age groups who have more difficulty in obtaining annual increases in earnings. From the cumulative gross income diagram on the right, we can make an assessment of the contributions which John Citizen makes to society in the form of national insurance and income tax during the course of his lifetime.

A measure of John Citizen's savings can be made by assuming that throughout his working life, it will be about 11 per cent of disposal income, which was the national average in 1982.[8] The same national statistic shows that these savings were made up to 7 per cent for life insurance and superannuation, with 4 per cent being for personal and household savings.

Thus, we are now able to estimate the distribution of the income which John Citizen earns during his working life between the ages of 16 and 65. This is summarized in the table below:

Distribution of John Citizen's Cumulative Income

	£ (000)	%
Consumer spending	290	64
National insurance contributions	41	9
Income tax	89	19
Insurance and superannuation	23	5
Personal household savings	13	3
Gross earnings	456	100

Inevitably, any plan for wider share ownership will involve John Citizen in purchasing shares over a substantial period of time and, in due course, we shall need to consider if such purchases are within his financial capability.

Principles and Concepts

Having established the nature of share ownership and of John Citizen's economic environment, we can now consider the principles that will form the basis of our plan. Our aim will be to create a system that will:

(a) represent a further stage in the evolution of our democracy;

(b) encourage John Citizen to invest his savings voluntarily in our wealth-creating society;

(c) be sufficiently stable to enable people to participate with confidence and without anxieties;

(d) ensure that those who have the use of John Citizen's savings remain accountable to him; and

(e) provide benefits for John Citizen, but at the same time ensure that he understands more fully than at present the responsibilities of shared ownership.

The adoption of these principles will necessitate some radical changes in the nature of share ownership and in John Citizen's perception of his role in the community.

The present system of share ownership has evolved in order to meet the requirements of present-day investors. Only a small proportion of the population is directly involved, and it would be surprising if the same system would be equally applicable in circumstances in which the vast majority of the people were taking part. It is essential that the system be relatively stable, and for this to be so, we need to create a nation of investors—not speculators. There can be little doubt that many purchasers of British Telecom shares were motivated by the prospects of an immediate capital gain. Before we contemplate motivating the vast majority of our citizens in this way, it might be well to remember that such visions of quick riches were the cause of the South Sea Bubble.

We have defined an investor as one who is motivated to purchase shares in order to secure a legitimate entitlement to a proportion of the profits of a company. John Citizen's rewards should not be dependent on selling his shares at the most appropriate time. Also, we need to provide the means by which he can invest his savings. If our aim is universal share ownership, substantial numbers of new shares will need to be made available continuously.

To meet these requirements, we will adopt the measures proposed elsewhere[9] for the abandonment of the current practice of companies being able to retain part of their profits. They will be required to seek any new capital by further investment from new and existing shareholders. The effect will be threefold: the asset value per share would not increase (and thereby the price would become more directly dependent on profitability), substantial numbers of new shares will be created, and the accountability to shareholders would be improved.

Accountability is the essence of democracy. It therefore must be the keystone for any system of national share ownership. This means, in effect, developing the provisions of the Limited Liability Act, whereby the board of directors are responsible to the shareholders as a whole. The authority of the annual general meeting, therefore, needs to be amplified and extended.

If we are to develop the function of the annual general meeting, a number of changes will need to be made. In particular, the use of proxies should be severely curtailed without reducing the rights of any shareholder to record his vote. At the same time, the large institutional shareholders who cast their votes in a particular direction should be seen to be accountable to the body of shareholders for their decisions. Thus, a proper record should be made of all votes cast at the annual general meeting. These and other provisions will be a part of the plan to be described later in this essay.

Taxation has undoubtedly played a major role in shaping our social evolution. We have seen that the growth of home ownership and pension provisions have been stimulated by taxation policies. Similar taxation incentives will be necessary if we are to develop a system of national share ownership. Changes in taxation need to be made, based on the duality of John Citizen's income factor and personal capital factor. John Citizen's liability to tax should be seen to identify the two accounts. The income account should be clearly seen as being subject to tax, but the personal capital account should be regarded as savings and not subjected to tax constraints. Transfer from capital to income should incur tax, but the reverse transition of income into personal capital should be tax-free.

We have already established that John Citizen may have entitlements from capital funds apart from any personal capital. Such capital, as, for example, that accumulating in an employer's pension fund, already receives the benefit of tax concessions. It is acknowledged that the promotion of such funds by employers in the past has been a major contribution to our social welfare, but the time may be now appropriate for participation in such funds to be no longer a condition of employment. In that event, John Citizen could use the income release for the purchase of shares with the same tax concessions as are presently applied to his pension contribution. The difficulties of phasing out such schemes are great but not unsurmountable. Nevertheless, we should be moving in the direction of John Citizen being responsible for his own personal investment to provide his eventual pension.

The adoption of the plan will necessitate changes of perception, not only by John Citizen but by all concerned with share ownership. There is a need for a self-learning process of education. Although we have already dealt at some length with the issue of accountability, this cannot be divorced from the equally important necessity of accepting responsibility. The responsibility of John Citizen as a shareholder arises directly from his role as a part owner of the business.

To meet this requirement, it is proposed that a code of practice should be published, identifying the responsibilities of not only John Citizen but also the institutional shareholders as well as company directors. Such a code of practice would not be mandatory but would have an educational influence. In particular, it should encourage individual shareholders to form "shareholders associations," as a means of adopting a responsible representation at the annual general meeting. In the case of smaller companies, such an association would be based on a national organization, but a regional organization could be adopted by the larger companies.

A Plan for National Share Ownership

Our deliberations have now reached a point where we can make specific proposals in the form of a plan. It is convenient to group these proposals in relation to education, changes in taxation, and changes in company law.

(1) *Education*

  (a) A code of practice to be published, possibly by the Department of Trade and Industry, on the rights and responsibility of shareholders. It should specify that although John Citizen, as a shareholder, has a right to a share of the profits of the enterprise, he also has a responsibility to record a vote at the annual general meeting. The code should establish the right to participate in a shareholders' association.

(2) *Changes in Taxation*

  (a) Income invested in share purchases to be exempt from income tax in recognition that such purchases produce further income.

  (b) The annual tax return to identify a personal capital fund, being the aggregate value of purchase of shares for which income tax relief has been obtained.

  (c) The exemption from capital gains tax of gains below £6300 to be removed on all capital realized on assets for which income tax relief has been obtained. In the case of realization of an asset that had not been subjected to income tax relief, then only the capital gain would be subject to tax as income.

  (d) Corporation tax to be increased initially to offset any loss to the Exchequer in the initial development of the plan, but to be reduced as the return of tax from investment income increases.

  (e) Any monies realized as a result of shares for which tax relief has been obtained to be treated as income for tax purposes.

(3) *Changes in Company Law*

  (a) Profit after tax to be fully distributed to the shareholders.

  (b) Companies to be required to annually seek fresh capital from the public.

  (c) Companies to maintain a register of the votes of shareholders cast at annual general meetings, which should be readily available for inspection during normal business hours.

(d) Proxies to be limited to those with justifiable reason for not attending the annual general meeting. Such reasons should be identified in the code of practice, and the intention to use this provision should be notified to the registrar of the company at least one week before the annual general meeting.

(e) Proxies could be deposited with the company registrar with instruction on how the vote should be cast. Such proxies deposited in this way would not be discretionary.

(f) Proxies could also be deposited with a named individual, who would be attending the annual general meeting but should not be a member of the board. In this case, such proxies could be discretionary.

(g) A record of the proceedings of an annual general meeting to be prepared by the company secretary and to be available within one week of the meeting. The record would include details of any resolutions and the numbers of votes cast for and against. It should also accompany the annual report and accounts for the following year when they were later circulated to shareholders.

Final Commentary

The plan is designed to fulfill two basic requirements: to generate a sufficient number of shares, and to provide sufficient incentive to purchase them. Clearly, this depends on creating a demand for the capital that is within John Citizen's capacity to meet.

We have seen that the total value of the stock market is of the order of £100 billion. The average earnings of the industrial sector[10] for the last 12 months has been 9.5 per cent per annum, providing a dividend yield of 4.0 per cent per annum. Thus, 5.5 per cent of earnings was retained as additional capital, which under the plan would mean that £5.5 billion per annum of new capital would need to be generated. Thus, with an adult population of 40 million, this requirement could be met with an average annual saving of £138 per head. It is clear from our assessment of John Citizen's finances (Table I) that this would be within his saving capabilities.

At the same time, an essential feature of the plan is the tax relief on this investment. On the assumption that the relief is at the standard rate of tax, the cost to the Inland Revenue would be £1.6 billion per annum. Nevertheless, John Citizen's personal capital fund will eventually be used to produce additional taxable income. A measure of the order of magnitude of this additional revenue can be obtained by considering a hypothetical situation. Let us assume that all the citizens who had obtained tax relief on share purchases commenced to use the income from their personal capital fund after 20 years. The average personal capital fund would be £2,766 (i.e., 20 x £138) and would be generating an income of £262 (i.e., 9.5 per cent). This would produce an annual tax contribution of £76 from each of the 40 million personal capital funds. Such a contribution would amount to £3 billion per annum. In practice, part of this revenue will be generated in less than 20 years if John Citizen uses the income from his investment in his lifetime, or over 20 years if his personal capital fund is inherited by beneficiaries. Nevertheless, the model demonstrates that while the Inland Revenue will need to increase taxation in the short term, the plan will more than compensate for this by additional revenue in due course.

At the same time, acceptance of the plan will have consequences other than stimulating wider ownership of shares. In particular, there will be a major effect on the British economy. There can be little doubt that management of business in the United Kingdom since the war has lacked the vitality shown by our overseas competitors. One reason has been that British management has been able to obtain capital too easily. Under the proposals contained in the plan, management will have to fight to obtain capital by a process which ensures examination, argument, and justification. Such a process will ensure that some projects will not earn the support of shareholders, and it follows that an increasing proportion of the available capital will be available to managements who can show themselves to be the most effective. There can be little doubt that a schism has developed between the individual shareholders and the institutional shareholders because of the belief that changes in management occur as a result of debate behind closed doors in the institutions. Under the plan, this schism will be swept aside and individual and institutional shareholders will have a common purpose in making management of British industry more efficient.

So far in this essay, we have not considered the political implication. We have identified that we are involved in an evolutionary system and there can be little doubt that, in due course, our democracy will require the economy to become accountable to the people. At the present time, state ownership will continue to be an alternative to the proposals identified in the plan. Once national share ownership is established, however, the system will become self-protective. The John Citizen who is a socialist is not likely to change his basic political philosophy, but at the same time, having accepted national share ownership as an alternative to state ownership, he is likely to influence the policy of the Labour Party. Equally so, an expansion of share ownership without accountability would eventually fail and bring Conservative policies into disrepute. It is these pressures that are likely to ensure that all major parties ultimately will accept national ownership of shares.

Notes

1. John H. Plumb, *England in the Eighteenth Century.* Baltimore: Penguin Books, 1951.
2. John Moyle, *The Pattern of Ordinary Share Ownership 1957-1970.* Cambridge: Cambridge University Press, 1971.
3. The Stock Exchange. *The Stock Exchange Survey of Share Ownership.* London: The Exchange, 1983.
4. The Stock Exchange. *The Changing Face of Share Ownership.* London: The Exchange, 1986.
5. Central Statistical Office. *Annual Abstract of Statistics, 1967.* London: The Office, 1967.
6. Central Statistical Office. *Annual Abstract of Statistics, 1985.* London: The Office, 1985.
7. Central Statistical Office. *Social Trends, 1970.* London: The Office, 1970.
8. Central Statistical Office. *Social Trends, 1984.* London: The Office, 1984.
9. Stuart M. Speiser, *The USOP Handbook.* New York: Council on International and Public Affairs, 1986.
10. Central Statistical Office. *Financial Statistics, 1986.* London: The Office, 1986.

15

UNIVERSAL SHARE OWNERSHIP THROUGH DONATED AND ACQUIRED SUPERSTOCK SHARES

by

Jeremy S. Bradshaw

Editor's Note: *Jeremy S. Bradshaw of Wells, Somerset, winner of third prize in the British competition, is a first-year student at the London School of Economics. Previously, he was the winner of the Sainsbury Essay Competition on wider share ownership. He uses the Super-Stock/Kitty Hawk Model as a starting point, but proposes an innovative two-track plan for "donated" and "acquired" shares, the former resembling Dr. Terry Mollner's "trusteeship trusts" described in Chapter 12. Bradshaw sees USOP as a substitute for the welfare state, and advocates reduced taxes, increased work incentives, and vigorous privatization.*

ABSTRACT

The government's privatization program is a recognition of people's need for an individual stake in society, but it fails to provide genuine universal share ownership. Britain is suffering from a stagnant society with competition stifled by interest groups in and outside Parliament. The rule of law must be reasserted through "principled" legislation. Low income tax with a 25 per cent maximum must be implemented. The welfare state should be dismantled to allow for financial independence, and competitive education and health care (emphasizing preventive medicine) must come. The government must create a pool of "USOP shares" from the capital required by the leading 200 or so London-listed companies, which it guarantees to the lending banks.

Two types of shares would emerge—"donated SuperStock" and "acquired SuperStock." Donated shares, paid for by proceeds of privatization sales, would be given by the government to all those under 18 annually to finance their health, educational, and general needs, particularly in later life in times of unemployment, sickness, and the like. Acquired shares would be issued according to the SuperStock model and would pay for themselves out of their own earnings. The government would aim to give about £20,000 of acquired shares to each adult, irrespective of wealth, status, or income. These shares would pay for themselves within about seven years. Needy recipients—the unemployed and pensioners—could opt for smaller amount of donated SuperStock instead, or a combination of both. The incentive would be for them to allow their shares to increase in capital value and live off the dividends. But with low taxes, the system would encourage work or employment of entrepreneurial talents. Initially, employee share ownership would be encouraged by tax incentive. Privatization would be reformed to benefit USOP.

Individual share ownership in Britain has been reborn. The idea has captured the imagination of the public. It is a sea change of fundamental importance.

—Nigel Lawson in addressing
the WSOC, London, 1985

The recognition by the Thatcher government of the basic proposition in any society that the individual needs to feel a sense of identity, a sense of achievement, and, above all, a sense of belonging has undoubtedly been of "fundamental importance." This is an acknowledgment of the fact that all human beings must possess a stake in the community in which they live and thus enjoy directly the fruits of their labor.

However, universal share ownership is not so much part of a political or economic creed as an essential anthropological, psychic requirement of the social animal—the human being.

Underlying the philosophy of the government's privatization program has been the classical liberal belief that the role of government is essentially to ensure justice, peace, and protection. Coupled with this has been the belief by some that government, by and large, is an impediment to the efficiency and competitiveness of industry.

Unfortunately, the success of privatization in providing a genuine democracy based on universal share ownership has been very limited. While pursuant to the British Gas sale there may exist around 7 million shareholders, the startling reality is that out of a population approaching 60 million, only 800,000 citizens possess shares in over *six* companies. So, as John Kay of the London Business School puts it: "If you want genuine share ownership, you want people buying bits of Amstrad, Marks and Spencer, and ICI—not just holding a few shares in British Gas or the TSB."

Privatization has been a success in that the government has rid itself of the responsibility for the performance of certain industries. An important aspect of privatization is the interest it has generated among the different classes of society, particularly the workers in the newly privatized industries. According to Dewe Rogerson, around 65 per cent of shareholders now come from the middle socioeconomic groups, compared with 46 per cent in 1983. But as Edgar Palamountain, chairman of London's Wider Share Ownership Council (WSOC), recognizes: "Statistically, it's a breakthrough, but there's a lot of work to be done yet."

Man must be forced to be free.

—Rousseau

For any radical plan of universal share ownership to be enacted, it is essential to point out to both the British politicians and the general public the principles involved, and its foreseen benefits for our prosperity, liberty, freedom, and democratic way of life. This means instilling hope into people. As Ralf Dahrendorf stated in "The New Liberty," his 1975 Reith Lecture: "If you have no hope there is hardly any incentive for sustained change."

Dahrendorf goes on to say:

> . . . representative government has been transferred into a gigantic
> and confused bargaining process between organized groups. . . . We

will not have the New Liberty unless we create a new kind of effective general public which guards and develops the roles by which we decide on our affairs . . . but the constitution of tomorrow is going to look different from yesterday's and today's.

It is my firm belief that the Universal Share Ownership Plan (USOP) will never be implemented unless the sinister opposition of those interest groups that have ingratiated themselves with key officials in the British government—indeed, the Parliament itself (in its most obvious form, sponsored MPs)—is overcome. A basic solution to this may be that an undertaking be extracted from all parties in the state, confirming that the maintenance of liberty and the rule of law is *the* (or at least *a*) cardinal principle of government.

The "rule of law" is the absence of arbitrary power. It means in Albert Dicey's words, "equality before the law," so that, "Be you ever so high, the Law is above you" (Thomas Fuller). Alas, in this century the law has become riddled with inconsistencies and contradictions so that the idea of liberal or natural rights, as expounded by John Locke, has been eroded.

In his book, *Lectures on the Relation Between Law and Public Opinion in England,* Dicey illustrates that by the Trades Disputes Act of 1906, a privilege of freedom from prosecution had been wrongfully extended to all trade unions. This is a privilege not possessed by any other person or body in the United Kingdom and the first time such an act had been passed by an English Parliament.

According to Graham and Clarke in their recently published book, *The New Enlightenment—The Rebirth of Liberalism,* this legislation:

> . . . opened the way to the emergence of a modern politics of accommodation in which parties win office by appealing to a coalition of interest groups with whom they compete for electoral favor by offering tax reliefs or some exemption from general rules.

For USOP to succeed we must recognize that there must be no favors given to one section of society at the expense of another, irrespective of present status, wealth, or income.

Since USOP ultimately is concerned with increasing the individual's liberty and freedom, it is essential not only to establish new bastions of democracy, such as universal share ownership, but to *rectify extant* impediments inherent in our society. For example, I believe our liberty has been threatened by Parliament in this century through its preoccupation over detail in the law-making process and a lesser concern with principle. Thus, the work of the courts has been made infinitely more difficult, especially as the jury (another pillar of liberty) is liable to be quite baffled by complex and "unprincipled" legislation.

The 1980 Employment Act is a prime case of a piece of "unprincipled" legislation. It provides that a work force is entitled to a closed shop if 80 per cent vote in favor of one. And so, the principle that the closed shop is wrong has been replaced by Mill's "tyranny of the majority" and, hence, the individual's freedom to choose is violated.

Therefore, all USOP legislation must heed the mistakes of the past. It should adhere to John Stuart Mill's principle of liberty: ". . . the only purpose for which power can be rightfully exercised over any member of a civilized community, against his Will, is to prevent harm to others."

> There is practically no single factor which has contributed more to the prosperity of the West than the relative certainty of the law which has prevailed there.
>
> —Frederick Hayek

In my plan for USOP, the priority of the government would be to put an immediate end to the welfare state—a creature that like a cancerous and uncontainable growth has become despised and criticized by most and understood by none. USOP offers the chance of ending "the sickness of an overgoverned society," to borrow Walter Lippman's phrase, in which government spending on Social Security, education, and health represents well over 50 per cent of the entire budget and, in numerical terms, equals nearly £2,000 per capita.

The USOP I envisage will be based on the principle of the Kitty Hawk plan espoused by Stuart Speiser, in which he suggests the top 200 or so companies listed on the London stock exchange finance all future capital growth through issuing a special stock, "USOP shares" or Super-Stock. The government would "pool" these shares and provide a guarantee to the lending banks, who would provide the necessary funds to pay for the shares, the theory being that SuperStock would probably pay for itself within about seven years.

Outline of Steps for Achieving USOP

(1) Decrease the tax rate immediately with a maximum rate of 25 per cent and thereby increase work incentive.

(2) Implement legislation producing Speiser's suggested pool of USOP shares from the best performing "big" companies quoted on the London stock exchange. The number may be recommended by a Royal

Commission's findings. The number and composition may vary over a period of time to reflect the performance of companies—i.e., profitability and growth.

(3) The USOP shares will divide into two categories:

(a) *Donated SuperStock.* Fully paid shares *given* by the government to individual citizens; and

(b) *Acquired SuperStock.* Unpaid shares that individuals receive, but only possess fully when the shares have paid for themselves and the interest owed to the lending banks.

Both types of shares will be non-transferable and non-voting. Conditions as to the selling of donated SuperStock will be laid down by the government. The acquired SuperStock will be saleable once fully owned by the individual citizen.

(4) The government will assign a specified amount of donated SuperStock—say, £1,250 worth—to every child under 18 on every birthday up until the age of 18. The income from these shares will be used by the parents or guardian of the children to finance their health care, education, and general welfare, thus replacing such welfare provisions as exist presently and widening the scope for choice by the parents.

These shares will provide the basis of future "USOP generations," and will be their safeguard against unemployment, poor health, and other such times of financial need. The government will determine the age at which these shares may be voluntarily sold. Perhaps the age may be 18 or 21 years, or alternatively the government may allow only a specified percentage to be sold each year—say, between 18 to 21, or possibly to 23. To discourage selling, the government may tax the sale of shares heavily, but government should avoid placing a tax on the dividends of donated SuperStock received by children.

(5) The government will systematically dismantle the millstone of a welfare state, terminating over a period of time the National Health Service, the whole educational establishment, and all Social Security payments. The speed with which this is enacted will depend upon the time taken to sell off existing assets to newly founded independent health and educational trusts. The aim will be to create an entirely privately operated health service, emphasizing preventive health care in a *competitive* environment. Responsibility for all educational facilities will effectively move into the private sphere, with fee-paying schools and higher education institutions (including universities) supplying precisely what the market forces of supply and demand dictate.

The government will use the capital raised from selling off these assets to fund the cost of the donated SuperStock and the transitional phase of moving into an entirely free-market economy.

(6) The role that acquired SuperStock will play will be essential to the object of providing all citizens with USOP shares. The government should aim to provide a set value of acquired SuperStock to all over 18 years. I suggest a sum in the region of £20,000.

Present recipients of Social Security benefits or state pensions will qualify, however, as "needy recipients" and therefore will be able to apply for donated SuperStock. In other words, they will be able to possess immediately shares which in themselves will offer both an income in the form of dividends and great potential capital growth. The penalty for receiving donated SuperStock in place of acquired SuperStock will be a large reduction in the overall amount of SuperStock allotted to that individual. So, if the government were to propose giving £20,000 worth of acquired SuperStock to all individuals, then perhaps those who opted for the maximum allowable number of donated shares would receive only £8,000 to £10,000 SuperStock in all.

This system is advantageous because needy recipients would have an incentive *not* to sell their donated stock, but rather to benefit from its capital growth and the income from its dividends. Therefore, idle, unemployed individuals may feel an added incentive to work (especially as the tax system would encourage it) or to put their entrepreneurial talents to the test. Older pensioners may understandably opt for their quota of donated shares, as waiting approximately seven years for acquired shares may be unrealistic.

A sliding scale should be formulated, enabling needy recipients to opt for only a percentage of donated stock, and so allowing them some acquired stock. The smaller the amount of donated stock, the less the overall loss in terms of the initial capital outlay of the shares will be. For example, if £2,000 of donated stock is demanded, then out of a possible £20,000 worth of acquired stock the individual would receive, say, £15,000 to £16,000 of acquired stock. The beauty of this system is that the needy will not necessarily be losing out by opting for donated stock. If they do not spend all of it, they will benefit from the capital growth and future dividend income.

Because of the limits of the total amount of USOP stock available, all citizens promised USOP shares will receive small amounts each year. But there will be a slightly weighted allocation system favoring all individuals in their 50s, so that they will receive full possession of £20,000 worth of shares sooner than the younger generations. Of course, future generations with the financial independence inherent in USOP share ownership will be able to determine their own retirement age.

(7) The government will vigorously pursue privatization, but with one fundamental difference: 80 per cent of new issues will be allocated to USOP with 20 per cent going to the stock exchange. In this way, the government will be financing part of its USOP program while ensuring that all citizens benefit from previously nationalized industries.

(8) When USOP shares are sold, they will revert to the USOP pool. Should the pool find that in the process of time it accumulates unpromised SuperStock, it may be designated to charities on a rota basis.

(9) The government should encourage a plan such as that outlined in Weitzman's *The Share Economy,* whereby employees receive part of their income as a predetermined percentage of the profits, say, a third. However, the government should seek to encourage employees to purchase shares in their own workplaces by extending especially devised tax incentives. For example, the government could reduce the tax rate by 1 per cent on the income earned on the shares of an employee's own company for a period of two or three years up to a maximum amount of £3000 to £4000.

(10) The government should ultimately reduce and eventually replace donated SuperStock by acquired SuperStock in that donated stock will have served its primary purpose of allowing the immediate dismantling of the welfare state and the educational and health services. Moreover, taxes will be reduced further by the reduction in government expenditure. The weighting system (giving priority to approaching pensioners) will also be eradicated after a period of time, enabling every citizen to receive a specific and equal percentage of new USOP shares annually. At that point, a review of USOP should take place and its future be reevaluated, particularly in regard to integrating USOP shares with the normal trade shares on the London stock exchange.

16

TOWARD WIDER SHARE OWNERSHIP: THE NATIONAL SOCIAL WORK SCHEME (NSWS)

by

Susan Potterton

Editor's Note: *Susan Potterton of Moreton Morrell, Warwickshire, is a housewife, trained as a geologist and mathematician. She describes herself as a small shareholder and a history buff. Mrs. Potterton uses some features of the SuperStock/Kitty Hawk Model, including the reservoir of annual corporate capital additions, but rejects others. She ties eligibility for USOP shares to performance of social and community work, thus anticipating the topic of the present 1988 essay competitions in the United States and Great Britain.*

ABSTRACT

This essay seeks to make wider share ownership an achievable aim by introducing a scheme that:

- uses ordinary shares;
- obtains the approval of the overwhelming majority;

- is simple;

- benefits industry and the economy;

- gives the unemployed new drive;

- is approved by the stock market; and

- offers secure investment.

It achieves these aims by:

- opening up the scheme to the unemployed, the handicapped, the housewife, the pensioner;

- giving them social work which is not presently carried out;

- creating a pool of shares to pay for such work and allowing these shares to be traded in the normal way;

- redirecting the education and training infrastructure to improve the quality of the labor pool;

- making the City—London's equivalent of New York's Wall Street—and the people realize that share ownership by many leads to a greater interest in the economic well-being of the country by those who at present have no influence on and little stake in the existing system.

Aim and Introduction

The aim of this paper is to devise a plan for wider share ownership that will stimulate the economy without resorting to confiscation or increased taxation. The plan outlined will suggest a three-pronged approach:
(1) The introduction of share ownership to targeted sectors of the populace, linked with the problem of unemployment.
(2) The education of the population to have a sense of ownership of, and identity with, the nation's economy.
(3) Making investment in shares as acceptable as investing in building societies, transcending politics.

Any effort to promote wider share ownership comes up against problems which are inextricably linked with the mosaic of politics and economics—the complexities and anomalies of the welfare state, unemployment, and the stock market itself. The danger is that a plan, which takes on a more and more complex nature in order to confront all these problems, may strangle itself. Thus, before coming up with any scheme that is simple, workable, worthwhile, and so able to obtain the approval of the overwhelming majority, the main obstacles and some historical experiments should be studied.

Shortcomings in the Present Situation

The present situation related to jobs, unemployment, welfare benefits, taxes, and the stock market has many shortcomings. Here are some that affect schemes to establish wider share ownership.

(1) *The Welfare System.*   With each new government, the system becomes more cumbersome and the infrastructure increases in complexity. However, two types of benefits stand out as being effective in meeting real needs: child benefits and mortgage tax relief. It is the aim of this essay to come up with another such benefit, offering the automatic (but earned) opportunity for share ownership to those with the least ability to acquire shares by purchasing them with "disposable" income after meeting daily living expenses.

(2) *Unemployment.*

    (a) People are taxed into unemployment when the unemployment benefits are similar to take-home pay. With such pay scales, many companies find it almost impossible to fill vacancies, even though unemployment is high. Many long-term unemployed are also participating in the informal economy by doing jobs off-the-books and cannot afford to work legitimately for less than, say, £180 per week.

    (b) Unemployment benefits are not conditional on doing any work.

    (c) The welfare system cannot prevent abuse of benefits. Many part-time workers are paid out of the till while also drawing the dole.

    (d) The rate of change in manufacturing and services is accelerating faster than the national capacity to deliver trained employees. The unskilled section at the bottom of the labor pyramid is being joined by increasing numbers of semi-skilled and redundant workers, who could only fill new jobs demanding higher skills through massive investment in retraining. Thus, public-work programs will never be more than a short-term palliative for unemployment. Many women are left behind by technology when they opt out for several years to undertake the very important task of bringing up the next generation.

(3) *Shares.*

    (a) PEP (Personal Equity Plan). The underlying weakness is that the small investor enjoys exemption from capital gains tax up to £6,300 per year, and probably pays the lower rates of income tax, so the main beneficiaries would be those who have already used up their exemption and use the PEP to gain further tax relief. This leaves out the majority. PEP should be abolished immediately.

    (b) Employee Share Ownership Schemes. Various types of incentive have been provided to encourage wider share ownership among employees. The resulting improvement in productivity, profits, and other psychological and material advantages to employees and management has been well documented. While this is a good way of combating intensifying foreign competition through increased productivity, there are two major disadvantages:

        (i) All taxpayers are underwriting a selected group of workers—namely, those who have jobs with successful companies, the shares of which have value over the long term.

        (ii) Housewives, the unemployed, pensioners, the disabled, and young people of voting age (but engaged in further education) cannot participate in such schemes.

These employee share ownership schemes, therefore, must be implemented in parallel with, and complementary to, a plan for wider share ownership among those not able to participate in the former.

(4) *The Stock Market.*

    (a) Although there are more people with a stake in the stock market than ever before, there are millions more still conscious of looking in on the feast from the outside, including those who do not identify their future pensions with the strength of the stock market in which their contributions have been invested. They do not see beyond the City's visible symbol, the stock market, and all the national and international earning power and mobilization of capital to strengthen the industrial base that it represents. They see only the profits made from speculation. Pension funds and other institutions are the opposite of direct and individual ownership, and this faceless capitalism is in danger of squeezing out the individual.

    (b) The building societies, on the other hand, have been successful since they project an image to the public of security, accessibility, and simplicity of dealing. Because of the approval of the overwhelming majority, they have transcended politics.

(c) Many people feel insecure about how to buy shares and where to seek advice. People favor such ordinary, familiar institutions as the neighborhood branch of their bank for their personal financial dealings, and are put off by the idea of going through a stockbroker. They also distrust investing in an unfamiliar medium.

(d) There is opposition from the City to a multitude of small investors because of the system of individually registered shares and the paperwork it would generate, as well as the question of profitability. But this is probably not an insurmountable problem.

(e) The volatility of the stock market makes it too risky for the poor person. This is the biggest single obstacle to be overcome by any proposed scheme of wider share ownership. To target wider share ownership only at those who have more than £5,000 invested in the building societies, does not address the problem of the inequities in the present system.

(f) Distributing new government privatization shares free to the entire adult population is not the answer either. Not only would this method fail to engender the feeling of everyone having a true stake in the system, but the poorest would tend to sell off their shares, thus re-establishing the traditional patterns of ownership and incomes.

(5) *Taxes.*   The tax system is not neutral between different forms of savings and investment. A very important aspect that the stock market must take advantage of, and publicize in conjunction with promoting a wider share ownership scheme, is that while interest on capital invested in building societies is taxed at the source (as are dividends), there is the £6,300 capital gain exemption for investments in the stock market. This must be incorporated in any effective scheme for universal share ownership.

A Page from History.

Just as today there are many reservations about the present welfare system not working as it was originally conceived, a similar situation existed at the time of the Speenhamland Poor-Relief System of 1795 with disastrous consequences.

In order to contain increasing unemployment, a farm laborer's wages were made up to a minimum living wage by a supplement from the parish. The farmers gained by paying lower and lower wages while smallholders, who paid property taxes but did not employ anyone, bore part of the burden but gained nothing. The laborer, finding that industriousness would not secure him a better wage and that laziness still guaranteed him a minimum wage, became less productive.

The rates had to be quadrupled in 20 years to bear this burden. Farmers and landowners paid in rates what should have been paid in wages, but received much less productivity for it. In the end, the farmers paid one-third and the parish two-thirds of the wages. There was no inducement for a worker on supplementary poor-relief to increase his skills. The system was abolished on the principle that a man must maintain himself by his own exertions.

Main Arguments for a New Scheme

While *The USOP Handbook,* outlining the Kitty Hawk Universal Share Ownership Plan, has stimulating ideas for this essay contest, it has certain limitations:

(1) The plan gives people shares with no contribution from them. People do not appreciate what they have not worked for.

(2) The Labour Party raison d'etre would be threatened by a raw USOP (Kitty Hawk) proposal or any similar proposal. This must be defused by obtaining massive popular support for any such scheme so that it would not be stillborn by political attacks.

(3) Twenty years is far too long to wait for the benefits, especially since the shares would be non-negotiable and essentially fixed in capital value.

(4) While unemployment is a separate issue, it is also an enormously significant factor in the consideration of the USOP scheme. By merely paying the unemployed with USOP shares, the actual problem of unemployment is not dealt with. Were the USOP scheme to be put into practice, it would lessen the pressure on any government to make a serious effort to solve this problem. It would merely be an alternative method of coping with the burden of the dole bill.

(5) The Kitty Hawk plan has all the makings of becoming impossibly complicated while having the best of intentions. Shares that have so many restrictions and qualifications can hardly be called traditional shares. The plan would hardly lend to meaningful partici-

pation in capitalism if one's shares were non-transferable and non-voting. The plan would thus have all the appeal of "owning" the nationalized industries.

(6) By separating the two types of shares, the stock market (open market) share base will not increase. It would only serve to put a higher premium on the "real" shares, and the "them and us" syndrome would be preserved.

In order for a plan for wider share ownership to succeed (taking child benefits and mortgage tax relief as successful examples to emulate), it must:

- use ordinary shares with no qualifications or restrictions;

- have the approval of the overwhelming majority in order to withstand changes in government;

- be simple to administer;

- achieve the twin aims of benefiting both industry and the economy as a whole, as well as the populace at large, especially the targeted sections of the community;

- have the willing support of the stock market; and

- offer security.

The Plan Proposed: National Social Work Scheme (NSWS)

Eligibility.   In the area of unemployment, we need to separate the need to survive from the need to work. Any system of taxation and welfare should ideally protect the unemployed, but allow them a net addition to their standard of living if they do work of any kind and at any level. This plan would cut at right angles through the social structure of the country and be open to all registered on the welfare system.

The Work.   All those registered on the welfare system would have the opportunity to improve the quality of their lives (and that of the community as a whole) by being paid in scheme shares for vital work needed in such areas as human services, environmental protection, and education. The overall success of the plan requires a very carefully structured and well-thought-out national scheme of work (perhaps encompassing applications from charities and the like) so that it is not a piecemeal conglomeration of make-work jobs.

Financial Basis.   Such work would be paid for in ordinary shares, representing new capital for the expansion of the industrial base, and also privatization of government-owned companies. These shares would be available from a pool so that a steady work program can be maintained. The financial basis of the scheme shares is to be a simple one with all NSWS shares of new capital provided by private funding but guaranteed by government.

The danger in such lending is that due to government guarantees, the lending institution need not be as scrupulous about the security of the loan as it would be without such a guarantee. The scheme gets around this because the people earning the scheme shares will have a free choice of shares. A poor risk would be unpopular, and since the shares are ordinary tradeable shares, the law of supply and demand—i.e., share price—will govern. All new capital sought from the private sector and in the privatization of government-owned companies would have a very substantial allotment of new shares for the wider share ownership pool.

Direct Participation in the Economy. A very important point is that since the shares would be earned in the ways described above, the holder would not only place an intrinsic value on them because they were genuinely earned. In selling them on the open market, he or she would become part of the stock market system through his or her own effort. The question of how to get the widest participation and sense of identity of the people with the economy is answered.

Such a self-perpetuating system would stimulate the economy and the nation's people. The words of a black woman being interviewed in February 1986 on Radio 4 inspired my determination to write this essay: "Equality does not mean anything to a person who has had no opportunities—it's a 'pie in the sky' idea." This would be her opportunity.

Effect on the Economy. To earn the shares in this scheme, the work being performed should not interfere with the normal economy, or infringe upon the earning capacity of any business nor threaten the employment levels of a business or government institution. The obvious areas are community betterment and charitable work. This has sometimes been the stumbling block of the American "workfare," and was the cause of the failure of Speenhamland.

Voluntary Basis. There would be no pressure at all on those who do not wish to work. They would merely forego the opportunity to earn shares. This would solve the problem of political pressure, where no one is able to criticize certain sectors of the unemployed population for fear of being labeled uncaring. The scheme would exclude wage earners without penalizing them. In general, the poorer sectors of the population are far better off than those of a century ago, but there is still a large gulf between the rich and the poor, between the haves and the have-nots.

Untapped Resources.   Pensioners are marvelous people, totally underutilized and a growing segment of the population. They collectively represent the brains and brawn that worked for what we have now. The youth are full of ideals that develop into all the wrong emotions so easily. They too must have the opportunity to advance themselves through their own work. Housebound women, who bring up the next generation or care for elderly or sick relatives, would automatically be raised from a low social status to a higher one by being paid with NSWS shares.

Women.   A common factor in the success of the child benefit and mortgage relief schemes is that the people on the receiving end of the former are mainly women. A very sizeable proportion of the present shareholding public are women. In all cases, although these women may or may not be working, they are not naturally formed into interest or pressure groups, such as those industrial leaders fear with trade union ownership. This is a big factor in reducing resistance against universal share ownership. The question of whether the recent coal miners' strike failed because the majority of women played a behind-the-scene role (not wanting to lose their homes) has relevance in this context.

Education.   As an adjunct to the NSWS system, there is an urgent need to raise the quality of the labor pool and to make more of the unemployed employable.

The City.   Of course, many changes would have to come to the City. By popular demand, the stock market would have to become more "user friendly," probably educating the public through the media. A computerized system would have to be devised to deal with the paperwork engendered by so many shareholders.

Stability of the Market.   The plus side would be that, as with the institutions that are locked into the stock market, the new investors (investing the sweat of their labor, so to speak) would be tied to the British system, which should make for a more stable market. This should go a long way toward solving the security worries that separate the building societies from the stock market by such a wide gulf.

A more stable market could decrease speculation. Financial gains through speculation do not promote jobs or productivity. Stability in any market should increase yields by decreasing interest rates, so that benefits are tied more to profits than to speculation.

Share-Owning Pattern.   It would be natural for some people to revert back to old habits and sell their shares (but, hopefully, not all). However, the old traditional pattern of share ownership would have been altered radically, and there would develop a gradual evolution— rather than a revolution—toward the concept of universal share owner- ship.

17

A PRACTICAL EXPERIMENT IN UNIVERSAL SHARE OWNERSHIP

by

Jack B. Grant

Editor's Note: *Jack B. Grant, CSS, MSW of Giffnock, Glasgow, was educated at the University of Glasgow and at Tulane University, where he received a Master of Social Work degree in 1968. He served as industrial relations officer for Imperial Chemical Industries Ltd. and as a consultant, lecturer, and demonstration project director in community work and social services, most recently at the University of Glasgow. Grant would use the SuperStock/Kitty Hawk Model as the basis for an experimental program in the depressed Greater Easterhouse District of Glasgow (population 60,000). He would distribute "community shares" and identify their source as part of the general public's tax funds and savings, rather than as charity. As this is written (early 1988), he is actually attempting to implement such a program in Greater Easterhouse, thus giving our 1986 essay competition its first practical test. His hands-on experience with the problems of the working poor and the unemployed provide valuable insights from the standpoint of the depressed areas.*

ABSTRACT

This paper discusses USOP as an economic plan to combat poverty and is contrasted with plans to create a trade union bank in 1971 and political proposals made in 1983. It is argued that there is sufficient theory to warrant a practical experiment, and there is a proposal for an ideal site in the Greater Easterhouse District of Glasgow.

The essay discusses some of the problems that an experiment will encounter. There is special focus on the psychological impact with emphasis on education, communication, and ideology.

Proposals are made to locate the initial sources of funds from finance already made available by government, the EEC, and the regions through grants, loans, and inducements to attract industry to development areas. Also suggested are new sources of funds, namely, 10 per cent of VAT and the millions of unclaimed Social Security benefits.

Criticized is the opinion of Robert Lekachman in *The USOP Handbook*,[1] who recommends that instead of universal share ownership, we should move toward more decent provisions of Social Security. Failure of British experiments in Social Security and welfare are noted. USOP is favored as a method for dealing with the crises caused by deterioration in levels of income for millions in the face of growing productive power.

Building Institutions for Economic Democracy

The immense and impressive work that has gone into developing the concepts of the Universal Share Ownership Plan (USOP) is a breathtaking example of the level of creative thinking that Western democracy badly needs if it is to survive its growing economic and social crises.[2]

In 1971, I proposed the establishment of an investment bank, whereby trade unionists could engage in capital formation to help save existing enterprises and enable trade unionists to participate in the management and rewards of successful companies. Had the idea been adopted at the time, over £1.5 billion could have been saved by members, to which one must add profits from banking operations. Plans for developing investments in the insurance business could also have contributed substantially to the bank's income. Unhappily, although there was grassroots interest, trade union leaders refused to listen. In 1984, however, Unity Trust was established as the first trade union bank. With aims similar to those I proposed in 1971, it is now in the process of developing plans for employee share ownership (ESOP).

The thinking and emotions that influenced the creation of Unity Trust should be carefully analyzed in order to understand the processes by which change occurred—how particular trade union leaders, previously fixated in outmoded ideology, came to accept the need to participate as mature partners in the economy.

There is now a sense of urgency. In a 1983 paper, I wrote:

> The declared aim of our modern democratic society to be based on justice and fairness is far from reality. In the course of exercising our freedoms we have, in effect, created three nations—the owners and controllers of resources, those who are at work, and those who are out of work and are totally dependent on state aid. . . . The need to plan policies that can embrace economic change, productive efficiency, *and* human welfare has never been so imperative since the war. We have *no* policy to deal with labor availability—except a policy of disposal via redundancy and unemployment. The ranks of the Third Nation are therefore being swelled by skilled workers from every walk of life—a growing mass of disillusioned and confused men and women and a younger generation denied the prospects of adult independence. . . . We seem well on the way to achieving a measure of social chaos unequalled [in] this century—at a time when we have the greatest opportunity man has ever had of creating and distributing wealth.[3]

USOP has gone a long way to answer the problem of how to include the non-working population in an economic plan. Until now, I envisaged a solution by political means, and in the above paper, pointed out that the "third nation" contained 15 million people who, if they could act together, could form an overwhelming political lobby to bargain for economic improvement. This plan would now seem to be unnecessary in the face of a workable economic plan on the scale envisaged by USOP.

Sufficient theoretical preparation seems to have been accomplished to experiment with USOP in order to gain the necessary practical experience upon which evaluation can proceed. The main theme of this essay will, therefore, be devoted to preparing the groundwork for such an experiment to take place.

I predict that the most crucial battle will take place in the realm of ideas and beliefs. Communication can be bedeviled by labels that haunt both sides of the economic divide. Such phrases as "making everyone a capitalist—or socialist" reflect the fears, disdain, and opposition of people who have suffered decades of economic deprivation and of those who have experienced insecurity while succeeding in the harsh competitiveness of the modern economic jungle. Ideological confrontation has produced the communication and tools of conflict with scant attention paid to any prospect of cooperation. If we are to win the battle of ideas, we must present the plan in pragmatic terms and avoid the language that perpetuates the "them and us" divide. To make the plan digestible for the majority of the British population, the following is proposed: The sources of funds should be identified for what they are—as savings and taxes accumulated by the banks and the government from people's own savings and contributions.

On the government side, a percentage of the Value Added Tax (VAT) that the government collects on the sale of goods and services should be returned each year to accumulate in a USOP fund. Total net proceeds from VAT in 1984-85 were £18,535 million. Ten per cent of this could be returned to the taxpayers to enable the trustees of USOP to purchase "community shares" in the 1,000 or so most successful companies. Since a portion of the taxes they have paid is now being returned to them, people will not feel they are receiving charity (which, of course, they are not). This is very important in view of the stigma people continue to feel in respect to claiming what they are entitled to under Social Security.

Indeed, during 1981-82, there were £836 million of unclaimed Social Security benefits,[4] and here is yet another source of funds for USOP. This would return to the people that to which they are entitled and therefore is not charity.

With regard to the return of VAT, the government will not lose, as has been pointed out elsewhere. USOP shares will begin to replace the direct grants, loans, and inducements the government already makes to industry. Government could also gain by the generation of new jobs, producing taxes on earnings and VAT on increased purchasing power.

A Regional Approach

Likewise, the millions spent by regions (from local taxes) and from the EEC (which provides matching funds) to attract industry, especially to the heavily depressed areas, could be handed over as USOP shares rather than as grants and financial inducements at present. Once again, local residents will feel that it is out of their tax contributions that the shares are being bought and thus is not charity. Additional capital can be negotiated from banks and loans guaranteed as outlined in *The USOP*

Handbook.

Excluding bank loans, the sums that could be made available are:[5]

National Account:	£2.8 Billion per Annum (10 per cent of VAT plus Unclaimed Social Security Benefit)
Regional Account:	£5.024 Million (Economic and Industrial Development Budget)

There would, therefore, be sufficient funds available for the experiment to take place in one or two regions and to pinpoint one district in each for a combined special development program. An area that has all the characteristics of extraordinary high unemployment, high levels of Social Security payments, a housing repair crisis, and high expenditure on health and welfare services is the Glasgow district of Greater Easterhouse with a population of 60,000.

This area would be ideal for the experiment since it has already attracted the notice of the EEC as well as a concentration of resources by the region, but with few fundamental changes to the economic structure so far. The following statistics[6] show only too clearly the levels of deprivation:

March 1986 (Scotland): Per Cent Unemployed and Claiming Benefit

Total:	15.9	Male:	19.5	Female:	11.3
Easterhouse:	40.0	Male:	35.0	Female:	45.0

The region itself is keen to engage in any initiative that would relieve the crushing burden of poverty in Strathclyde. It has recently proposed the use of £5 million from its own pension fund for investment purposes in order to promote employment. It has also pioneered a scheme for subsidizing wages to enable companies to engage more labor, and has set up more than 50 projects to help community initiatives (mainly in the provision of badly needed social and community services). Other sources of finance are:

- Scottish Development Agency

- Glasgow District Council

- Manpower Services Commission

- The Department of Employment

- EEC Social Fund

- European Regional Development Fund

- Urban Aid

- Pension Funds

With the availability of several billion pounds, it will become possible to develop a major project to attract the expansion of existing successful enterprises and new enterprises into the area of Greater Easterhouse. The offer to these companies of easy access to finances by means of USOP Shares, together with other inducements (such as rate-free premises and employee wage subsidies), should make Easterhouse an ideal site for industrial expansion. Such easy access to finance, much of which can be given as grants and the remainder as low-interest loans[7] to purchase USOP shares, could offset high interest rates, currently inhibiting the use of borrowed capital by new enterprises. As pointed out in *The USOP Handbook,* availability of new capital for investment and for raising productivity would not contribute to inflationary pressure. USOP shareholders will also be on par with existing stockholders who "under government grants and tax credits, own new capital without investing any more money."[8]

Organization

The USOP Handbook provides an excellent framework for creating the organization necessary to operate the plan. The following are important elements:

The experiment not only must be adopted by central government and the Strathclyde region but by major Scottish banks and the companies one would hope to attract. USOP must have an appeal to *all* as opening up a new era in economic progress. The trade unions must obviously be major partners, while Unity Trust, the trade union bank, may wish to undertake a key role. I have deliberately omitted the role of political parties as I believe that the idea will gain cross-party support. Participation at all levels of negotiation and organization must be reserved for members of the local community who will become USOP shareholders.

Communications

The main resource for providing education and publicity to the district would be the Regional Council. It has the organizational structure, stretching into the community to engage in public education and community work, and for listing the collaboration of all the agencies that would be involved, including central government departments and the EEC. As the largest region in the U.K., Strathclyde has the infrastructure of technical, professional, and physical resources to support the project. Above all, it has the *will*, as evidenced by its research studies and its anti-poverty strategy for the 1980s.[9]

Education should take the form of simple, straightforward description and, where possible, role-play should be employed. The message that charity is *not* involved should be emphasized. Abstract political meanderings should be avoided at all costs. Education of the public at large will obviously require a major effort.

Problems

Inevitably, problems will arise concerning the non-voting element in the plan, whereby USOP shareholders will be unable to directly influence management by using their combined voting strength or by selling or transferring their shares. This, and USOP's relation to any ESOP that might be developed, are some of the good reasons for launching an experiment.

Questions to whether income from USOP should affect continued rights to welfare benefits will require detailed study and negotiation with the central government. Since current levels of maintenance are grossly inadequate and require major reassessment, my own recommendation would be to allow the welfare recipient's income to rise without any claw-back until a satisfactory level of income is achieved. The USOP experiment can therefore be used to answer fundamental questions about the levels of income required to obliterate poverty.

Argument

I accept the fact that in an economy experiencing successive technological revolutions, income from employment will no longer be available to millions of previously employed persons. Without income from their labor, workers ought to share in the wealth produced by robots and capital investment. The maintenance of *income* is crucial not only for basic human needs but also to provide the growing markets that advanced technology makes possible. Capital may no longer need labor to produce its wealth, but it needs a well-paid community to consume its products. USOP provides a *peaceful* means for radical redistribution of wealth "without confiscation or the imposition of taxes"—the only major alternatives which in the past have provided not only conflictual but have singularly failed to eradicate the great divide between the "haves" and "have nots," irrespective of the opposing political shades of successive governments. Opponents of this argument will no doubt plead that the reasons for failure were due to weaknesses in the application of political dogma and that if "pure" or "extreme" measures were taken, then their proposals would work. Well, there are ample examples of economies where extreme measures are used, but the cost is usually paid for by the loss of civil and political rights.

Since USOP will eventually guarantee a large proportion of a worker's earnings, the introduction of USOP into the U.S. economy will give it an advantage over countries which do not adopt the plan. The advantages would be the relaxation of high-wage demands and the lessening of wage inflation, together with the removal of psychological barriers to higher productivity. It is important for Britain, therefore, to take a lead in the introduction of USOP in order to be able to compete with possible developments in the United States.

On the general question of a shorter working week, I agree that USOP can become an ideal bridge, ensuring that income is not exclusively tied to hours of work, but is directly related to the returns of investment and higher productivity. This would be a matter for detailed study by both trade unions and employers, as would the proposal that redundancy be handled in the way undertaken by several states in the U.S. (where rather than reducing a work force by 20 per cent, the working week is reduced to four days with the fifth day paid for by unemployment benefit).

The recommendation by Robert Lekachman[10] that instead of share ownership, we should move toward more decent provisions of social benefit (via Social Security) fails to appreciate that as long as the "have nots" are made to feel that they are a distinct "problem"—to be aided by welfare provision—such identification is, by itself, stigmatizing, labeling, and therefore self-defeating.

Further, the manner by which welfare provision has to compete with other items in the national budget (such as defence) will always ensure a low priority for welfare. For employment incentive purposes also, governments can claim that welfare incomes must not rise beyond a certain point so that minimum wages are not affected.

The most recent experiment in Britain to alleviate the poverty that continues to affect those on welfare benefits was undertaken between 1969 and 1978. Known as Community Development Projects (CDPs), this cost the government 5.5 million pounds at the time. The aims were to ensure that there was the fullest take-up of welfare benefits in cash and in kind and to create services and fill gaps in others so that the populations concerned (in 12 different poverty areas) received the maximum in benefits and services. These projects were to no avail—poverty still pervaded these areas after completion. The reasons were obvious. There were no basic changes in the economic structure and people still remained stigmatized, this time because of all the attention they were given. Their mere address prevented them from being considered for a job!

Conclusion

Poverty, being relative, requires a multi-dimensional equalization process, beginning with equality of opportunity in incomes. Why should only a portion of the population suffer the cost of industrial reorganization? With old industries contracting, thousands of workers bear the cost in redundance to make way for technological improvements and the creation of new industries.

When new industries appear, they are predominantly capital intensive, and so the economy is caught up in a process of continuous job displacement—yet only a percentage of the population bears the cost. Why should a person who is disabled or becoming old require less to live on than the lowest of the low paid worker? Is he or she not in just as great a need for income as before, or at least in as great a need as that of the average earner? And why should he or she not "earn" the equivalent of an average wage? There is no reason why this cannot be done in an affluent society. It is our ideas and false values that create the problems upon which we construct immense bureaucracies and spend so much time and money in trying to find solutions.

The money that industry needs each year (24 billion pounds in Britain) will be invested in the names of the community at large under universal share ownership and will at least guarantee that between 7 and 20 years, the income from such investment will be broadly spread among those who until now have not gained a penny from capital investment, but whose taxes and savings have hitherto made it possible for only a small percentage of the population (approximately 6 per cent) to reap all the benefits.

It is my earnest wish that those who are interested in pursuing USOP should now feel that the time is ripe to launch such an experiment.

Notes

1. Robert Lekachman in Stuart M. Speiser, *The USOP Handbook.* New York: Council on International and Public Affairs, 1986, p. 154.
2. Speiser, op. cit.
3. Jack B. Grant, "Proposal for Unemployed and Pensioners' Trade Union." Unpublished paper, 1983.
4. Data from Department of Health and Social Security (DHSS) Information Office, Edinburgh.
5. Strathclyde Regional Council, "Annual Report and Financial Statement 1985/86." Glasgow: Chief Executive's Department, The Council, 1986.
6. Data from Strathclyde Trades Union Congress (STUC) and Strathclyde Regional Council, Glasgow, n.d.
7. See Speiser, op. cit., p. 43, for example of low interest rates available to large corporations.
8. Ibid., p. 67.
9. Strathclyde Regional Council, *Social Strategy for the 80s.* Glasgow: Chief Executive's Department, The Council, n.d.
10. Lekachman in Speiser, op. cit., pp. 154-55.

18

THE SMOOTH FLIGHT: UNIVERSAL SHARE OWNERSHIP AND THE SUSTAINABLE ECONOMIC SYSTEM

by

David Hill

Editor's Note: *David Hill of Rothesbank, Nemphlar, Lanark, is a chartered mechanical engineer who has worked for such companies as Austin, General Motors, and Rolls Royce Aero. He also served on the Trade, Industry, and Economics Panel of the Scottish Liberal Party.*

His essay analyzes the SuperStock/Kitty Hawk Model and explores the reasons for its primitive aerodynamic status. He provides it with turbojet thrust by linking USOP to ESOP, with the USOP fund standing as guarantor of ESOP share values up to their tangible asset values. His concept of limited life of title to capital assets, measured by the real life expectancy of those assets, is similar to ideas expressed by Shann Turnbull (see Chapter 6). But Hill applies this principle uniquely to serve as a basis for linking USOP and ESOP as well as improving the entire system of capital formation. He also addresses the environmental impact of USOP.

ABSTRACT

The essay begins with a condensation of the USOP Kitty Hawk plan taken from Stuart M. Speiser's *The USOP Handbook.*

It then goes on to develop means of linking USOP with employee share ownership, and explains how with suitable innovations to accounting procedures it could be possible to do this without committing the government (as guarantor for USOP) to excessive risks. Essentially, this is done by linking the face value of ESOP shares with the value of the plant. The essay explains that this is feasible with small to medium firms, although not for large ones.

A further measure for making share face values more in step with the reality of the production facilities they represent is suggested. It is explained that this would (a) make shares easier understood by the masses who, under USOP, are going to own them; (b) make redistribution of wealth a continuous process; (c) result in a more continuous creation of new capital, thereby aiding USOP; and (d) enable the monetary system to cope with an expanding, steady state, or even a temporarily diminishing economy. In this context, the possible effects of "limits to growth" are briefly explored.

The essay concludes by describing the attractiveness of USOP to various shades of political opinion and makes the point that its potential for coping responsibly with environmental pressures is one of its prime virtues.

Introduction

"You get no marks for trying." This principle is indoctrinated into every youngster who takes up a career in engineering. Unless his or her pet ideas are actually developed into something useful, they will sink without trace and will earn no credit to their originator. In the field which covers the interaction of economics and society, the same principle applies, although it is rarely so brutally expressed. Much good creative thinking has failed to produce the effect it deserves, and has had no impact. The concept of universal share ownership has the potential to avoid this fate. It could "earn marks."

Western-style capitalist democracies give to all their members a combination of freedom, justice, and affluence which, as far as we can tell, surpasses anything achieved by previous civilizations. Nonetheless, they do have certain defects, even to the extent of containing the seeds of their own destruction. There is a widespread view that the defects are systematic rather than ideological, and are to do with the tendency within present day capitalist systems for wealth, and with it power, to accumulate unevenly into the hands of too small a proportion of the population. Spreading capital ownership more widely, even universally, is seen by many as a way of averting the consequences of this self-destructive tendency, and still further improving the degree of freedom, justice, and prosperity available to all. And because universal share ownership comes, so to speak, in a variety of flavors with which to attract a variety of political tastes, its chances of being successfully implemented are good.

Governments throughout recent history have tried physical redistribution of wealth by various methods. Some, like communism, have concentrated on confiscation and control of property by the state. Naturally this has provoked strong opposition from the wealthy, to the point of bloodshed and increased oppression, and when redistribution has been achieved it has usually failed to bring about a significant improvement in the conditions of ordinary people. Alternatively, governments, such as that of the U.S., have distributed newly won agricultural lands to pioneers, subject only to provisions that the pioneers should hold the lands for a minimum time and work them. Unfortunately, the benefits of this strategy have usually been temporary—title to the lands tending eventually to accumulate within a few hands.

The Kitty Hawk Model

To avoid these pitfalls, and to achieve a self-perpetuating mechanism of wealth redistribution, several thinkers have come up with schemes that build the existing highly effective capitalist monetary system into it a way of spreading ownership of capital widely among the community. Best known are the various employee share ownership schemes of which several thousand operate in Europe and America. However, these can only spread shares among those in the population who work in commercial enterprises, which, moreover, must be of a certain minimum size. Less well known, but of potentially even greater significance, are those schemes that aim to spread share ownership to all the citizens of the country in which the scheme operates. A radical and well-thought-out example is that described by Stuart M. Speiser in his *USOP Handbook*. Speiser names his plan a "Kitty Hawk" Model after the first flightworthy airplane. As with the Kitty Hawk, it embodies enough of the vital ingredients to make it an effective, operable scheme, but he considers that it needs developing and fleshing out in order to operate really well.

The heart of the Kitty Hawk Model of universal share ownership is in the method of creating, and assigning ownership of, new capital. When a company is investing in a new wealth-producing plant, it raises the money (at least partially) by selling new shares. But under the present system, the only people who can buy the shares, and thus share in the wealth-producing potential of the new plant, are those who already have capital in the form of savings or property which can serve as collateral. "Kitty Hawk" will establish a government-backed USOP (Universal Share Ownership Plan) fund which will guarantee loans to all members of the public on a quota basis for the express and sole purpose of buying shares in a portfolio of top companies whenever these companies raise new capital. It would work through the existing financial institutions that already finance and underwrite loans for new ventures. The difference would be that the financial institutions would hold the new shares in escrow for their individual owners until the dividends on the shares had paid off the debt plus a handling charge. The new owner would then assume full ownership of the shares. All legitimately raised capital is self-liquidating in the sense that it is expected to pay for itself and, moreover, there is little danger of the shares not paying off the debt. It is, however, to guard against this unlikely situation that the government, rather than the individual, stands guarantor. On past experience, it can be said that with good management, the risk to the taxpayer is minimal. But the vast numbers of people who would otherwise never have share ownership, and benefit from the profits thereof, will gradually acquire this kind of wealth. The scheme does not envisage that holders of USOP shares would have voting rights, nor would they be able to sell their shares.

Functionally, the USOP scheme is workable. It has been costed out thoroughly and has stood up to scrutiny by competent authority. Why then is it regarded as a "Kitty Hawk" Model rather than a ready-for-service jumbo jet? The answer must lie not in the general outline, but in the sophistication of its details, its finer implications, and in the general readiness of the public to make full use of it.

There is little justification for a plan to redistribute the title to wealth just because a few intellectuals have a theological belief that the world should be so ordered. What must be achieved is the spreading around of the real benefits—both material and psychological—of ownership of wealth, and the avoidance of the corrupting influence of large accretions of wealth with its concomitant power within the hands of a few without accountability. To do this, the practical details must be designed so that the plan is self-sustaining in its day-to-day workings and able to cope with periods of economic growth, stability, or recession. It must also address itself to relationships between the individual and the system at all levels.

Linking USOP and ESOP

One area where the relationship between the individual and the capital he uses is easily perceived is in Employee Share Ownership Plan schemes (ESOPs). However, the Kitty Hawk Model envisages that the stocks that would be allocated would be those only of selected large, established companies—what Speiser terms "SuperStock." Furthermore, SuperStock would not carry voting rights. Fair enough. The system is to be government guaranteed, and the taxpayer must be protected from dodgy setups that would seek to "milk" the scheme. This does, however, leave the SuperStock shareholder remote from his holdings. Can SuperStock somehow be linked to employee share schemes (ESOPs), so that at least those members of the community who work in companies where ESOP would be relevant may not only have title to the capital wealth of the nation but a sense of involvement too?

If SuperStock were to be issued, not directly but by means of a voucher that must be spent on SuperStock through a recognized source, then it would be easy to rule that those who actually worked in one of the listed companies would receive employee shares in their own company as part of their allocation. They would have superior voting rights to a degree dependent on the rules under which their company operated. But what of the large number who worked in those public companies not of the elite that qualified to issue SuperStock? They too would have to use their vouchers to buy shares in their own company. However, these people need protection from fraudulent or incompetent management and not total protection. That would remove some of their incentive to take an intelligent interest in what "their" management was up to, and to use their voting powers if need be. But there is no reason why employees of small to middling sized companies should bear a disproportionate risk compared with the holders of 100 per cent Super-Stock. Certain accountancy techniques could make it practical for the government-backed USOP to offer substantial guarantees to ESOP holders without letting the taxpayer in for a significant burden. These techniques would be aimed at defining the money value of a company in a convincing way. Among large and stock market-quoted companies, the financial world carries out a continuous valuation by virtue of the share price offered in the daily trading of the stock market. This valuation is based largely, if not entirely, on the expected earning power of the company under question. It is influenced by market conditions, management personalities, possibility of impending takeover, rumor, scandal, and the mood of the stock market. In a minor way, the replacement value of the plan occasionally is a factor.

Government ESOP Guarantees Based on Plan Value

This last remark is not intended to be cynical. While it is straightforward to put a cost on a large plant, it is not easy to put a money value on it as an artifact. Take, for example, a plant manufacturing the universal chemical feedstock, ethylene. Technically, the bigger the plant, the more efficient it is and therefore the more potentially profitable. So everyone in the ethylene line builds the biggest plant they can. At the time of writing, there is only a smallish number of ethylene plants in the world, but even so, there are more than the world really needs. So if you tried to sell one, what you would get for it, if anything, is problematical. It has no logical value.

However, firms below a certain size do not have ethylene plants or similar non-saleable material assets. Small- to middle-size firms are rarely unique or even unusual in character. The tools of their trade, while often custom made, have a market value since there are plenty of similar firms who would buy in the event of a sell-out. To a fair degree of accuracy, it is possible to assess the value of their assets. Since nearly all of the plant would be readily saleable in the event of liquidation, it is also likely that the plant would represent a higher proportion of the firm's share value than would be the case with a large company. It is the value of this plant (and other tangible assets), perhaps at a slightly generous valuation, which would be the basis of the government's backing of employee share ownership via USOP SuperStock.

It would be necessary to establish within small non-SuperStock companies an accounting routine to keep the face value of existing shares close to a predetermined relationship with plant and tangibles value. Since the ESOP shares are not tradeable, their face value will not vary outside the control of the company. It is a matter of keeping track of tangible values through recording costs of new and replacement plant, wastage due to wear and tear, and also variations in working capital, stock in trade, and so forth. In order to keep the workload on the ac-

counting staff within limits, it would be necessary to establish and refine
rules of thumb and simple procedures that would work most of the time.
Possibly computer routines could do most of the work with very little
more information than is currently fed to accounting computers. Over
the years, discrepancies would occur due to the accumulation of small
errors. It would then be necessary for a reconciliation exercise to be carried out to correct these discrepancies. This could be a management
decision. Or it could be the legal right of unions, shareholders, consumer
bodies, tax authorities, or the USOP body to demand the exercise, as
experience dictates.

Since the earning value of a good company not only depends on its
plant but on additional factors, such as good will and trade or technical
knowledge, employee shares would have a high earning power. Good
will is such an ephemeral asset that it would be totally unrealistic for
an institutional guarantor to be expected to take it into account. Technical knowledge is a more difficult matter, and the consideration of its
value is a topic in itself. The sad experience of Rolls Royce in 1971 was
put down in some quarters to the failure of financial institutions to fully
value technical know-how. It could well be that employee investors
would make a better stab at it. However, it would not perhaps be appropriate in the early stages of USOP-guaranteed ESOP to take into account knowledge value, but such a step could be borne in mind as a
future development.

Employee shares, then, in terms of the earning power of a good
company, would usually be undervalued by normal commercial or stock
market standards. In the event of failure and subsequent liquidation of
a small/medium company, it would therefore not be overgenerous to
compensate ex-employees with an allocation of SuperStock in exchange for their employee stock. To recompense itself, the government
would seize the assets and sell them for the best possible price. The
position of other creditors would not be much different; they are already
at the end of the queue as it is.

To summarize, employee shareholders of a firm with a USOP-
backed scheme would then be on to a good thing, if the firm did well;
they would get a higher return than straight SuperStock. If it did badly,
they would see their returns fall. That, after all, is what employee participation is about. If their firm folded altogether, they would be
protected, but since their shareholdings represented only the tangible
asset value of the firm, they would receive USOP SuperStock only to
that value. The government, through its backing of USOP would not be
let in for too much of the taxpayer's money since it would normally

have worthwhile plant to dispose of.

USOP Shares and Obsolescence of Assets

We have talked of relating the face value of shares to the asset value of smaller companies operating employee share ownership. But something of a similar nature must be done for all shares. If, through USOP, we are to build a nation of shareholders, moreover, shareholders who feel some affinity with the activities to which these shares relate, we must make the monetary system of which shareholding is a part more easily understandable. It must be seen to mirror reality. And one question that shareholders will ask is: "What happens to shares when they grow old?" Reality is that the plant, which the original shares purchased, wears out, crumbling to rust. The knowledge so painstakingly gathered becomes merely the hardcore foundation for fresher, newer, more comprehensive knowledge. In other words, the Second Law of Thermodynamics rules. So all shares must obey the same law. A simple finite life, as with a simple self-liquidating loan, is probably not appropriate. It would be too inflexible, and if the asset it represented was still good, who would own it? It would be better for a share when issued to be assigned, like a radioactive particle, a half-life. At the end of this time, it would be gathered in and a share of much lower value tendered in payment. This share would also have a half-life, and so on. Within limits, managers would have a say concerning the half-life they would offer on new stock and the face value of the "second half-life" stock, thereby building in flexibility and enabling the stock to mirror more nearly the real state of affairs. All shares, including existing ones—not just USOP and ESOP ones—would conform to this rule.

This would be easily understood by the majority of new shareholders created by USOP, whereas the present system of writing off history through company restructuring, liquidation, systematic inflation, and so on is only understood by chartered accountants and trained economists (and, some would say, not even fully by them).

The constant weathering away of the stock, or rather its paper symbol, would result in rather more new stock being available for the USOP. Companies, released from the burden of paying full dividends on stock that represented old and worn assets, would be able to be less inhibited about raising new capital.

It would also achieve the redistribution of wealth without confiscation. No doubt the rich, who are at present "featherbedded" in that the paper title to their wealth has a theoretical immortality, unmatched by the transient nature of much of their real possessions, would protest otherwise. But the rich as a class have a noticeable tendency to preach to the poor about facing up to reality, and it would do no harm to remind them that they too should enjoy a similar discipline. Unlike the confiscation of wealth demanded by socialism, the constant recirculation of the title to productive capital would apply to all classes, from those with the bare USOP holdings to those who had bought or inherited large shareholdings by ordinary commercial methods.

No one would be discouraged from attempting to become rich by legitimate methods; the beneficial effects of Adam Smith's doctrine of "enlightened self-interest" would still apply. The glamor of the rich—their Ferraris, their graceful yachts, the handsome horses, the patronage of arts and sports—would still be there for us all to enjoy. (The writer is not rich, nor does he have expectations.) But our enjoyment would be cleaner and less tinged with envy for knowledge that they, like us, would have to "keep at it" to retain their comfortable situation.

Limits to Growth

Limitation on the life of title to productive capital gives the USOP and ESOP another very significant strength. It enables the monetary system to cope with an economy which is either stable or even shrinking in conventional accountancy terms. Although a continuously expanding economy is the aim of all Western democracies, and is generally thought by most serious commentators to be feasible at least in the short to medium term, it would be irresponsible to ignore warnings about the effects of "limits to growth."

There are two main schools of thought (perhaps schools of anxiety would be a better term) on limits to growth. One is the environmental one, which recognizes that Western industrial society has, to date, based its expansion on the consumption of energy, much of which comes from finite sources. These resources are certain to become exhausted some day, although when is debatable. Also, most industrial processes have side effects, some of which are deleterious and have to be faced up to. Remedying these may retard growth.

Social limitations to growth are also significant. There is a limit to the amount of food a family can eat, the clothes they can wear, the amount of sports or culture they can find the energy to partake of. There is a limit to material demand. Above a certain level, an individual's expenditure and his/her salary expectation is largely based on psychological needs, the need to gain status—or not to, as the case may be.

In addition, there are periods of growth or even shrinkage brought about by natural trade cycles.

Universal share ownership helps a free enterprise economy to deal with these phenomena with the minimum of distress to its members. A free enterprise economy without USOP finds it difficult to deal with reductions in demand. A drop in demand due to natural cycles, or to higher prices caused by a shortage, leads to cuts in overtime or laying off labor. It is the poorer members who are usually cut back, and they are the ones who spend the higher proportion of their incomes on consumables. So demand falls still faster. A Keynesian government intervention may be necessary to reverse the slide.

USOP, either by itself or in conjunction with a self-adjusting welfare boost scheme, such as the tax credit plan put forward by the British Liberal Party, would have a restraining effect on these swings. Those who suffered a loss of earnings due to small natural recessions would, by virtue of their USOP income, still have money to spend, and the demand effect would be less exaggerated.

It must be said that even a non-growing economy can be, contrary to what many economists seem to assume, a very vigorous one. Environmental effects, even if they become powerful enough to limit growth as conventionally measured, will demand intense economic activity. We may have to run hard in order to stand still. Social limits through concentrating people's demands on less rational satisfactions than plain food, clothing, and shelter will lead to a fickleness of the market. Fashion will create demands. These may conflict with environmental impacts. We are not in for a quiet time.

Because universal share ownership, especially with the elaborations suggested in this essay, would aid the continual creation of new capital as the economy is required to do new things, and make palatable the phasing out of old capital, it represents an unparalleled opportunity. It offers the opportunity to avert the existing self-destructing latency in free world capitalism, and to cope with new demands from totally changed economic circumstances.

Political Appeal of USOP

It can succeed because it is a political device which, with some variations of emphasis, can appeal across a wide spectrum of political thought. The USOP is not an "ism." It is a set of changes to the rules of the monetary system, and can be popularized as such. It is helpful here, toward the end of longish essay, to stress this point. The monetary system and the economy are not the same thing, although they are linked. The best economists instinctively know this, but rarely if ever put across the crucial differences when talking to laymen. The economy consists of people doing things to provide themselves with food, shelter, clothing, education, sport, and culture. It is organic, it develops partly by mankind's efforts and partly by the circumstances of nature. Attempts to circumscribe it by central planning have not been very successful.

A monetary system, however, is a purely man-made thing. It is a quasi-mathematical set of rules to try to monitor the economy and to help man make better decisions about the economy. A well-developed monetary system exercises a degree of control over the economy. If sufficiently elegant, a monetary system would result in the economy to which it refers being completely self-sustaining and self-adjusting by virtue of the information it supplies to, and the pressures it exerts on, all the members of the economy.

This presumably is the dream of monetarists, although there is little to suggest that we are anywhere near achieving a monetary system of anything like the requisite degree of sophistication. However, USOP brings that state a step closer, and must therefore be welcomed by monetarists.

But USOP does not need to offend those of socialist leanings. True, it does not greatly, if at all, increase state involvement, but it does offer a way of redistributing wealth, and, moreover, as a continuous process. And it puts the means of production into the hands of the masses.

Meanwhile, conventional conservatives should be happy that there is nothing in USOP to hinder—and everything to encourage—the acquisition of wealth by the individual due to his or her own efforts.

And to this writer, perhaps its potential for coping responsibly with the environmental pressures, but without detriment to the good quality of life we enjoy in the West, is the most attractive feature of USOP.

19

EVERYONE A SHAREHOLDER

by

Hazel V. Taylor

Editor's Note: *Hazel V. Taylor of Orpington, Kent, holds an Honors Degree from Cambridge University and a Ph.D. from Oxford University. Qualified as a chartered accountant, she has been audit manager and senior manager for a major international accounting firm, and has also served in a line management role in corporate banking. Taylor's essay uses existing plans (privatization, Personal Equity Plans, ESOP, etc.) as the foundation for imaginative new schemes, such as using trading stamps to promote consumer share ownership and issuing shares to government employees that will enable them to profit from the efficiency of the agencies in which they work. She stresses the roles of education and voluntary share purchasing programs.*

ABSTRACT

The productive assets, ownership of which is to be spread, are identified first as the human assets and second as physical manufacturing, extractive, and transportation assets. Education is key because of the need to train people to contribute to the economy and to understand and share the benefits of ownership.

Taxation provides a captive audience to be exploited. Taxpayers could be granted an ownership interest in government assets by a choice in where their taxes are spent. In our consumer society, potential exists for investment in suppliers of goods by way of consumer shares. These would be allotted with priority given to consumers of those goods. Especially designated discounts on purchases would accumulate until minimum investment levels were reached.

Employee shares as remuneration should be extended to include government employees, using new securities for each department related to its performance. Non-incorporated bodies would create a second tier of equity for employees' remuneration and outside investors. New small businesses and reduced burdens on private companies will increase assets and spread their ownership from the few to the many. Recent changes are a start from which to build these ideas, retaining always a balance of risk versus reward.

"First catch your hare. . . ." was the wonderfully practical instruction with which Mrs. Beeton commenced her well-known recipe for jugged hare. When addressing an essay subject concerned with spreading the ownership of Britain's productive assets, one is irresistibly drawn to this analogy, for how indeed are these productive assets to be captured? Lest we become too rigid or unimaginative in our thinking, let us first consider in the broadest sense the nature of our nation's productive assets.

The Victorians were the first to establish that Britons had a great pioneering spirit and the drive and enthusiasm to go out and conquer far horizons. Of course, it is unfashionable in the current climate to dwell overmuch on the Empire, and there was indeed much to regret in the subjugation of nations and peoples, not to mention economies, to our foreign culture and religious beliefs. Yet one must not lose sight of the inner driving force that fueled the great adventure—a force that brought back not only material treasures but also enriched knowledge and broadened thinking, enhancing the returning traveller's mind. This same pioneering spirit and quest after the unknown manifests itself in the great British inventors who, time after time, have made the scientific, technological, and lateral thinking breakthroughs which other nations have exploited. Thus, our first class of productive asset must be our people, embodying all the qualities which are theirs from a rich and varied history.

In our largest corporations and companies, the highest value is often placed upon the people who have the skills to make those organizations flourish. The question of human assets is not a frivolous one. Human asset accounting has even been the subject of papers in the accounting press. When one considers the major professional firms, whether they be accountants, solicitors, or surveyors, it is even more striking that the productive assets are very largely the individuals who make up that firm with little contribution from the necessary, but low-grade, periphery of word processors, computers, and other office accoutrements.

Our first asset, therefore, comprises our people, who are also those to whom those assets should belong. This interdependence is pivotal to the success of our strategy, and the concepts of this essay flow from this as their origin.

Productive assets include every class of factory and machinery used in manufacturing to add value to raw materials. Manufacturing has always been at the heart of the industrial strength of a nation. How sad it is to see the wastelands of our northwest Midlands. Where once tens of thousands of employees labored in productive industry in its simplest sense, now only one-tenth as many are laboring and the dole lines are lengthening. If the ownership of these assets were only in the grasp of the people who depend on them, this decline could somehow have been averted. But these assets cannot individually be spread among the people. They must be owned by larger entities through which an organized ownership can function. Again, we are speaking of companies and of corporations which hold these assets. Thus, our task is to devise ways by which these companies can become more generally owned.

The extractive industries have never been more prominent and, indeed, more central to our economy than they are today. The oil and gas production equipment in the North Sea is without doubt a productive asset and an attractive one; no problem here in enticing investors to share its ownership. But look to the coal mines: sophisticated machines claw and wrench the black, dull, combustible deposit from its ancient resting place. Yet who would wish to join in ownership of these unprofitable operations? Talk is only of how to reduce the losses, knowing that profits cannot be earned while costs of extraction exceed the price in the market place. Profound questions must be answered and the answers put into practice before such productive assets as these can be enthusiastically sought after by the people.

Last in the catalogue of productive assets that deserve a special mention are the freight and ocean services. Transport of goods across country and overseas is fundamental to productivity. These assets were once a jewel in Britain's crown and still the ocean transport companies survive, but the merchant navy is now sadly depleted. Ownership of these assets broadly spread among ordinary people can be achieved. This gives hope for a better future prospect, where the people whose livelihood depends on particular productive assets are also those who have a say in their development. As in any democracy, the wider the spread of ownership, the more protection is gained from narrow interest groups who do not always consider the wider effects of their actions.

Let us now come to the strategy which can bring to fruition these hopes and benefits. Any plan must begin as an idea and the next part of the essay will explain these ideas. If we are to consider the broadest possible spread of ownership and best chance of reviving the economy, then the first priority is to capture the imagination of the people. How can this be done, not just for employers, not just for the employed, but for everyone? Thinking of what we all have in common, in Britain we are born to the great privilege of an education supplied to all, regardless of circumstances. Much debate may rage as to the quality of that education and whether it achieves all of its objectives, but nothing can take away the discovery of knowledge, be it a little or the gateway to great academic achievement. So the first idea follows this shared privilege given to all: one must begin with education. Unless our people know of their heritage, of their industrial strengths and weaknesses, of the scientific and artistic skills that exist, of the part they themselves can play, they can never want (or even perceive a need) to own these assets and fulfill their own role to the full.

Education is necessarily oriented toward the academic studies, yet the skills which are needed in practical situations are sadly often the most neglected. Even today, few schools offer economics as a subject as readily as physics or chemistry, French or German. Geography is often illuminating on the industries of Finland or France, yet may fail to set Britain's own industry within context of both Europe and the world. So let us promote an education that will equip our children—the governors and lawmakers of the future—to understand and build up the British economy, as the governors and lawmakers of the past (of whatever political color) have failed to do. Let us also educate our children to develop their skills and potential to the full, perfecting the first element of the strategy—our human assets.

Now to turn to other common denominators of the great mass of the British population. We all live in communities, whether a widely flung rural area, a suburb of London, or the inner city of Liverpool. Here then is another idea: bring ownership of the productive assets of the area first to the people of the local community. This is related to the existing concept of employce share ownership, but can be widened not only to embrace employees but those who depend on local industry. Many would be willing to share the ownership of their own community's productive assets and gain a voice in its progress. Such a scheme could be administered by local government bodies, acting as coordinators to bring together the present owners and managers of the local business with those who wish to invest in it.

Nothing, it is said, is certain in life except for death and taxes. We all pay taxes, whether on income we earn or as value added tax on everyday purchases. Here again is one of the great common denominators of the population. Ideas again flow from this common factor, ways in which to harness this captive audience. Let us propose that a proportion of income tax be set aside for investment by individuals in national assets. On a broader front, perhaps income tax could be waived on certain investments to encourage wider share ownership. Another idea would be to nominate one-fifteenth of the 15 per cent value added tax as a returnable amount at the option of the ultimate purchaser, as an investment in the producing company.

We already have substantial investment by the government in taxes they collect from us, for example, in service industries, the heavy burden of funding the National Health Service. Yet we do not feel a sense of personal investment in our health service; we feel instead a forcible depletion of the salary or wages check with apparently no very tangible or constructive results. One of the problems for the taxpayer is the limited accountability of government over how the taxes are spent. Only the ultimate sanction of voting the ruling party out of office can shift policies with which the people disagree. A plan for allocation of income tax and other taxes to specific government functions, with an element of choice by the taxpayer, would result in a more specific accounting for the stewardship of this money.

Further answers may lie in a devolution of such services as the National Health Service to a local investment/local benefit basis. No one wishes to see areas of relative affluence enjoy far better health care than those of the inner cities, but this need not be an insurmountable problem. Resources could still be equalized on a national basis, but still preserve an element of optional investment by the individual taxpayer. A portion of, say, the national insurance contribution could be nominated as an investment in some specific health area, perhaps on a rotational basis. If anyone doubts that health care is both a productive asset and vital for revival of the economy, only consider the fundamental importance of the human assets and their well-being to both productivity and economic health. Nor need we only consider health care; other services, such as law enforcement and public transport, could be usefully brought within a scheme of partial ownership and direction by the general population with many potential benefits from local rather than merely national implementation.

Considering again the activities and circumstances common to us all, one which leaps to mind is the purchase of goods for the home. We all go out at some time and buy a refrigerator, television, furniture, or stereo system. Broadening this further, leisure activities involve greater or lesser expenditures—the keen sportsman will require new equipment; the gardener, tools; the fisherman, new rods and lines. In short, we are a consumer society and all the signs are that this past Christmas has brought credit purchasing to an all-time high. Two separate trains of thought emerge from this: the first is the source of potential among consumers to invest in those who supply them. This idea is certainly not a new one; companies have traditionally invested in their competitors in order to obtain information with a view to expansion by acquisition. Further, many invest in suppliers for similar reasons and to secure their sources of supply. There seems to be no good theoretical reason why we, who consume goods so freely, should not also share in the ownership of the suppliers and manufacturers.

The second train of thought is the growing importance of credit business and of the whole financial service industry to our economy. Any plan to spread the ownership of Britain's productive assets and revive its economy must not neglect the enormous earning power of these invisible contributors to economic health. The problem, of course, in both the above thoughts is the inaccessibility of the suppliers and financial service industries to direct investment by their consumers. That this can be overcome has been shown dramatically, although not uncontroversially, by the privatization of British Telecom and British Gas. Here we now have a considerable distribution of ownership of assets in a supplier to a cross-section of its consumers. The complications arise because of the previous nationalized status of both, a separate argument that will not be debated here. The principle at stake is the ownership by consumers of a part interest in their supplier.

There are a number of ways in which this idea could be progressed. One idea would be to increase the share capital of a supplier company by introducing a new class of shares to be known as consumer shares. These could be subscribed for only by consumers able to evidence that they were such, with priority assigned in share allocation to appropriate bands of spending on the goods supplied. One could imagine special rights being conferred on consumer shareholders, such as the right to be balloted for their opinion on any major step contemplated by management, or in principal diversification out of traditional areas to new ones, either at home or overseas. This may seem revolutionary, but it in no way contravenes the spirit of wider share ownership and could well provide an incentive to those who we would encourage to own those shares. Following the vouchers for services piloted by the privatization issues, a further extension of special rights for consumer shareholders could be selective discounts on goods sold or distributed. The old idea of trading stamps, given by supermarkets for value of goods purchased, could see a renaissance if the objective was to achieve a sufficient number of stamp-filled books to exchange wholly or in part for an allotment of consumer shares in the supermarket. Doubtless, there are many motorists who would soon be able to accumulate sufficient stamps for consumer shares in, for example, British Petroleum.

An alternative means of promoting ownership by consumers of their suppliers would be to gradually accumulate a holding of convertible unsecured loan stock by means of discounts on purchases. This would carry rights of conversion to equity at some future date in the usual way, once a sufficient discount had accumulated to generate a minimum stockholding, for example, £100. Building societies could perhaps obtain business out of the transaction by holding discount amounts in restricted access saver accounts until the minimum holding level was reached. Any consumer who did not want to take the benefit of the discount in this form could choose to forfeit it, but clearly this would be quite unattractive by comparison. It is easy to see how the concepts involved could be extended to consumers in the insurance field by means of discounts based on insurance premiums. Alternatively, there could be an option to take a no-claims bonus in the form of shares in the insurer, instead of as a cash reduction of the premium. Banks and building societies could adapt the methodology to suit themselves and might well see an opportunity to further market their own services in share dealing for customers.

For those among us in full-time employment, the concept of receiving remuneration by way of employee share schemes is attractive. A relatively large number of such schemes already exist and have shown that positive benefits in earnings per share and market capitalization accrue when there is significant employee shareholding. This need be no surprise, as the element of motivation and incentive to an employee for having a personal financial stake in the progress of his employer is a powerful factor. Certain safeguards and tax consequences of these schemes have been well documented elsewhere and therefore are not reiterated here. Thus, it only remains to promote the implementation of such employee share schemes across a broader spectrum, both by publicizing proven benefits to employers and by attracting the interest of employees to their own chance to share in their employer's creation of wealth.

What, then, of employees in government employment? It seems inappropriate that while those in the private sector can enjoy remuneration in the form of shares, public employees cannot. It appears that there is no reason why government securities should not be issued to employees of government bodies as part of their remuneration package. While one may argue that such securities do not confer ownership of the assets involved, new issues could be designed to confer benefits on the employee investor in proportion to the performance of the government body involved. It would fit well with the concept of taxpayers' investment through such taxations as national insurance contributions. Benefits could be realized through the greater incentive to improve overall performance.

This leaves the question of remuneration of employees of other non-incorporated bodies, such as partnerships. Again, the basic principle of a personal financial stake in the equity of the business would be desirable, but this is presently restricted to the partners. Some employee remuneration schemes in such partnerships already recognize the need to relate the rewards earned to the success of the firm as a whole. As in the case of employees of government, ownership of the business in the direct sense as shareholders cannot be achieved, but there is room to devise new forms of sharing in the business which would give some form of stake to employees, perhaps by creating a second tier, known as an employee tier of equity. This need not be restricted to employees but could accommodate investment by other outside parties. The rights attaching to the secondary tiers would necessarily be restricted as the partners would retain management control of the firm. Concepts such as these require work to evolve a detailed form acceptable to the entity in question and subject also to tax implications. Nevertheless, it would take only one determined and farsighted partnership to bring about a successful employee ownership scheme for many others to follow.

While on the topic of individually owned businesses, it would be well not to forget the thousands of private companies registered in the

United Kingdom. All are bound by company law just as much as the largest listed company, albeit with some relaxations and reduced disclosure requirements. These companies are the embodiment of a wide ownership of Britain's productive assets. The smallest grocer's shop may be a company, its shares owned by a small group of family shareholders. In this respect, Britain exceeds its European neighbors by the sheer numbers of privately owned businesses it can boast. The concept of wider ownership of our resources can be related to these businesses; they should be encouraged; unnecessary restrictions and lengthy filings should be reduced to more appropriately match the needs of both the company and its creditors and debtors. The nonsense of a full audit requirement for the tiniest company should also undergo a more critical assessment.

Having moved through the realms of ideas and imagination, one must next consider certain practicalities of the strategy. In assessing where we are and where we have still to go, we should build eagerly on the positive elements which already exist and move forward from them. Thus, much has been written on the government's new Personal Equity Plans ("PEPs") introduced in the 1986 Budget. The PEPs are not perfect, but they are a step in the right direction and so are to be welcomed. At last, tax benefits are available to ordinary people investing up to £2400 a year in shares, subject to a minimum holding period. The limitations on the PEP concept lie mainly in the stipulation that the investments must be made through an approved fund manager. This pushes back the investment decision to a central body and limits the extent to which the individual investor can influence the makeup of his or her own portfolio. This drawback is in common with the unit trusts, where the investor is wholly in the hands of the professional portfolio manager, and indeed up to 25% of the PEP investment may be in the form of unit trusts. Already, however, the financial press has commented that the PEPs are probably most attractive to those who already have a portfolio of shares, as the annual exemption from capital gains tax would be more than adequate to accommodate most small investors' gains on their shares. To move forward from PEPs to even more encouraging tax benefits for small investors will be that much easier once PEPs are established.

Again, now that a first step has been taken, in future it may be possible to move to legislation similar to the Loi Monory of France, which places the tax relief upon new investments by individual shareholders in designated securities. However, one should not rely only upon tax incentives to promote wider share ownership, as there is a political price to pay: any tax concession or related tax-planning scheme has value only until new legislation supersedes it. Thus, the emphasis of our strategy must come first from a change in expectations of the population at large. This can be achieved mainly by education and, as mentioned earlier, it appears indispensable to provide proper grounding, not only in economics, but also in the personal management and academic skills needed to properly service commerce in Britain. More still is required. Already the big privatization issues of British Telecom and British Gas have greatly influenced the man in the street, and there is no doubt that the number of small shareholders was boosted. But as many observers have noted, owning shares in one or two entities alone does not create a portfolio, nor does it serve to ground the investor in the basis for making investment decisions.

The point here is the relationship between risk and reward. Only education can serve to equip a small investor with the rudiments of understanding of the risks he runs by owning shares. Here, the privatization issues and the sale of Trustee Savings Bank have almost done a disservice to the wider issues by creating the impression that shares, once purchased, can only increase in price and create gains. Of course, we all work toward that end, and the future prosperity of Britain depends on ensuring that industry grows profitably and creates wealth. Yet we must be aware that for every stock market gain there may be a loss, and the share that increases in price today may decrease tomorrow. The wise counsel must, therefore, be not to withhold ownership, but to be aware of both the risks and rewards of ownership.

This brings into sharp focus the need for protection of investors. Never has there been more publicity of this aspect of share ownership, nor more justification for concern as the "Big Bang" change in stock exchange practices takes effect. No one can yet say how effective the Securities and Investments Board will be, nor whether the Financial Services Bill will operate as intended. But any strategy to promote wider ownership of shares must be developed to reflect these new bodies and regulations as they evolve.

Although the forecast was that small investors would suffer higher commission rates on transactions after the Big Bang, actual experience suggests that this is not the case. With so many more players competing in the market for business of all kinds, the smaller investor is now being wooed by many different commission rate and transaction rate concessions. This reflects the overcapacity in brokering as the existing cake is sliced smaller and smaller, leading to a search for more business and more investors. These changes must act to stimulate the share-owning environment and will help to create conditions in which many of the ideas explained above will more easily take root.

Moving on from the risks and rewards of ownership, the practicalities of our political system introduce a further problem: the political risk. This element is a powerful force in a democracy where governments are elected for a five-year term. There is an inevitability that sooner or later the political color of government will change to a new majority party. This is a very healthy prospect and one which is a cherished safeguard of the system itself, yet it is not unalloyed joy to the proponents of apolitical schemes for the spreading of the ownership of our productive assets.

The topic of this essay competition prohibited both increased taxation and confiscation as means to the end. Both are not only contemplated, but widely promulgated by some political groups. Thus, one must realistically assess the effect of such action on plans for wider share ownership. Crippling blows could be dealt to the credibility of share ownership for the man in the street if his British Telecom shares were confiscated in a swing toward re-nationalization. There is no real need for share ownership in its broadest sense to be considered a privilege of moneyed classes or any similar simplistic ingredient to political polemic. After all, even in Communist China, ownership interest in collective farms has been shown to be an effective incentive to both productivity and the prosperity of the community. Thus, no fundamental political stand underlies the ideas set forth above, but only the gentle logic that those who own also care. Those who care commit themselves and their efforts more fully and efficiently to the success of their ventures. Unless, however, this gains widespread acceptance, the system that subjects our government to the votes of the people at least every five years may threaten the stability of plans implemented.

However, this is not cause for gloom, as the benefits of the wider ownership we have discussed will have a spiralling effect. Once a higher and higher proportion of the population is directly involved, its desirability to the remainder will increase proportionately. In this respect, there is an analogy with home ownership, which is desired by an overwhelming majority (and achieved by a majority) of Britain's population today. A recent National Opinion Poll showed that an estimated 14 per cent of the adult population own shares; the Wider Share Ownership Council's own estimate is nearer to 10 per cent. An objective of doubling this figure within two years, and doubling it again in the next five years, is a tangible target. In assessing this possibility, not only share ownership as it exists today needs to be considered. We also need to consider all the potential schemes that have been postulated to broaden both the concept and the practical expression of wider owner-ship among the people. We can look forward to the day when colleagues will compare their holdings of consumer shares in rival retail chains, or their holdings of employee remuneration securities related to the per-formance of their government department.

In summary, then, the stage is set both for a planned growth in wider ownership of Britain's productive assets and for a real revival in the economy. The focus for the change is upon the people whose skills and enterprise build the companies. Our task is to communicate with those people and share a vision of these benefits such that, whatever their political persuasion, those benefits are indisputable and the course of action clear.

20

THE NATIONAL ASSET FUND

by

Andrew Philip Stewart-Brown

Editor's Note: *Andrew Philip Stewart-Brown of Oxford received under-graduate degrees from Reading University (Agricultural Economics) and Oxford University (Theology). After teaching in secondary schools for seven years, he is now a business entrepreneur.*

Moving swiftly from Robinson Crusoe to the "increment of associa-tion" and the Henry George land tax theory, he proposes a National Asset Fund that would issue one "Share in Britain" to every citizen. The fund would receive shares from British companies that voluntarily donated them in consideration of low-cost loans for capital expansion. Thus, Stewart-Brown deals with the tricky problem of inducing busi-ness to participate voluntarily in distribution of USOP shares. Such voluntary plans as the National Asset Fund could probably be tested on a useful scale at negligible cost.

ABSTRACT

The essay seeks to explain some of the causes of the current mal-distribution of the ownership of productive assets in the U.K. and to explain why that pattern is self-perpetuating. It then proposes a method of producing a distribution which is fairer to all, namely, by forming a National Asset Fund which will yield dividends to every person. The dividends would build up over a period of decades. Once the distribution of income improved, the distribution of wealth would gradually normalize itself. As economic power is spread more evenly, poverty would be finally eliminated, as would the need for subsidies. Freed from the compulsion to earn money, all could find their own way more readily. The whole community would share in the benefits of unimpeded technological advance.

In 5,000 words or less, devise a plan for spreading the ownership of Britain's productive assets more widely among the people, and reviving the economy, without confiscation or increased taxation.

A practical plan has to address the question of persuasion. How can enough people be made to believe that this ownership should be distributed more widely? For if any plan should fail in this, it will end its days in one of the graveyards for lost economic causes—which are not empty.

It seems to me that the first point to be hammered home is the difference between the product of an individual's efforts when he works on his own and when he works in a community. If you take away the part that can be attributed to the work of his neighbors, both in the past and in the present, and reduce a person to the level of Crusoe, you can begin to appreciate the difference. Fifty-five million Crusoes, each on his island, could not produce a thousandth of our GDP. (Forgive the absurdity.)

The Increment of Association

At various levels of economics, this idea has been referred to as an increment of association. In the theory of international trade, it is commonly held to play a part. But considered nationally, it should be easy to understand that individual efforts are dwarfed, or rather their differences are dwarfed, by the effect of working together.

The ethical consequences are quite simple. Indeed, they are implicitly held by many. Once I heard a die-hard Tory say about a city salary of over £1,000,000: "Nobody can be worth that much!" Of course, the market could bear it but the disproportion was obvious. The same peculiarity is found in the distribution of wealth in the U.K., and it reflects the distribution of the ownership of productive assets: some 5 per cent of the people hold 50 per cent of the wealth. Everyone knows that the 5 per cent does not hold 50 per cent of the merit, talent, and intelligence. Perhaps they have less than their fair share of these qualities. But either way, they have a kind of power which is perfectly real and which is denied to the rest. It is arguable that this distribution of wealth vitiates the political equality we are all meant to enjoy.

People become very wealthy or gain huge salaries because they are in a position to appropriate for themselves disproportionate parts of the national increment of association. They sit in favored spots under the tree and find fruit falling into their hands. This is perfectly legal and not to be despised. But it does mean that the apples do not fall elsewhere. There are several well-known "favored spots." A monopoly in production, or the exclusive ownership of a fixed supply of some factor of production when faced with a rising demand; the control of the power of credit; and, more generally, the ownership of productive assets—all are such advantageous positions.

There are many ways of trying to even out the resulting distribution. A graduated income tax is clearly one. A system of subsidies—and there are now more than 20 million people in receipt of some state disbursement—is another. But the state in this connection is only operating a massive system of transfer. One reason for spreading the ownership of productive assets more widely among the people is this: the further such ownership extends, the more will receive an independent income from dividends and other sources, and the less the state will be burdened by the need to subsidize the poorer members of the community. There is a vast difference between receiving a check for supplementary, unemployment, or invalidity benefit and a dividend from shares in some public company. Although the benefits come "of right," the recipient of benefits designed for direct relief of poverty feels himself a suppliant. He has to meet conditions, such as having no more than £3,000 in savings; he ought to notify the bureaucracy when his circumstances change, but knows deception to be commonplace. In fact, the money he receives has strings attached which bind him into poverty. By contrast, the man getting dividend payments is free. The system of benefits is aimed at those in need, but has become so complicated and overburdened that it does not work efficiently. Furthermore, the indignity of being asked by some official how much washing and cleaning one had to do in order to receive some specific allowance should be obvious. Once there were people too proud and independent to take anything from the state.

But money is already being "given away" in vast sums in expensive and rather inefficient ways. Given that this is the case, and there are reasons why it must be so quite apart from the collective loss of individual independence, it would be a better idea to give it away equitably, efficiently, and cheaply. Ideally, each member of the community should be provided with an independent claim on the "increment of association" sufficient to sustain a good life. If the question of fairness should arise, the answer would run like this: just as no one can "deserve" a salary of £1 million a year, albeit able to "command" it, so no one can "deserve" grinding poverty, malnutrition, and misery. No normal human being enjoys a life of indigence. Who would choose to spend their life in poverty if given the freedom to choose?

Unfortunately, this point is seldom put to the test. Choice is a luxury possessed fully only by those who have independent means. As for the poor, they have to be seen as victims. Their situation may be compared to that of people at the bottom of a deep well, the sides of which are particularly slippery at the bottom. They look up to the light and hear those at the top giving advice and throwing down scraps of food. The only way to take advantage of any increment of association is by standing on one another's shoulders pyramid fashion, a procedure which can help few. At the very top, the sides are less steep and there are ladders and winches for the final step. The people who have escaped are firmly tied to fixtures in their surroundings to prevent a fall from riches to rags. Poverty is a trap in a more than purely fiscal sense.

Henry George

One of the people with an economic nostrum that is now almost dead and buried wrote a book in 1879 entitled *Progress and Poverty*. (Canaan, New Hampshire: Phoenix Publishers, 1979). His argument ran along the lines that the ownership of land was the principal means of gaining a private purchase on the increment of association. The greater part of the landlord's rent was strictly speaking an economic rent. That is to say, the difference between what a man could earn at the margin of production, given equal applications of labor and capital, and what he could earn on a site nearer the center was the economic rent. As a town or city was built up, George saw the process of land speculation happen over and over again, with central sites coming to command huge premiums over marginal sites. My own family made a fortune, long since dissipated, from owning two miles of beach frontage in Sydney, Australia. Because the advantage gained by the landlord had nothing to do with his own contribution to the welfare of his fellows, and everything to do with their presence and physical concentration, George believed that a tax should be placed on land (strictly site) values. Apart from the fact that it would "home in" on the values created by common effort, a land tax could not be shifted onto the tenant or any other party by the landlord. Taking the pure surplus of economic rent would no more cause a change in land-use patterns than doubling the taxation borne by some of the richer pop-stars would cause them to cease warbling. In theory, this tax is a free-marketeer's dream. The invisible hand will be just as able to do its job after as before its introduction.

There is good reason to believe that George identified one reason for the maldistribution of wealth, and his ideas are mentioned in some modern economic textbooks as an example in the equilibrium analysis of rent. But in the positivistic way of modern economics, the concept of economic rent is also applied to the earnings of labor and capital. The reward to and of the three factors of production is divided into transfer earnings and economic rent. The former is defined as the least the factor will accept—or its owner will accept—without transferring to another occupation. The latter is the rest of the return. Wherever a factor of production is in fixed supply and faced with a steady or rising demand, nearly all of its earnings will be an economic rent. Under this definition, the above-mentioned earnings of the pop-star are a surplus, an economic rent, which could be taxed away without altering the use of the communities' resources.

But there was another point George was at pains to make and he could not understand why it was not taken up by the economic pundits of his day. Perhaps his idea offended powerful interests. Nowadays the reason it is neglected is that it leads directly to a normative or ethical consideration, which cannot be admitted in a positive treatment of economics. George was not familiar, however, with a way of thinking that treated land, labor, and capital as co-equal factors of production. But he perceived that as settlements developed, land at the center of a community soon approached the state of a "factor in fixed supply," and an economic rent arose. But land itself was abundant and so the transfer earnings of labor were determined by what could be earned at the margin of production. Wage rates remained high in the early towns because a man could always go westwards and try his luck as a Crusoe of the plains. Or he could stay nearer civilization and enjoy the benefits of associating with his fellows from a distance. Indeed, in Alaska today, the government gives land to those who are prepared to build a house and support themselves on it for a few years. But in the U.S., when the land had all been bought and claimed, wages began to fall. Where there is no margin for labor, it will have to take the least it is willing to accept. Why should anyone endure poverty? Because there is no alternative within range. Where one exists, it will be taken. Many Highlanders were driven off their laird's lands in the 19th century by infamous agents whose names are still remembered today. They were forced to scrape a living on the seashore. When passages to Australia were offered at high prices and in appalling conditions, they were taken because there was no alternative.

When Marx wrote of the "Reserve Army" of labor, he was referring to the same phenomenon. And if you peel away enough pages of specious nonsense about the labor theory of value of class war between capital and labor, you may find a prescription, namely, the common ownership of the means of production. This may not be seen as a recommendation for the wider spreading of the ownership of productive assets, but it does suggest that if each member of the Reserve Army could be given the same sense of independence and freedom from subservience enjoyed by the settler for whom the margin presented a real opportunity for a good life, then one of the main phenomena which lent Marx's theories plausibility would evaporate.

The Reserve Army does not consist of the poor who "we always have with us." Those are the sick, the old, and the incapable. The Army consists of those who have been incapacitated. It is not only because the laborer cannot set up on the physical margin of production that he is rendered useless. An analogous situation exists with respect to capital. Anyone without money is almost by definition a bad risk. Quite ordinary people, distinguished only by being born in an area where money is scarce, find themselves below the threshold at which they could borrow the necessary funds for setting up businesses. Borrowing for consumption is easier, at least to get started. The criteria by which money is loaned favor those who already own productive assets and are formed by considerations of a bank's own rather short-term profit, instead of the interest of the community as a whole over the next generations. Likewise, no one seems to maintain that the international capital markets and the funds flowing through them have the long-term welfare of mankind at heart.

Importance of Credit

Yet money is another "thing" which owes its existence to the presence of a community. It is notoriously inedible when other supplies fail. As a means of exchange, it works wonders by facilitating transactions, but these are not comparable with the miracle which occurs when it is gathered in a bank. Roughly speaking, whenever I deposit ten tenners, the bank deems itself to have £1,000 to lend. This miracle is a commonplace to a banker because he knows that the original discovery that this was a safe procedure took place many years ago. As long as all his customers do not want to withdraw simultaneously, or rather as long as they continue to withdraw at the same rate, he can exercise the power of multiplying money with impunity. Essentially, he can multiply claims on the communities' wealth. Whether he writes out blank checks, creates a deposit in someone's account, or prints money to give to people, it is essentially the same. This power is hedged around with many restrictions and kept within certain bounds by the financial system. But although the banks have an aura of reliability, they have been the cause of great trouble when their lending policy has been governed by speculative adventures and short-term considerations. The recent decline in agricultural land values has revealed some overenthusiastic lending for unrealistic purchases. Take this as the middle of a scale, one end of which represents the collapse of the 1930s. At the other end, are loans made in the long-term best interest of the whole community. It is worth noting that the most successful and cheapest method of lowering the unemployment figures has been the simple donation of £40 a week in 50 installments to those who had been unemployed for more than six weeks, who could raise £1,000 to seed a business account, and who could think of a decent way of making money. After two years, some 60 per cent are said to be still employing themselves gainfully. The success of this simple distribution of free credit indicates the scope for real credit reform in reviving the economy.

The argument so far is that there are "commanding heights" in our economic system from which the system not only can be surveyed but also controlled. Those who occupy them have an advantage that they seldom exercise altruistically. Attempts to scale the heights by revolution, or to mitigate their effects be welfare arrangements, have not worked well, albeit the second is infinitely preferable to the first. The better way is submersion. But if the increment of association were to be properly distributed in the future, the heights would eventually disappear beneath the rising general level of wealth. It may be ridiculous to suppose that men will ever all learn not to covet their neighbors' property, but it is not absurd to believe that the rich can be prevented from grinding the faces of the poor.

"Shares in Britain"

The first step would be to form a national fund, called perhaps the National Asset, which would be composed of non-voting but dividend-bearing shares of Public Limited-Liability Companies (PLCs). This fund would be divided into roughly 55 million "Shares in Britain." The exact number would be the number of British citizens, perhaps including those who do not necessarily have the right of residence in the United Kingdom. The dividends would be distributed to citizens annually on their birthdays, beginning at age one. Until the age of majority, the dividends would be held in escrow, except perhaps for purposes of education. After that, the dividends would be regularly paid unless the citizen was convicted of a criminal offense, was sectioned under the Mental Health Act, or became chronically indebted. In these cases, the yearly dividend might respectively be applied to compensation, contribute to the costs of specialist treatment, or be directed toward repayment by order of court.

As far as possible, the fund would be administered by a body independent of government. Its task would be to distribute the dividend to each citizen at the right time. It would also have to receive and hold the shares of the PLCs until the dividend payment became active. These companies would be persuaded to provide them in the following way. Whenever they wished to raise capital, they would have the usual methods of the market available. They could have a rights issue, offering it first to their own shareholders at an attractive discount; they could get a loan from one of the banks, or raise it on the markets using one of thousands of instruments and agencies which are available. Alternatively, they could apply for a special loan from the Bank of England—or from another bank underwritten by the Bank of England. This loan would be cheap, well below the market rate, and it would have a condition attached. Non-voting shares of equivalent value to the loan would be lodged with the responsible body and would begin to yield a dividend when the loan was fully repaid.

The first problem which arises is the dilution of the existing shareholders' assets without their permission. The City has already begun to give way on this issue in the sense that it is in certain circumstances now possible for directors to increase the number of their company's shares without in each instance balloting the shareholders. Provided the shareholders have given general permission at the general meeting, the directors have a free hand for a year in the eyes of the law. Of course, they are meant to have the interests of their shareholders at heart. But some less scrupulous people cannot resist the temptation of a larger personal section of the pie and will take advantage of new powers.

It should be possible to make sure that shareholders of the selected companies invited to distribute their shares more widely would see their assets continue to increase in real value, but relatively they might suffer. The only factors to set against this are the cheaper money and consequentially speedier growth, the stimulating effect on the economy of wider income distribution, and the increase in general well-being. But there will be a way of making the special loans so attractive they would not be refused. If the companies raised the money they need by rights issues, as they sometimes do, they are accepting obligations of exactly the same financial kind as those they accept by putting shares into the National Fund.

The next automatic question would concern inflation. Cheap money will expand the money supply and cause the level of prices to rise. Once steps are taken beyond considering the effect of giving everyone an extra £1,000, the question of cause or causes for inflation is not easy. But it is arguable that the creation of money for industrial development and expansion is not inflationary in the medium term. In fact, it may not have any untoward consequences at any stage. The companies chosen in the first instance would be Alpha Stock material. They form a floating island upon which the rest of the economy rest. If they cannot be trusted to make good use of the community's credit, then nobody can. Their projects have to be planned in the international context and are governed by the movements of markets at home and abroad. It is virtually perfectly reasonable to give them an advantage financially. They could virtually be trusted with their own mints.

The companies eligible would be carefully chosen. There need not only be two categories. Several ranks could be established with a graduated set of advantages. The larger companies would undoubtedly be given a competitive financial edge, but this would be balanced by a wider and larger distribution of profits. As far as possible, smaller companies should be encouraged by cheaper money. Banks might be able to make borrowing for consumption more expensive than it is already in order to compensate for the expense of encouraging industry.

Furthermore, ordinary people have no say in the investment

decisions of their banks, although it is their collective economic power
that enables banks to multiply its deposits by a factor of about ten. My
economics professor used to jingle the coins in his pocket, trying to im-
press on his students that each of them, in conjunction with the rest of
the population, determined the shape and direction of the economy by
their particular purchases and sales. Every purchase of a commodity is
a vote for further production. The sum of the votes determines whether
it is produced or scrapped. But a sense of responsibility toward the next
generation does not enter many consumer calculations.

Nor do people in the ordinary way realize that they give banks great
power by using deposit and current accounts. If and when they do, banks
may find that just as non-interest-bearing current accounts are now considered a banker's fiddle, so investment policies may no longer be taken
for granted. The campaign mounted against Barclay's policy of South
African investment would have been far more effective if customers
could have switched banks by tapping out a few numbers on a home
computer terminal. The individual can now gain control over many
areas of life previously left to experts. What is most likely to happen is
a call by particular interest groups to supporters to patronize a particular
bank and thereby gain some control over its policies. Alternatively, a
range of new banks might come into existence, one for conservationists,
another for canal-users and so on. At a small cost to each individual
"customer"—he or she would probably have to accept a lower rate of
interest than the current one—funds could be found for many projects
that are not felt to be good risks. The government should give every en-
couragement to people to invest in causes they believe in, voting for
their vision of the future by using their money, and thus breaking the
banks' oligopoly over the power of credit.

As citizens generally became richer under the scheme of dividends
from a National Asset, the question of using accumulated funds responsibly would become more acute. Ways would undoubtedly be found to
use the credit power generated for purposes—some charitable—which
would benefit the whole community. Much money would need to be invested and a far wider range of instruments should be available. And
here the full potential of the plan for distributing the ownership of
productive assets more widely would appear. Groups or individuals
would begin to build up portfolios of shares in public companies which
would contain shares with full voting rights. The distribution of wealth
will begin to even itself out only when the distribution of income has
been made fairer by the issue of dividends over one or two decades.

If it is objected that the rich will be all the while becoming even richer, the answer is that the distribution would nevertheless be approaching statistical and moral normality. And if the income received yearly from the dividend were to be made subject to income tax, then those in the higher tax brackets would receive little benefit, at least until their accountants had been to work. Those in the middle tax brackets would receive a significant increase, but those who received the greatest benefit would be those who were outside the scope of tax altogether. As the level of dividend payment rose, the personal allowances should be raised correspondingly until they reflected the sort of sum the particular category of individual was able to live well on. At the same time, billions of pounds would no longer have to be paid out in benefits. The first to go would be supplementary benefit, which is related to means. Others tied to the national insurance scheme would be honored. They would need to be reviewed carefully; in principle, there should no longer be any use for them and they could be phased out or the contributions could be paid back. Much of the apparatus of bureaucracy would be dissolved and the state could give up the futile attempt to daddy its citizens throughout their lives.

Who Will Own the Robots?

The dividend would establish a minimum income below which it was hard to fall. The effect on wages would be powerful. As the level rose, the wage earner would become richer, having to pay more tax. There would be no pressure for widespread increases, unless people had to be tempted out of idleness. This seems unlikely in the short term, although the day may come when very few engage in work as we understand it. But in the meantime, the directors of industry would soon find that with a permanent and irreducible universal income, the resistance to automation would be reduced. The Western countries have had the capacity to produce far more than they need of every commodity for 50 years at least. This power was only displayed, and the truth of the matter revealed, during the last war. Once the political leaders took charge and directed the production, records were achieved in many fields. Nowadays the galvanizing purpose is absent, but the capacity has been increased. Human labor is scarcely necessary to most factory processes once the design and installation of the machinery is finished. Robots can work a full day without tiring or erring. They are the productive capacity of the future and whoever owns them will become most powerful in the economic sphere. At the limit when all the work that can be is automated, how many will be "out of work" and how will they be able to buy what is produced?

Their problem will be severe unless the problem of distribution is solved. Given a share in the ownership of productive assets, first in the National Asset holding shares of many automating companies, and then directly by investing the distributed dividends, no one would suffer hardship. For the first time, advances in technology could be used to ensure that the distribution of income and wealth corresponded fundamentally to our vision of justice and equity. Even now most of us enjoy wealth undreamt by our great-grandparents. The prospect that now presents itself is of fairly shared abundance.

21

BRITISH ESSAY ROUND-UP

As with the North American contest, there were more good British essays than we have space to reprint in full. Many of them covered some of the same ground as those published in Chapters 13 to 20. Several others contained ideas that are worth noting, however briefly.

Allan Thompson of Hartford, Chesire, a retired engineer with a Cambridge degree in mathematics, suggested that British companies be compelled to distribute all their profits, with expansion and new ventures to be financed by "rights issues," i.e., new common shares to be offered to existing shareholders. This would have several beneficial effects, according to the author. The shareholders would receive much higher dividends, and would retain some control over their company's operations; they "would not find themselves in a position where the company has built up so much spare cash that they do not know whether they own an industrial company or a financial one." Takeover bids would be more difficult to mount, while genuine mergers to the benefit of both companies would not be adversely affected. Management would be able to take decisions in their shareholders' interests without looking over their shoulders for predators. And a new market would arise for dealing in the rights to subscribe to the new common shares each time expansion is undertaken.

Thompson's proposal for full dividend payout is also a feature of the SuperStock/Kitty Hawk Model. Higher dividends make it possible for USOP shares to pay for themselves quickly. Eliminating cash hoards makes it feasible to finance expansion through issuance of new shares. This process can be further accelerated by elimination of the corporate income tax with individual shareholders paying the normal tax on the increased dividends. The concept of requiring management to go to the equity market each year for expansion funds is a conservative one, favored by Milton Friedman and Friedrich von Hayek because they believe it makes the market more efficient.

Christopher J. Budd, publisher of *New Economy Magazine*, contributed a vehicle for privatization, "The Britannia Fund," designed to open ownership of Britain's principal business assets to all citizens. The fund would be financed by a tax on turnover (gross sales) of all businesses, which Mr.Budd estimates at 1 per cent per year. This would enable the fund to acquire "the nation's assets" (such as British Gas and British Telecom) and remove them from the seesaw political game of nationalization/privatization. Britannia Fund shares would be available to all citizens, but they would not carry any voting power and would not be redeemable (although they would be transferrable). Budd further suggests that there be a fixed annual return on these shares. As he sees it:

> The Britannia Fund would achieve the economic ends (although possibly challenging some of the political doctrines), both of those who promote state ownership of the nation's assets and those who argue for privatization. The nation's assets would be kept under permanent and proper fiscal and business management—which includes profitable operation—but neither their control nor their profits would pass out of the hands of the people. The non-voting stock would assure this. . . . The Fund would replace public sector financing of businesses, thus alleviating the taxpayers' provision of subsidies.

Angus Hanton of London, an Oxford graduate who runs a small marketing company and manages investment portfolios, contributed some imaginative ideas on privatization. Instead of selling all the shares for cash (as in British Telecom, British Gas, etc.), part of the company could be sold to establish a market value and produce government revenue, and part could be distributed free in the form of USOP shares. Also, large companies, such as British Gas, could be broken up into local units so that a Newcastle resident could hold shares in a newly created Newcastle Gas Company. Hanton feels that competition for financing between the regional companies would impose a marketplace financial discipline. He also advocates privatization of productive assets held by local authorities, such as hospitals and leisure centers.

Larry Trimby of Bexhill on Sea, East Sussex, a chartered accountant and member of the Economic Research Council (London), also favors breaking up nationalized companies into smaller localized units for privatization, again using the example of British Gas. In his essay, "From Kitty Hawk to Concord 2000," Trimby suggests the formation of a Concord Bank and a Concord Insurance Company to facilitate the long-term credit needed to create USOP shares.

Aaron Nejad of London, who graduated with honors from the London School of Economics and also completed his doctorate in Industrial Relations there, advocates broader use of employee buyouts in privatization of nationalized companies. He analyzes the successful employee buyouts of National Freight Co., Victaulic Company (formerly part of British Steel), and Vickers Shipbuilding & Engineering Ltd. He sees employee buyouts as particularly useful in privatization of such declining industries as coal mining, steel manufacturing, and shipbuilding, which have losses or low returns on invested capital and therefore would be difficult to sell through the stock market. Selling to employees at a discount with favorable financing arrangements may be preferable to continuing expensive government subsidies.

A fascinating essay on worker ownership was submitted by Alastair E.H. Campbell of Muir of Ord in the Scottish Highlands, a recognized authority on the subject of worker cooperatives. Colonel Campbell's essay summarized the main points of his book, *The Democratic Control of Work* (Oxford: Plunkett Foundation for Co-operative Studies, 1987). He draws heavily on the successful experience of the Mondragon cooperatives in the Basque region of Spain, and similar results in Hungary, where workers banded together to initiate and finance production. His principal innovation is his theory of "risk labor":

> Since worker ownership is the reverse of capital ownership, the process of starting a business enterprise is also reversed. This means that risk capital has to be replaced by risk labor. . . . Workers desirous of starting a new enterprise can thus pledge the capital-creating capacity of their future labor. In order to do this, they may at first have to accept some reduction in their normal rate of cash drawings; but in return, they start creating their own capital in their own business.

Colonel Campbell's book is a rich source of information on how the credit necessary to finance such worker ownership has been provided and how the lessons learned from Mondragon and Hungary can be broadly applied in Great Britain.

Anthony M. McDermott of Altrincham, Cheshire, in his essay, "Shares for All," suggests the formation of a national lottery to increase investment in British companies and broaden share ownership. All British companies would be invited to join in the lottery by providing their shares as prizes. Each participating company would receive a share of the lottery profits, proportionate to the value of shares contributed to the prize pool. The winners would receive shares of all the participating companies.

I hope that some future essayists will take up Anthony McDermott's suggestion and calculate how much investment capital might be raised through lotteries, and how much stock ownership could be distributed.

BIBLIOGRAPHY

Albus, James S. *Peoples' Capitalism: The Economics of the Robot Revolution.* Kensington, Maryland: New World Books, 1976. (Note: This book is available in Great Britain from Mr. V.R. Hadkins, Social Credit Centre, 32 Totley Grange Rd., Sheffield S17 4AF, U.K.)

Azar, Edward E."U.S. Comprehensive Regional Policy for the Middle East," in Morton A. Kaplan (ed.), *Global Policy Challenge of the 80s.* Washington, D.C.: Washington Institute for Values in Public Policy, 1984.

_____. "Development Diplomacy," in Joyce R. Starr (ed.), *A Shared Destiny.* New York: Praeger Publishers, 1983.

Blinder, Alan S."Economic Policy Can Be Hard-Headed—and Soft-Hearted," *Business Week,* August 12, 1985.

Brittan, Samuel."Economic Viewpoint," *Financial Times* (London), July 4, 1985.

_____. "Thatcherism and Beyond," *Encounter,* April 1985.

_____. *Jobs, Pay, Unions and the Ownership of Capital.* London: Financial Times, 1984.

_____. "The Case for Capital Ownership for All," *Financial Times* (London), September 20, 1984.

_____. *The Rôle and Limits of Government: Essays in Political Economy.* London: Temple Smith, 1983.

Butler, Stuart M. *Privatizing Federal Spending: A Strategy to Eliminate the Deficit.* New York: Universe Books, 1985.

Copeman, George. *The Changing Pattern of Savings and Investment in the United Kingdom.* London: Conference of the British-North American Committee, June 1976.

_____. *Employee Share Ownership and Industrial Stability.* London: Institute of Personnel Management, 1975.

_____. *The Chief Executive and Business Growth.* London: Leviathan House, 1971.

_____. *The Challenge of Employee Shareholding.* London: Business Publications, 1958.

_____. *Leaders of British Industry.* London: Gee, 1955.

Copeman, George, Peter Moore, and Carol Arrowsmith. *Shared Ownership: How to Use Capital Incentives to Sustain Business Growth.* Aldershot (U.K.): Gower Publishing, 1984.

Copeman, George and Tony Rumble. *Capital as an Incentive.* London: Leviathan House, 1972.

Davenport, Nicholas. *Memoirs of a City Radical.* London: Weidenfeld & Nicolson, 1974.

_____. *The Split Society.* London: Victor Gollancz, 1964.

Davidson, Paul, Robert Lekachman, Ward Morehouse, and Stuart M. Speiser. "Symposium on Broadening Capital Ownership," *Journal of Post Keynesian Economics* (M.E. Sharpe, Armonk, New York), Vol. 7, No. 3, 1985.

Fay, C.R. *Co-partnership in Industry.* Cambridge: Cambridge University Press, 1913.

Ferrara, Peter. *Social Security Reform.* Washington, D.C.: Heritage Foundation, 1982.

Galbraith, John Kenneth. *Almost Everyone's Guide to Economics.* New York: Bantam, 1978.

Goodman, John C. "Private Alternatives to Social Security: The Experience of Other Countries," *Cato Journal,* Vol. 3, No. 2, Fall 1983.

_____. *Social Security in the United Kingdom: Contracting Out of the System.* Washington, D.C.: American Enterprise Institute, 1981.

Hamrin, Robert. *Managing Growth in the 1980s: Toward a New Economics.* New York: Praeger Publishers, 1980.

Heller, Robert. *Shares for Employees*. London: Poland Street Publications, 1984.

Jay, Peter. *The Crisis for Western Political Economy*. London: Andre Deutsch, 1984.

Job Ownership Ltd. *Employee Ownership—Why, How?* London: Job Ownership, 1985.

Joint Economic Committee of Congress. 1976 Joint Economic Report. Washington, D.C.: The Committee, 1976.

Kautsky, Karl. "Is Soviet Russia a Socialist State?" in Kautsky, *Social Democracy vs. Communism*. New York: Rand School Press, 1946.

Kelso, Louis O. and Mortimer J. Adler. *The New Capitalists*. New York: Random House, 1961.

_____. *The Capitalist Manifesto*. New York: Random House, 1958.

Kelso, Louis O. and Patricia Hetter. *Two-factor Theory: The Economics of Reality*. New York: Vintage Books, 1968.

Kelso, Louis O. and Patricia Hetter Kelso. *Democracy and Economic Power*. Cambridge, Massachusetts: Ballinger Publishing, 1986.

Keynes, John Maynard. *The General Theory of Employment, Interest and Money*. New York: Cambridge University Press, 1973.

_____. *How to Pay for the War*. London: Macmillan, 1940.

Low, Sir Toby (later Lord Aldington). *Every Man a Capitalist*. London: Conservative Research Centre, 1958.

Maital, Shlomo. *Minds, Markets, Money*. New York: Basic Books, 1982.

McClaughry, John (ed.). *Expanded Ownership*. Fond du Lac, Wisconsin: Sabre Foundation, 1972.

McClosky, Herbert and John Zaller. *The American Ethos: Public Attitudes Toward Capitalism and Democracy*. Cambridge, Massachusetts: Harvard University Press, 1984.

Meade, James E. "Wage-Fixing Revisited." London: The Institute of Economic Affairs Occasional Paper 72, 1985.

_____. "Full Employment, New Technologies and the Distribution of Income," *Journal of Social Policy* (Cambridge University Press, Cambridge), Vol. 13, Part 2, April 1984.

_____. *Efficiency, Equality, and the Ownership of Property.* London: George Allen Unwin, 1964.

Morehouse, Ward (ed.). *The Handbook of Tools for Community Economic Change.* New York: Intermediate Technology Group of North America, 1983.

National Conference of Catholic Bishops. "Catholic Social Teaching and the U.S. Economy," *Origins,* Volume 15, No. 17. Washington, D.C.: National Catholic News Service, October 10, 1985.

Perry, Jr., John H. *The National Dividend.* New York: Ivan Obolensky, 1964.

Schumacher, E.F. *Small is Beautiful.* New York: Harper & Row, 1973.

Speiser, Stuart M. *Ethical Economics and the Faith Community: A Practical Plan of Work and Ownership for All.* Bloomington, Indiana: Meyer Stone Books, 1988.

_____. *Supplement to The USOP Handbook. Shareholders in America, Inc.: A First Step Toward Universal Share Ownership.* New York: Council on International and Public Affairs, June 1986.

_____. *The USOP Handbook: A Guide to Designing Universal Share Ownership Plans for the United States and Great Britain.* New York: Council on International and Public Affairs, 1986.

_____. *How to End the Nuclear Nightmare.* Croton-on-Hudson, New York/New York: North River Press/Dodd Mead, 1984.

_____. *SuperStock.* New York: Everest House, 1982.

_____. *A Piece of the Action.* New York: Van Nostrand Reinhold, 1977.

Taylor, Kenneth B. (ed.). *Capitalism and the 'Evil Empire': Reducing Superpower Conflict Through American Economic Reform.* New York: New Horizons Press, 1988.

Turnbull, C. S. Shann. *Democratising the Wealth of Nations.* Sydney: Company Directors Association of Australia, 1975.

Von Thunen, Johann Heinrich. *The Isolated State.* (Abridged and translated from the 2nd German ed.) Oxford: Pergamon Press, 1966.

Weitzman, Martin L. *The Share Economy: Conquering Stagflation.* Cambridge, Massachusetts: Harvard University Press, 1984.

"Wider Share Ownership—Equality and Opportunity in an Enterprise Economy," SDP Open Forum No. 11. London: Social Democratic

Party's Working Party on Share Ownership, 1985.

Wisman, Jon. "Economic Reform for Humanity's Greatest Struggle," Chapter II in Kenneth B. Taylor (ed.), New York: New Horizons Press, 1988.